Tyler Boss

Dead Dog's Bite ™

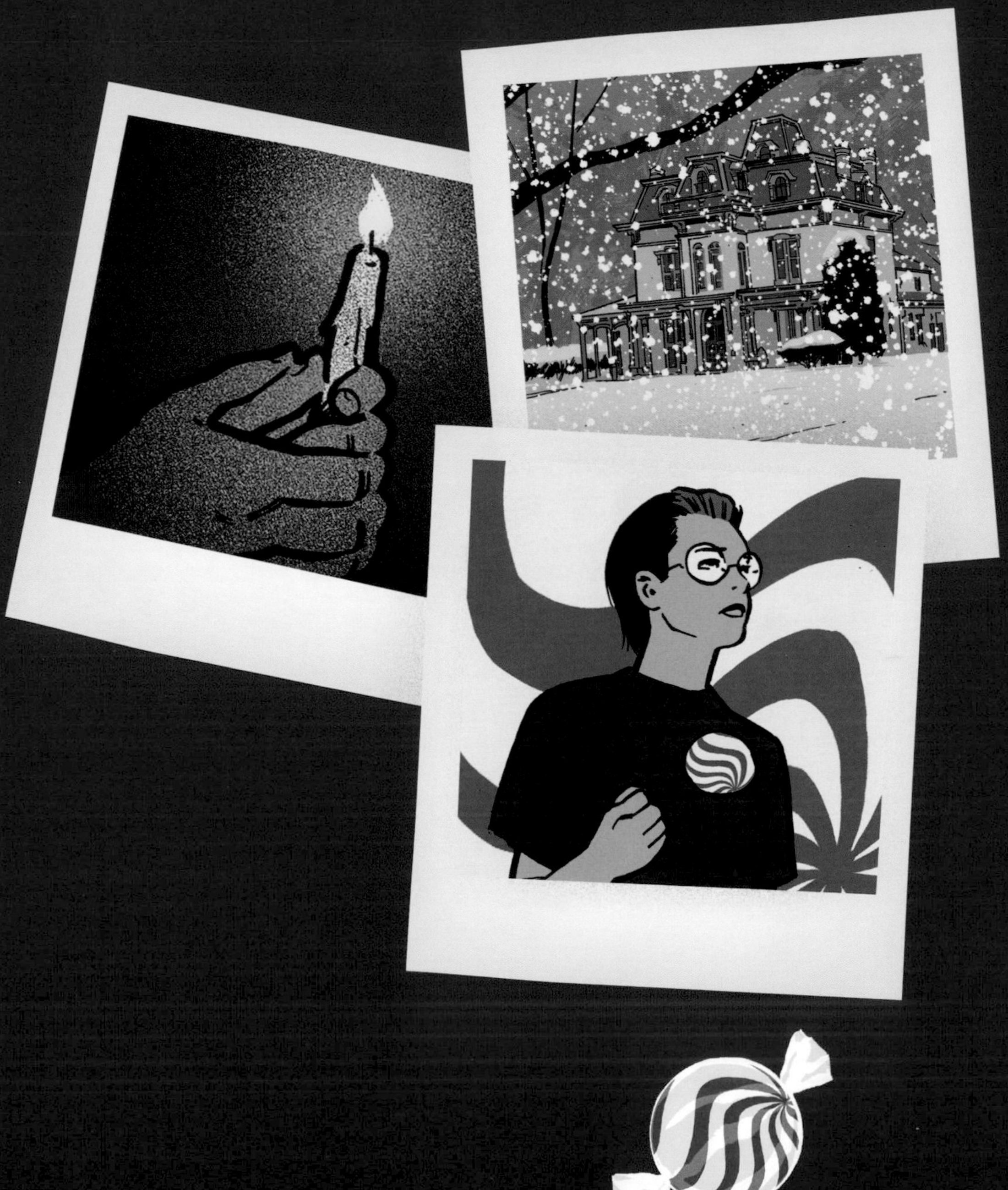

Dead Dog's Bite ™

Tyler Boss

Dark Horse Books

PRESIDENT AND PUBLISHER
Mike Richardson

EDITOR
Brett Israel

ASSISTANT EDITOR
Sanjay Dharawat

DIGITAL ART TECHNICIAN
Josie Christensen

COLLECTION DESIGNER
Kathleen Barnett

Special thanks to Ben Somers,
Peter Schmidt, and Gus Storms
for all of their help.

Published by Dark Horse Books
A division of Dark Horse Comics LLC
10956 SE Main Street
Milwaukie, OR 97222

Comic Shop Locator Service: comicshoplocator.com

This volume collects and reprints the comic book series Dead Dog's Bite #1–#4.

//////////

Library of Congress Cataloging-in-Publication Data

Names: Boss, Tyler, author, artist.
Title: Dead dog's bite / Tyler Boss.
Description: First edition. | Milwaukie, OR : Dark Horse Books, 2021. |
   "This volume collects and reprints the comic book series Dead Dog's Bite
   #1–#4." | Summary: "Cormac Guffin has gone missing. It's been three days
   and no one has seen hide nor hair of her. The police have nothing, and
   the townsfolk are acting more like a funeral procession than a search
   party. If Cormac has any hope of being found, it rests on the slouching
   shoulders of her best friend Joe. Joe will need her wits about her
   though because, like any story worth hearing, nothing is what it
   seems"-- Provided by publisher.
Identifiers: LCCN 2021010817 | ISBN 9781506714677 (hardcover) | ISBN
   9781506714684 (ebook)
Subjects: LCSH: Graphic novels.
Classification: LCC PN6727.B674 D43 2021 | DDC 741.5/973--dc23
LC record available at https://lccn.loc.gov/2021010817

First edition: September 2021
Ebook ISBN 978-1-50671-468-4
Hardcover ISBN 978-1-50671-467-7

10 9 8 7 6 5 4 3 2 1
Printed in China

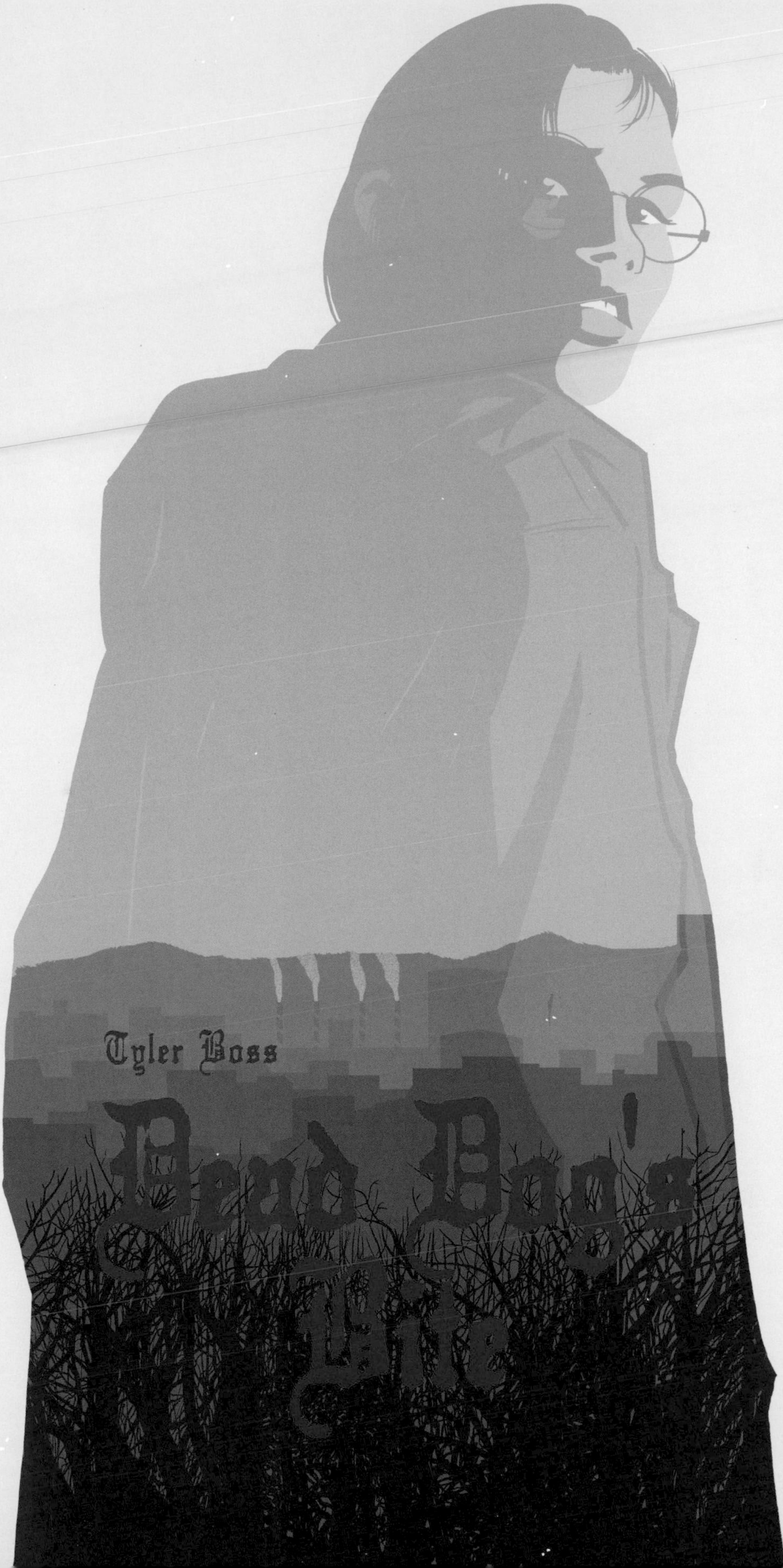
Tyler Boss
Dead Dog's Bite

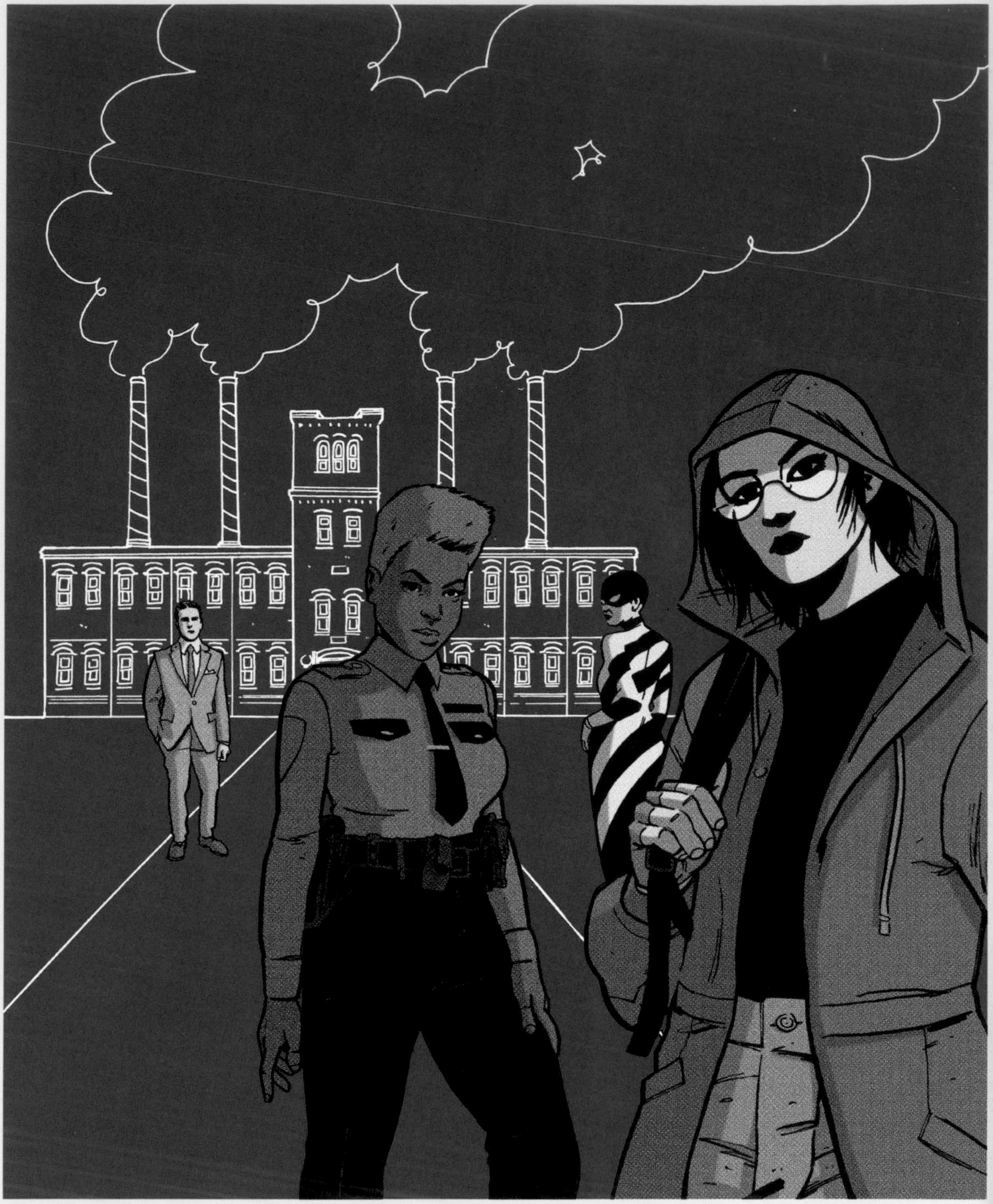

Tyler Boss

Dead Dog's Bite

Chapter One

"Shall I project a world?"
                                    --T.P.

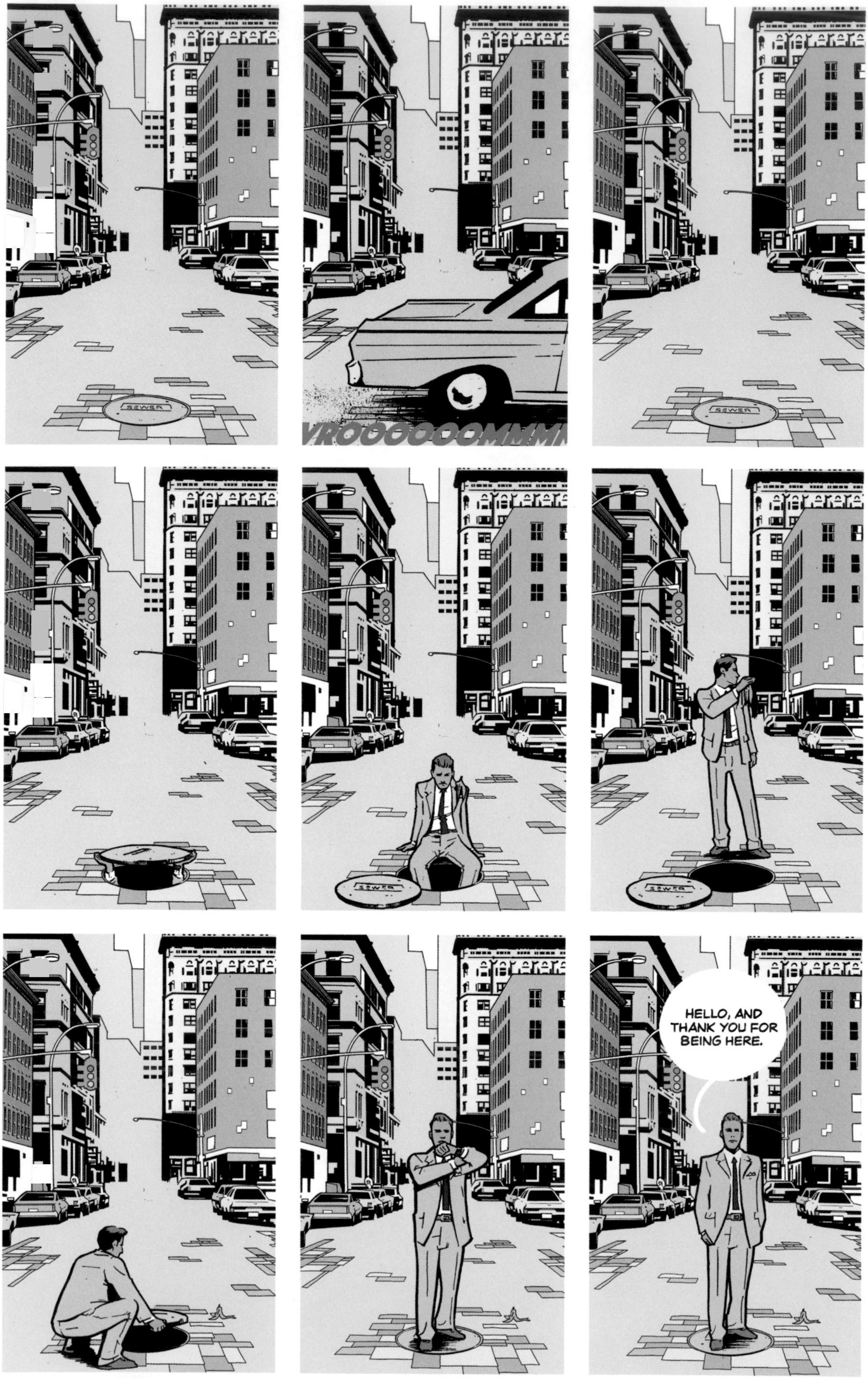
SEWER
VROOOOOOOMMMM
SEWER
SEWER
SEWER
HELLO, AND THANK YOU FOR BEING HERE.

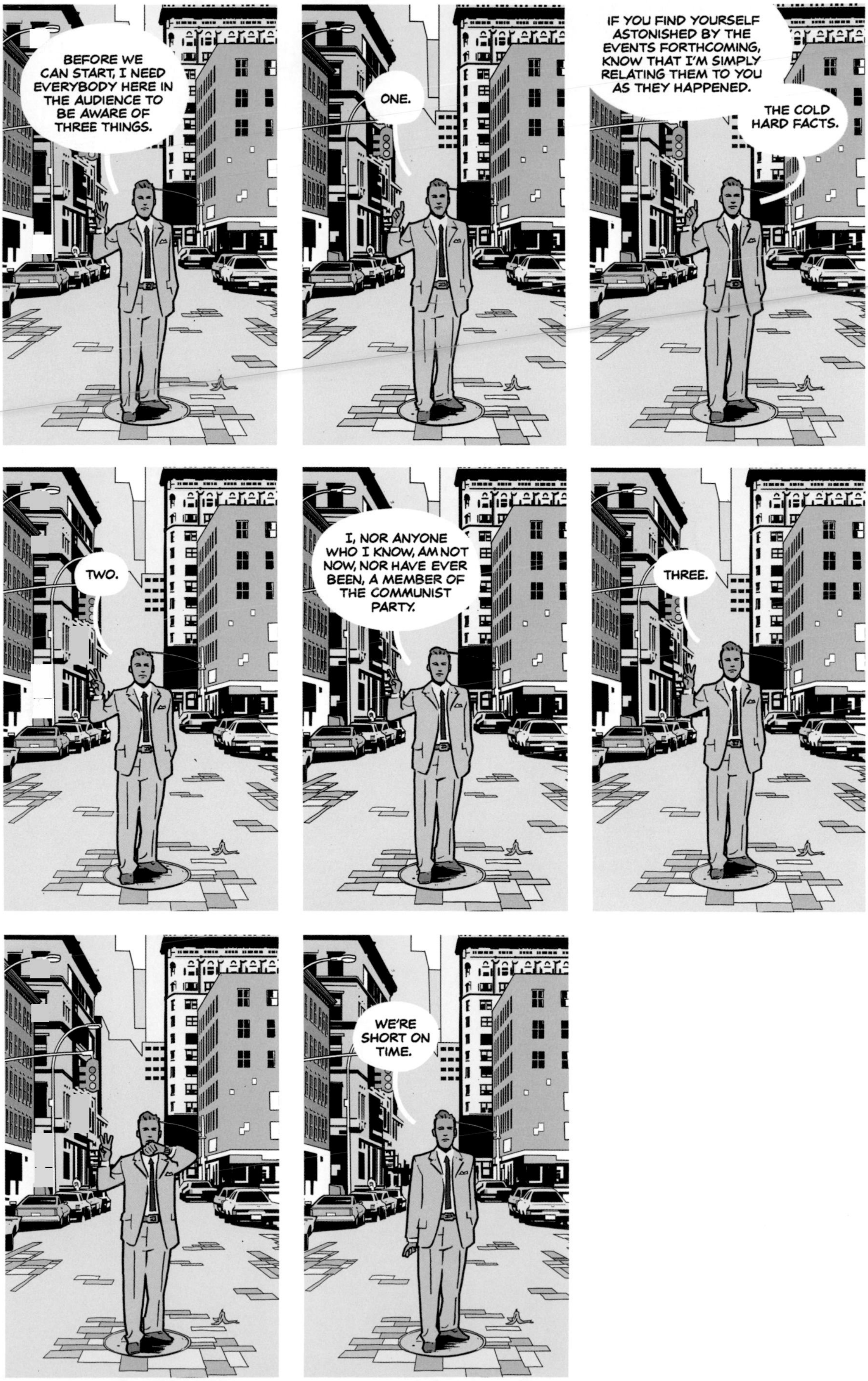
BEFORE WE CAN START, I NEED EVERYBODY HERE IN THE AUDIENCE TO BE AWARE OF THREE THINGS.
ONE.
IF YOU FIND YOURSELF ASTONISHED BY THE EVENTS FORTHCOMING, KNOW THAT I'M SIMPLY RELATING THEM TO YOU AS THEY HAPPENED.
THE COLD HARD FACTS.
TWO.
I, NOR ANYONE WHO I KNOW, AM NOT NOW, NOR HAVE EVER BEEN, A MEMBER OF THE COMMUNIST PARTY.
THREE.
WE'RE SHORT ON TIME.

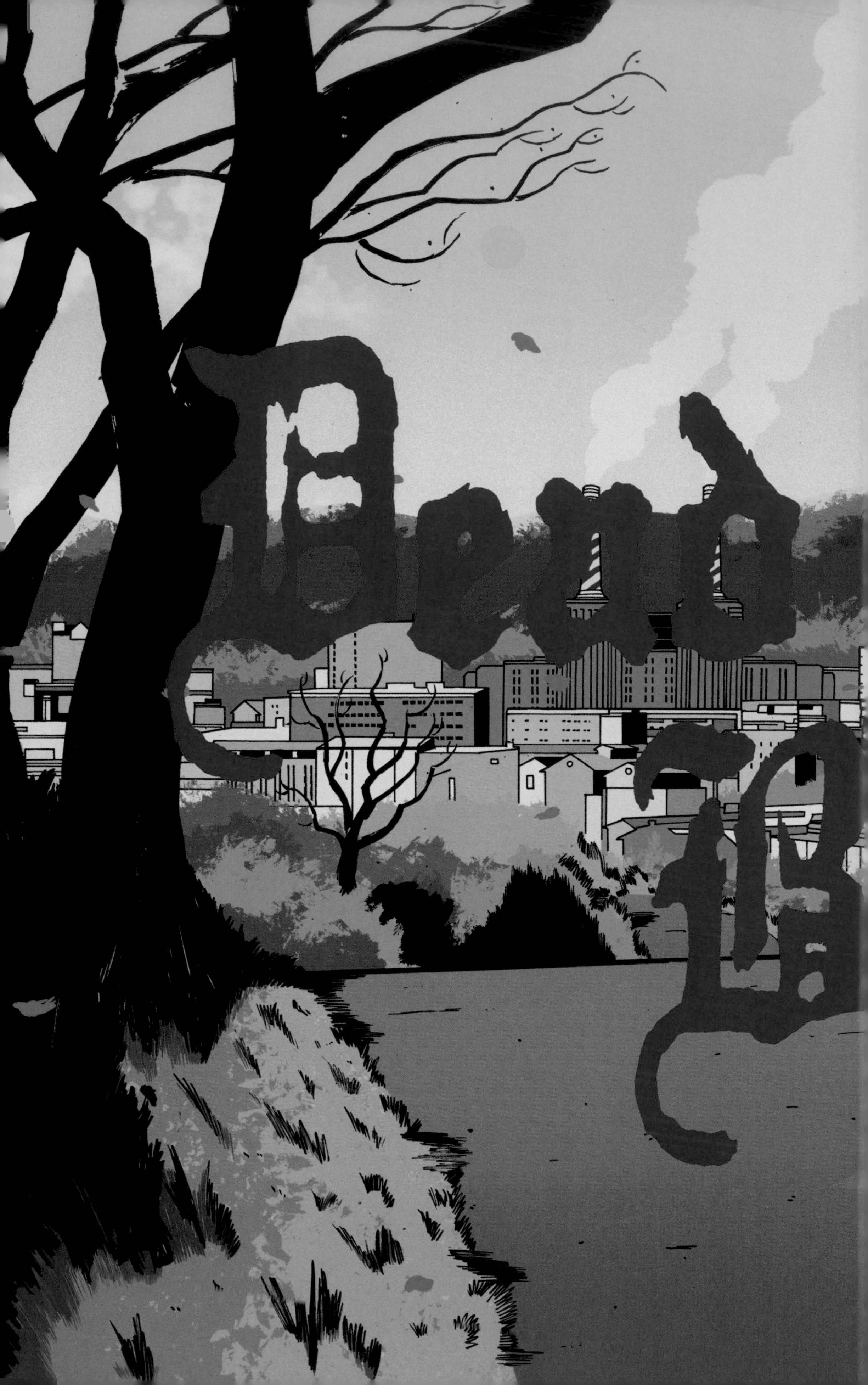

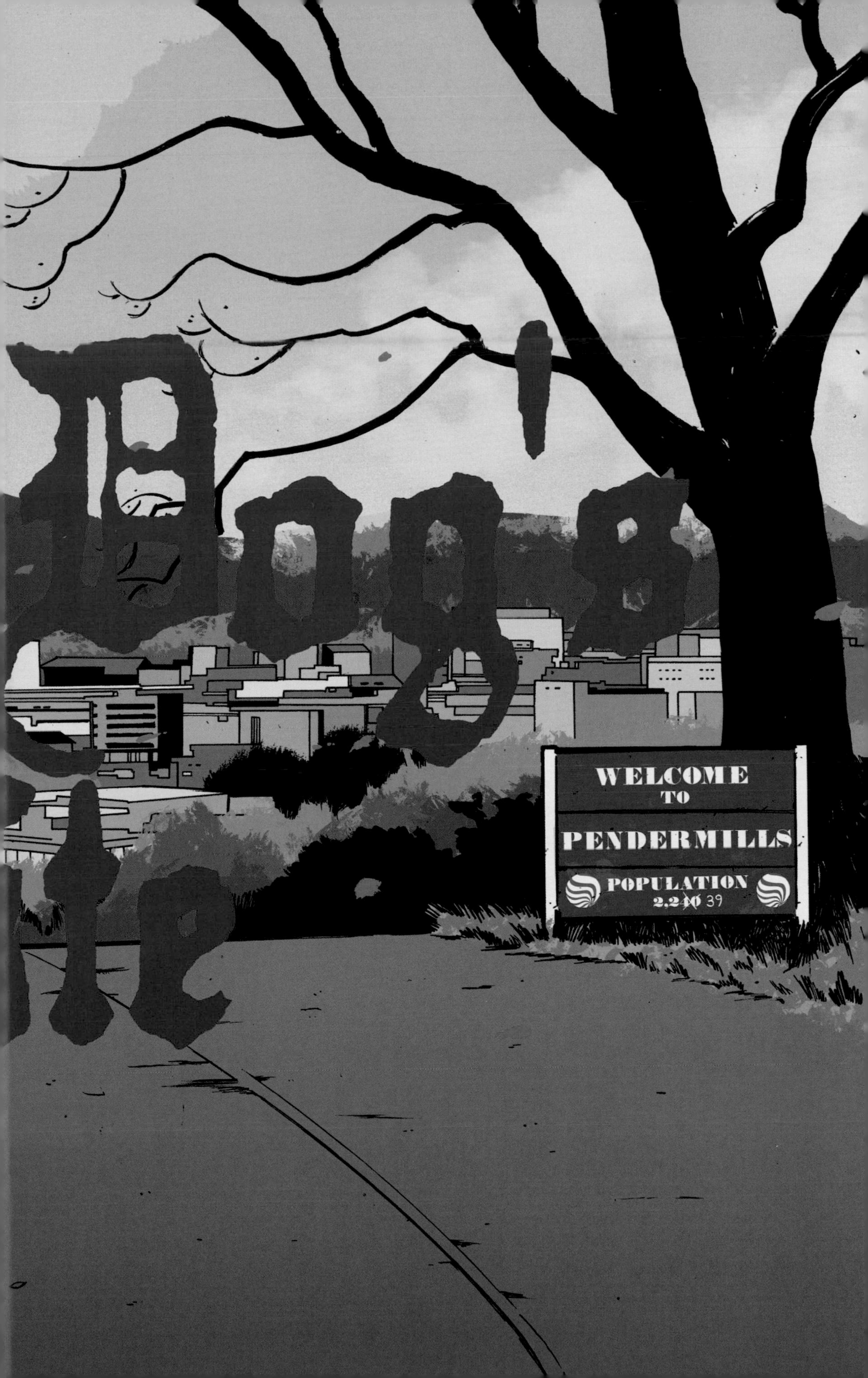
WELCOME
TO
PENDERMILLS
POPULATION
2,240 39

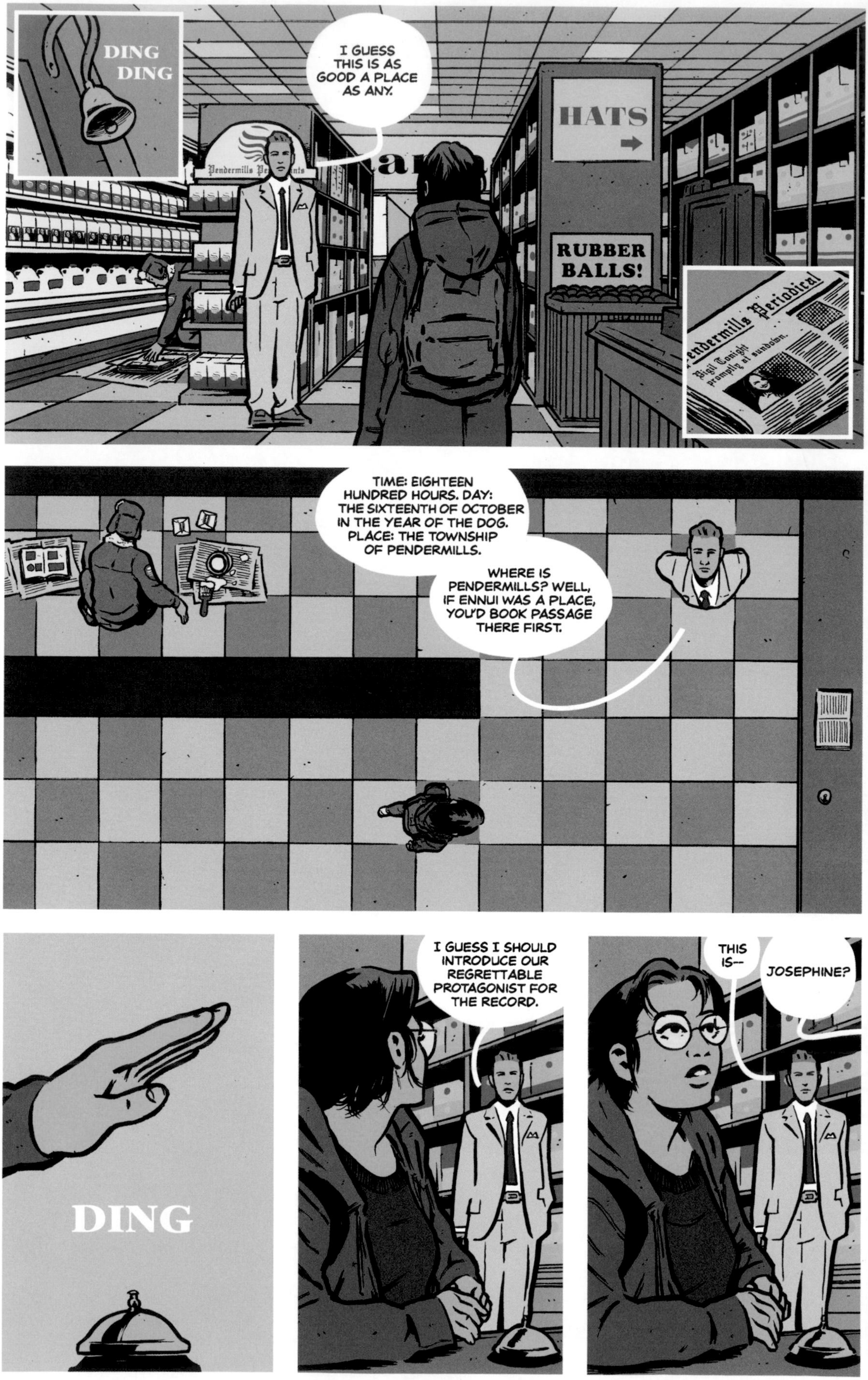
DING
DING
I GUESS THIS IS AS GOOD A PLACE AS ANY.
HATS
RUBBER BALLS!
Vigil Tonight promptly at sundown.
TIME: EIGHTEEN HUNDRED HOURS. DAY: THE SIXTEENTH OF OCTOBER IN THE YEAR OF THE DOG. PLACE: THE TOWNSHIP OF PENDERMILLS.
WHERE IS PENDERMILLS? WELL, IF ENNUI WAS A PLACE, YOU'D BOOK PASSAGE THERE FIRST.
DING
I GUESS I SHOULD INTRODUCE OUR REGRETTABLE PROTAGONIST FOR THE RECORD.
THIS IS--
JOSEPHINE?

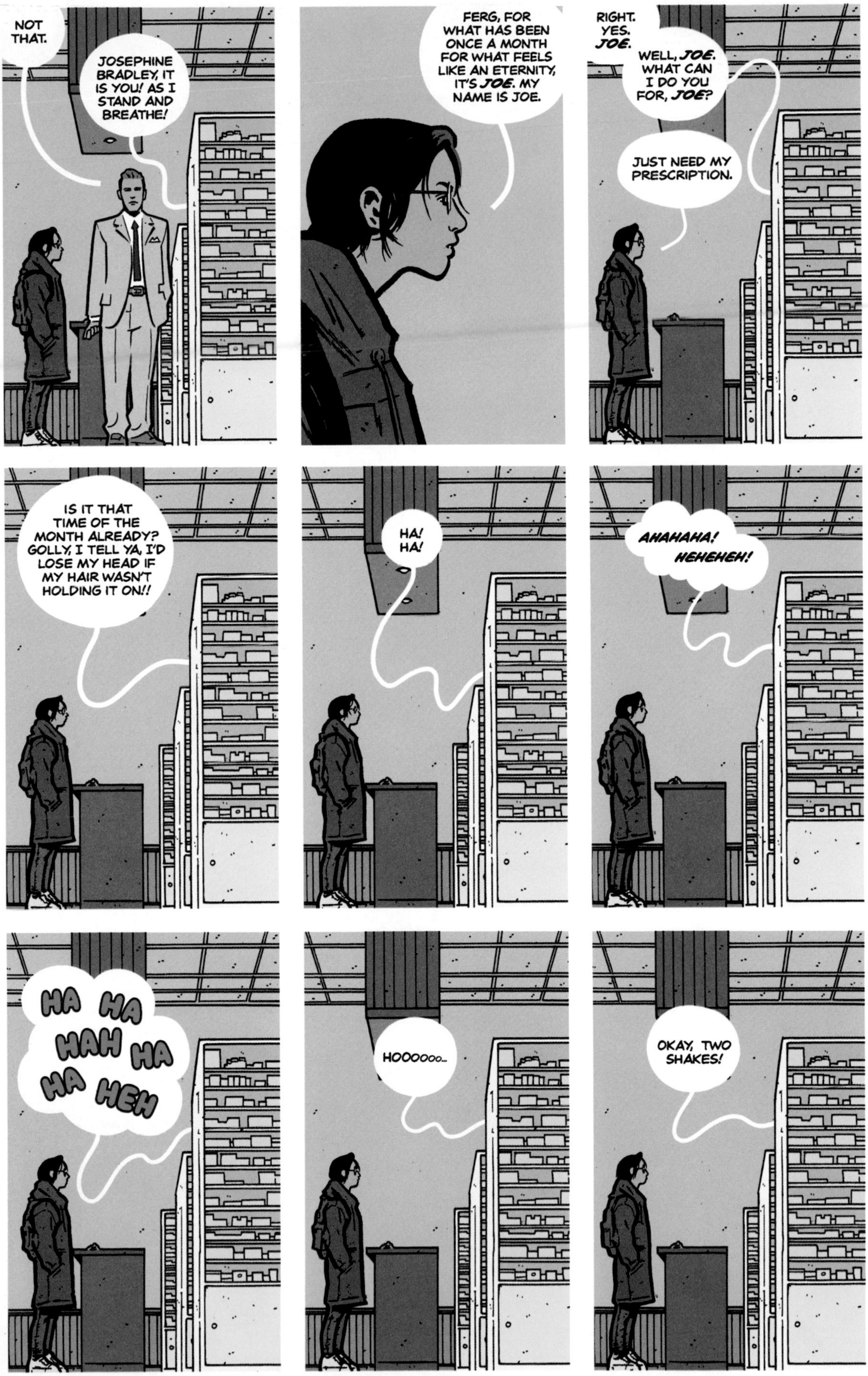
NOT THAT.
JOSEPHINE BRADLEY, IT IS YOU! AS I STAND AND BREATHE!
FERG, FOR WHAT HAS BEEN ONCE A MONTH FOR WHAT FEELS LIKE AN ETERNITY, IT'S JOE. MY NAME IS JOE.
RIGHT. YES. JOE.
WELL, JOE. WHAT CAN I DO YOU FOR, JOE?
JUST NEED MY PRESCRIPTION.
IS IT THAT TIME OF THE MONTH ALREADY? GOLLY, I TELL YA, I'D LOSE MY HEAD IF MY HAIR WASN'T HOLDING IT ON!!
HA! HA!
AHAHAHA! HEHEHEH!
HA HA HAH HA HA HEH
HOOOOOO...
OKAY, TWO SHAKES!

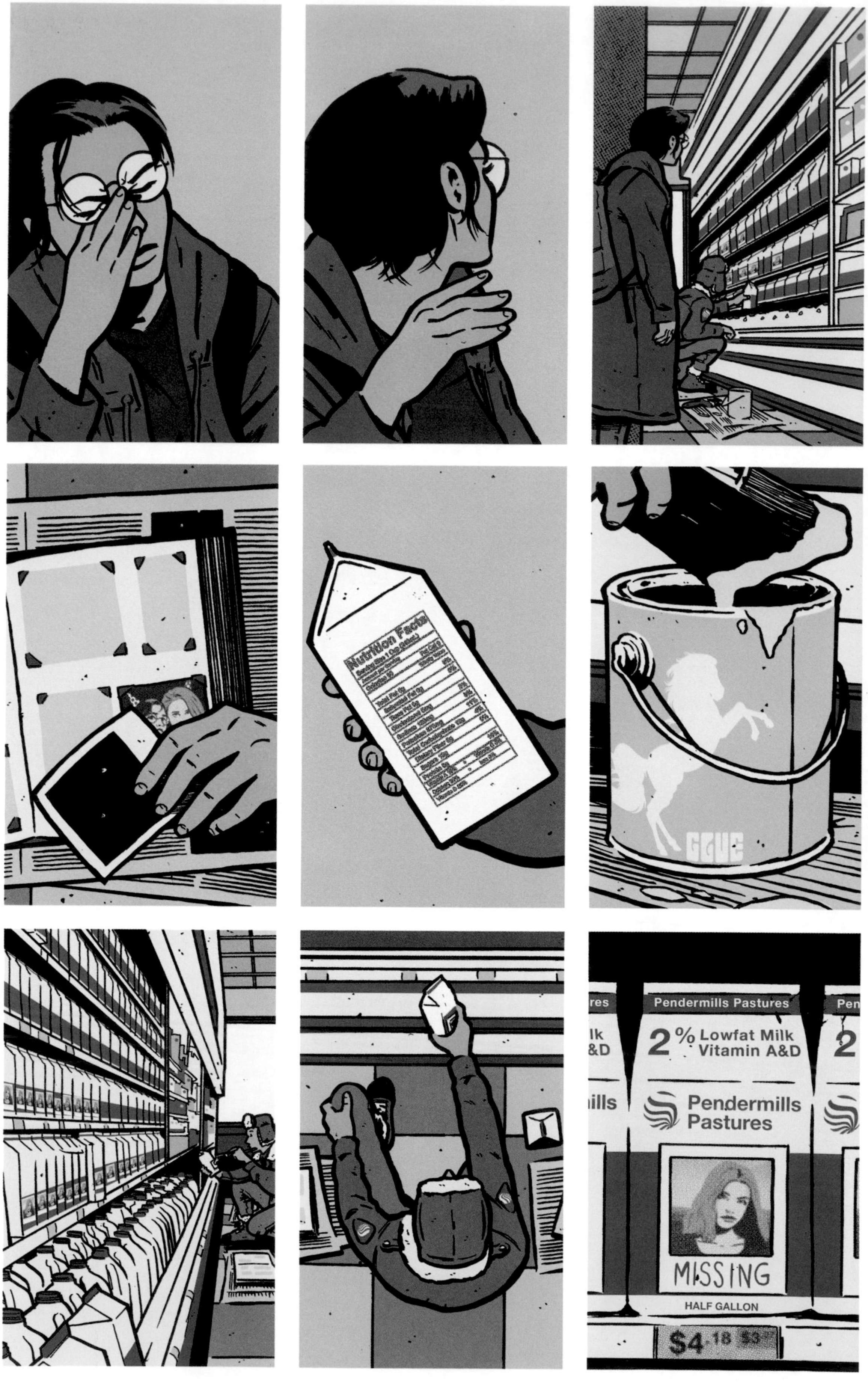
Nutrition Facts
GLUE
Pendermills Pastures
2% Lowfat Milk
Vitamin A&D
Pendermills Pastures
MISSING
HALF GALLON
$4.18

HOKAY, HERE WE ARE. ONE ORDER OF CARBAMAZEPINE WITH LAMICTAL ON THE SIDE, HOT AND READY TO GO!

WHAT'S WITH THE CASTS, FERG?

HM?

OH, MY CLAPPERS?!

IT'S A PRETTY CUTE STORY, ACTUALLY. I WAS IN A PUNCHING ACCIDENT WITH--

ALL RIGHT, FERG, THAT OUGHTA DO IT. NOBODY'S BUYING ANY COW'S BLOOD WITHOUT SEEING OUR MISS GUFFIN'S FACE.

WELL ALL RIGHT THEN. DEPUTY DUNAWAY, GOOD LUCK WITH YOUR INVESTIGATION! I'M SURE SHE'LL TURN UP NO WORSE FOR--

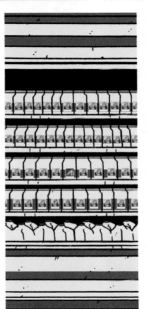

--THE DEAL WITH YOUR CLAPPERS ANYWAYS?

CLAPPERS?

OH, MY FLIMFLAMS! IT'S A PRETTY CUTE STORY, ACTUALLY--

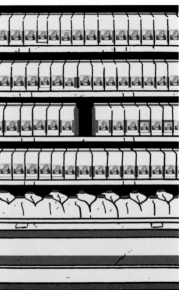

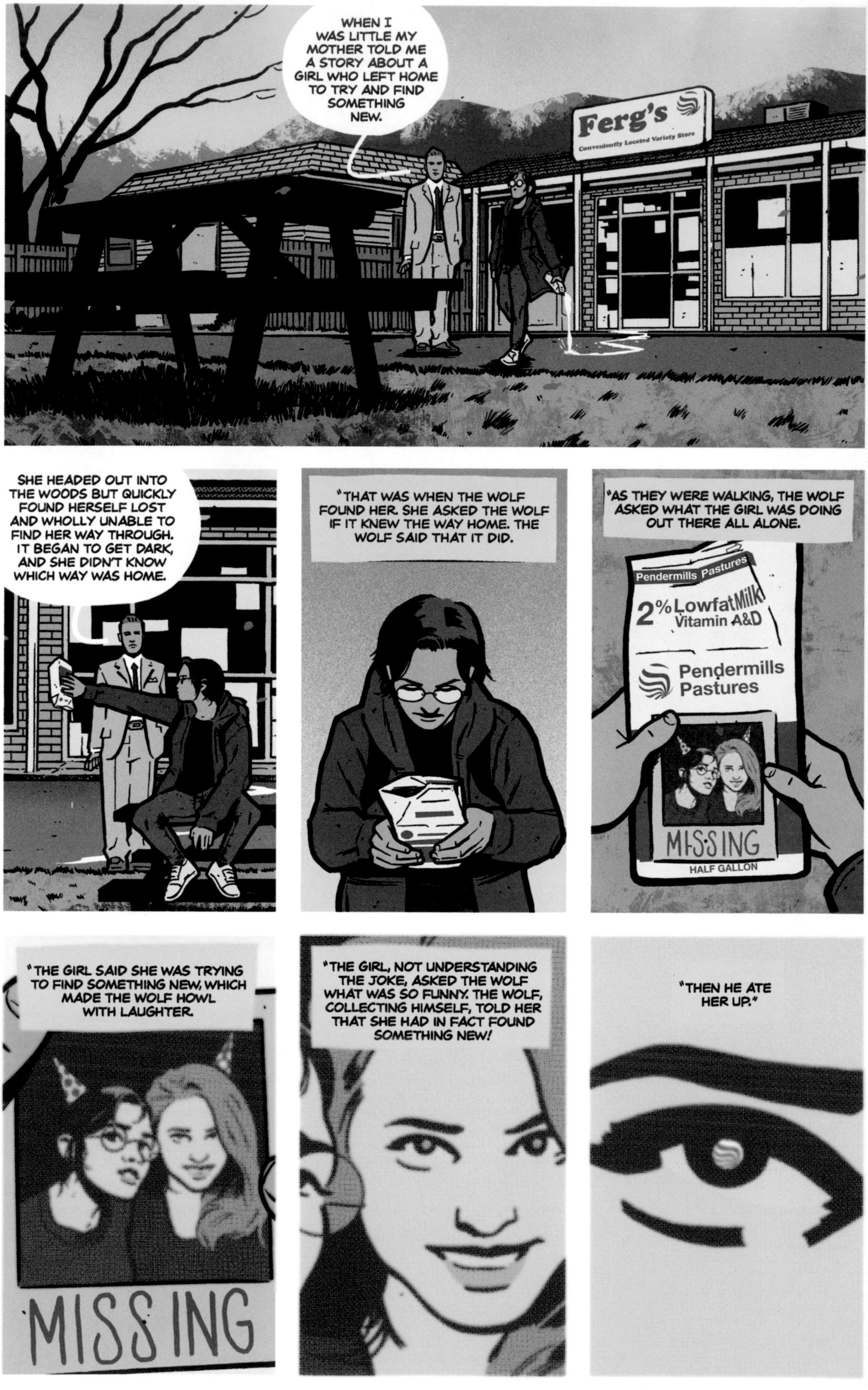
WHEN I WAS LITTLE MY MOTHER TOLD ME A STORY ABOUT A GIRL WHO LEFT HOME TO TRY AND FIND SOMETHING NEW.
Ferg's
Conveniently Located Variety Store
SHE HEADED OUT INTO THE WOODS BUT QUICKLY FOUND HERSELF LOST AND WHOLLY UNABLE TO FIND HER WAY THROUGH. IT BEGAN TO GET DARK, AND SHE DIDN'T KNOW WHICH WAY WAS HOME.
"THAT WAS WHEN THE WOLF FOUND HER. SHE ASKED THE WOLF IF IT KNEW THE WAY HOME. THE WOLF SAID THAT IT DID.
"AS THEY WERE WALKING, THE WOLF ASKED WHAT THE GIRL WAS DOING OUT THERE ALL ALONE.
Pendermills Pastures
2% LowfatMilk Vitamin A&D
Pendermills Pastures
MISSING
HALF GALLON
"THE GIRL SAID SHE WAS TRYING TO FIND SOMETHING NEW, WHICH MADE THE WOLF HOWL WITH LAUGHTER.
MISSING
"THE GIRL, NOT UNDERSTANDING THE JOKE, ASKED THE WOLF WHAT WAS SO FUNNY. THE WOLF, COLLECTING HIMSELF, TOLD HER THAT SHE HAD IN FACT FOUND SOMETHING NEW!
"THEN HE ATE HER UP."

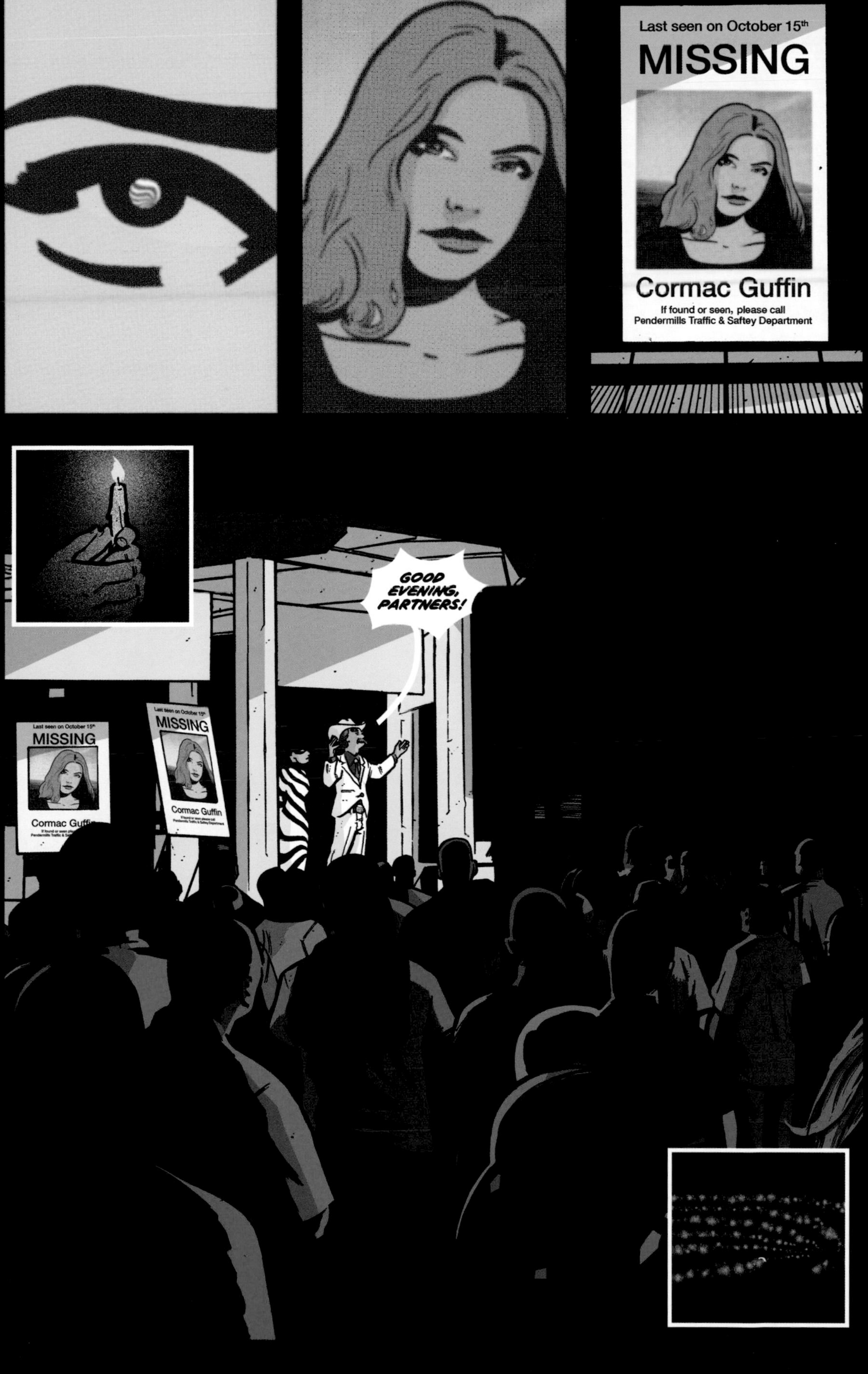
Last seen on October 15th
MISSING
Cormac Guffin
If found or seen, please call
Pendermills Traffic & Saftey Department
GOOD EVENING, PARTNERS!
Last seen on October 15th
MISSING
Last seen on October 15th
MISSING
Cormac Guffin

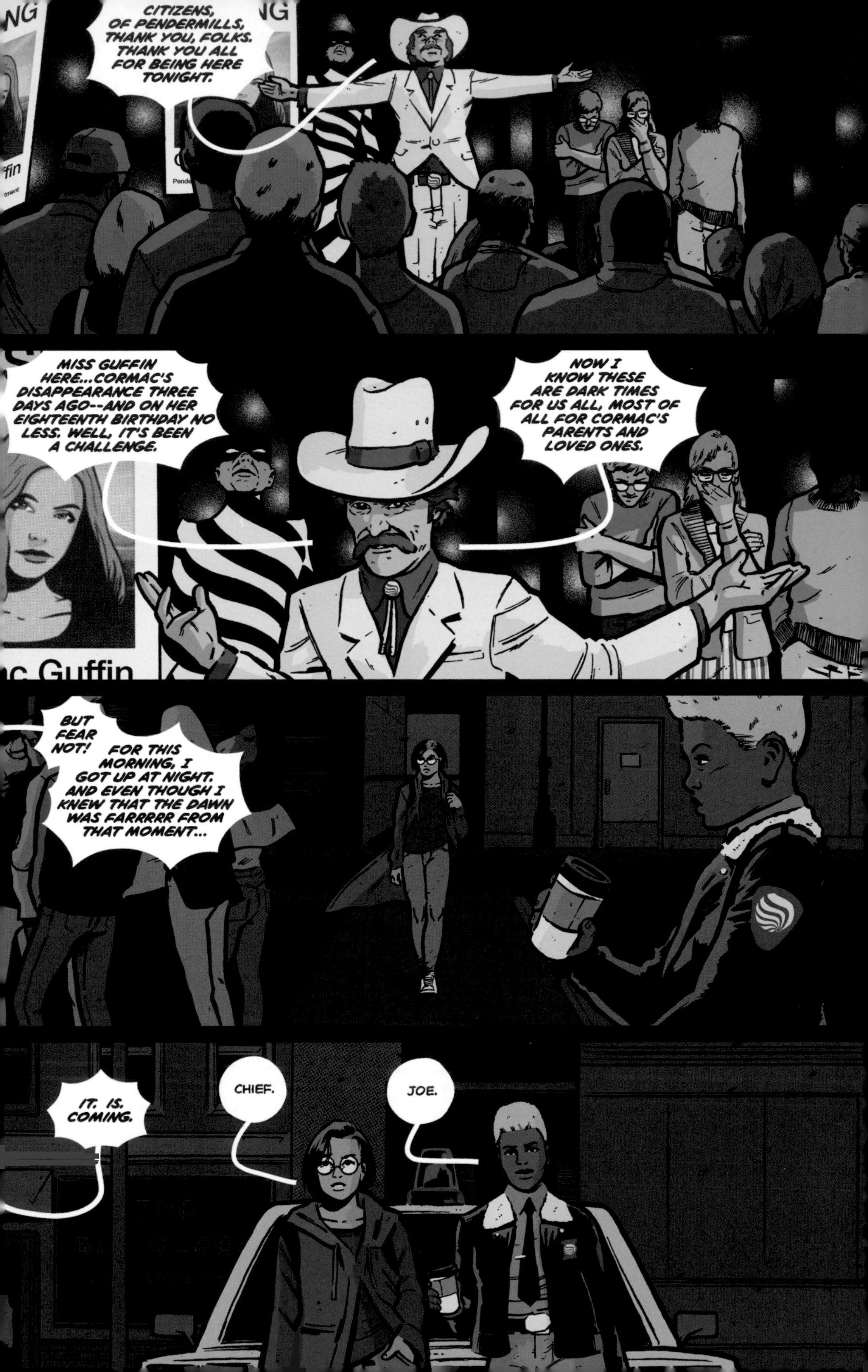
CITIZENS, OF PENDERMILLS, THANK YOU, FOLKS. THANK YOU ALL FOR BEING HERE TONIGHT.
MISS GUFFIN HERE...CORMAC'S DISAPPEARANCE THREE DAYS AGO--AND ON HER EIGHTEENTH BIRTHDAY NO LESS. WELL, IT'S BEEN A CHALLENGE.
NOW I KNOW THESE ARE DARK TIMES FOR US ALL, MOST OF ALL FOR CORMAC'S PARENTS AND LOVED ONES.
c Guffin
BUT FEAR NOT!
FOR THIS MORNING, I GOT UP AT NIGHT. AND EVEN THOUGH I KNEW THAT THE DAWN WAS FARRRRR FROM THAT MOMENT...
IT. IS. COMING.
CHIEF.
JOE.

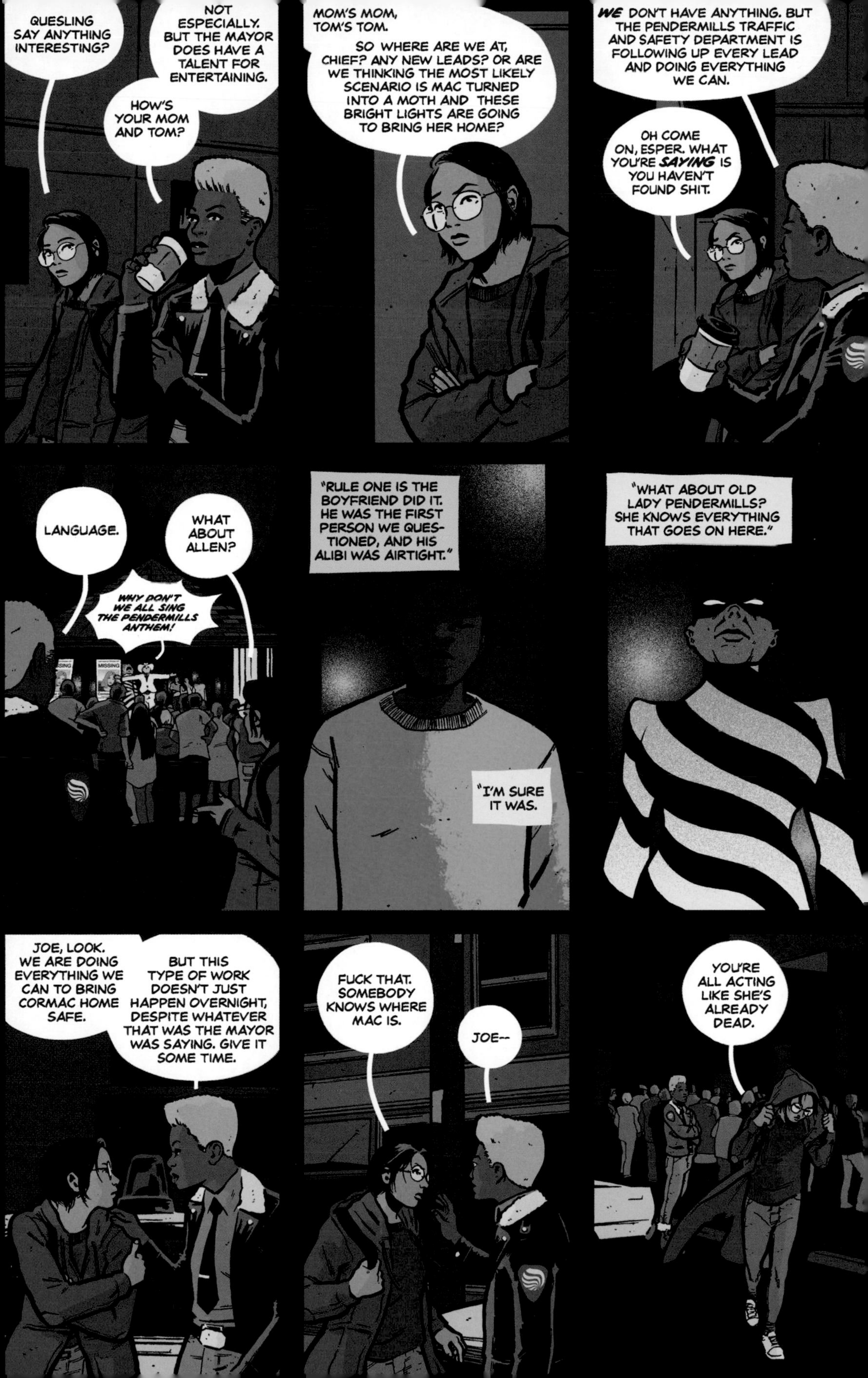
QUESLING SAY ANYTHING INTERESTING?
NOT ESPECIALLY. BUT THE MAYOR DOES HAVE A TALENT FOR ENTERTAINING.
HOW'S YOUR MOM AND TOM?
MOM'S MOM, TOM'S TOM.
SO WHERE ARE WE AT, CHIEF? ANY NEW LEADS? OR ARE WE THINKING THE MOST LIKELY SCENARIO IS MAC TURNED INTO A MOTH AND THESE BRIGHT LIGHTS ARE GOING TO BRING HER HOME?
WE DON'T HAVE ANYTHING. BUT THE PENDERMILLS TRAFFIC AND SAFETY DEPARTMENT IS FOLLOWING UP EVERY LEAD AND DOING EVERYTHING WE CAN.
OH COME ON, ESPER. WHAT YOU'RE SAYING IS YOU HAVEN'T FOUND SHIT.
LANGUAGE.
WHAT ABOUT ALLEN?
WHY DON'T WE ALL SING THE PENDERMILLS ANTHEM!
MISSING
MISSING
"RULE ONE IS THE BOYFRIEND DID IT. HE WAS THE FIRST PERSON WE QUES- TIONED, AND HIS ALIBI WAS AIRTIGHT."
"I'M SURE IT WAS.
"WHAT ABOUT OLD LADY PENDERMILLS? SHE KNOWS EVERYTHING THAT GOES ON HERE."
JOE, LOOK. WE ARE DOING EVERYTHING WE CAN TO BRING CORMAC HOME SAFE.
BUT THIS TYPE OF WORK DOESN'T JUST HAPPEN OVERNIGHT, DESPITE WHATEVER THAT WAS THE MAYOR WAS SAYING. GIVE IT SOME TIME.
FUCK THAT. SOMEBODY KNOWS WHERE MAC IS.
JOE--
YOU'RE ALL ACTING LIKE SHE'S ALREADY DEAD.

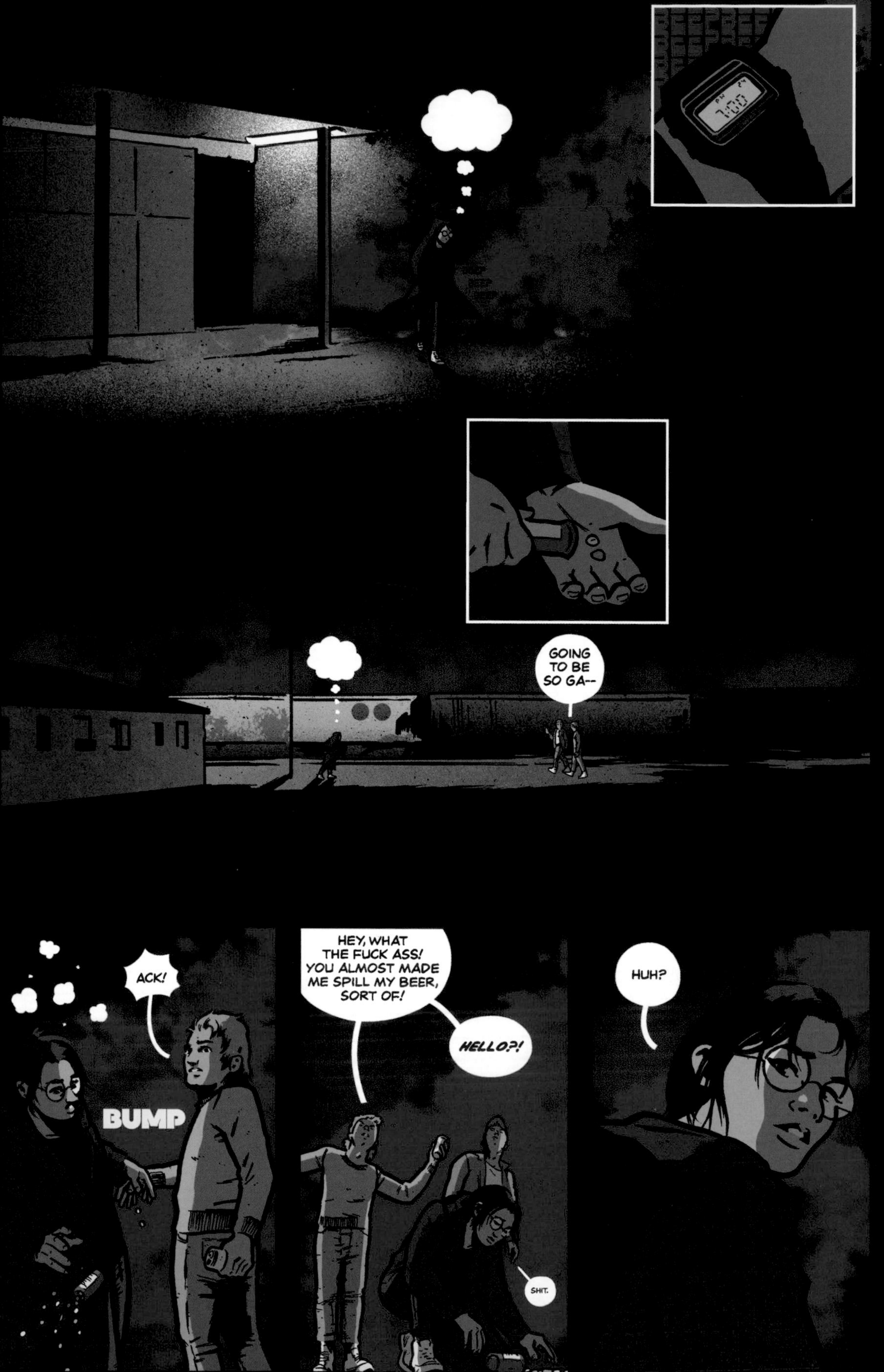
GOING TO BE SO GA--
ACK!
BUMP
HEY, WHAT THE FUCK ASS! YOU ALMOST MADE ME SPILL MY BEER, SORT OF!
HELLO?!
SHIT.
HUH?

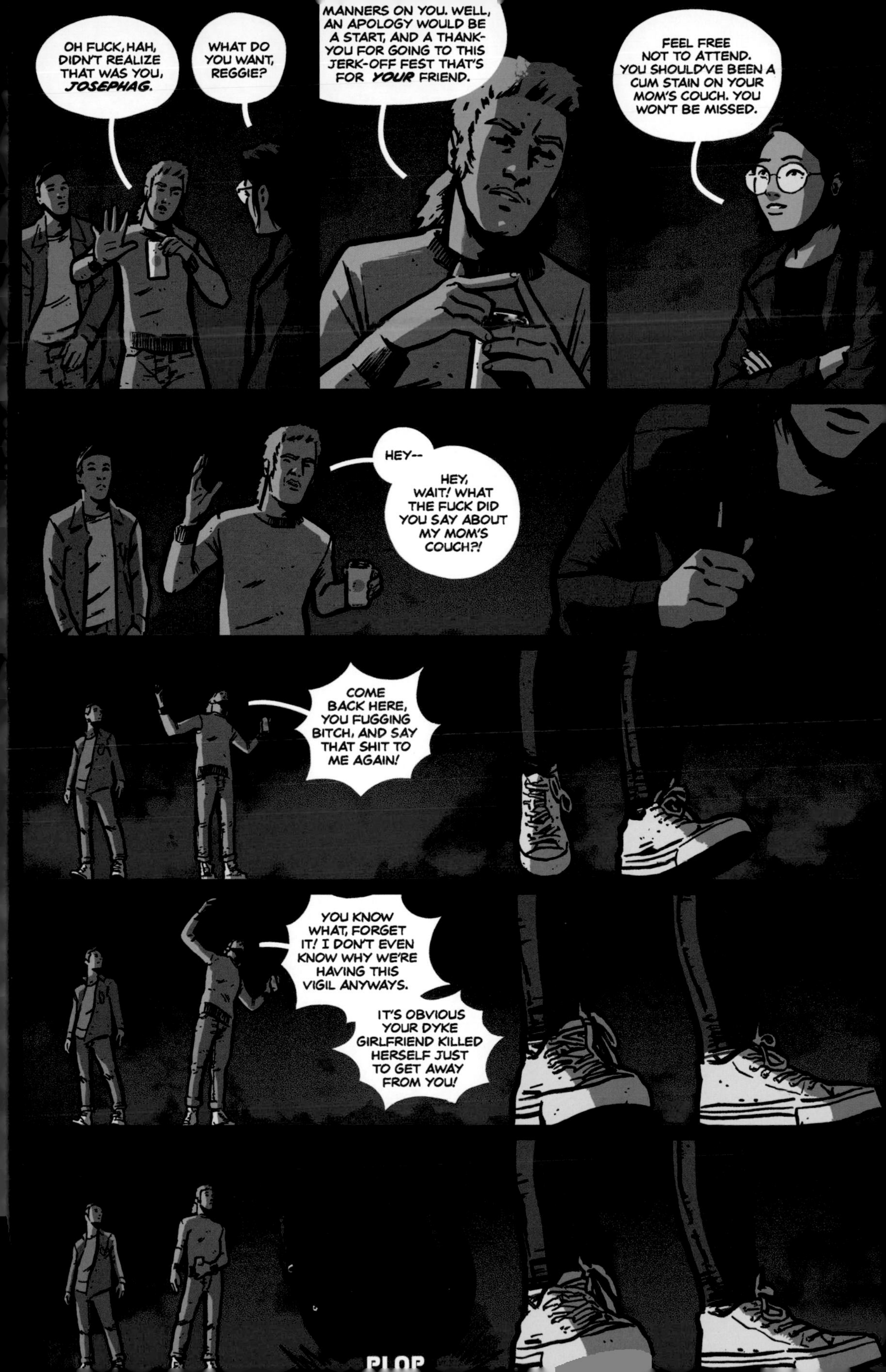

OH FUCK, HAH, DIDN'T REALIZE THAT WAS YOU, JOSEPHAG.
WHAT DO YOU WANT, REGGIE?
MANNERS ON YOU. WELL, AN APOLOGY WOULD BE A START, AND A THANK-YOU FOR GOING TO THIS JERK-OFF FEST THAT'S FOR YOUR FRIEND.
FEEL FREE NOT TO ATTEND. YOU SHOULD'VE BEEN A CUM STAIN ON YOUR MOM'S COUCH. YOU WON'T BE MISSED.
HEY--
HEY, WAIT! WHAT THE FUCK DID YOU SAY ABOUT MY MOM'S COUCH?!
COME BACK HERE, YOU FUGGING BITCH, AND SAY THAT SHIT TO ME AGAIN!
YOU KNOW WHAT, FORGET IT! I DON'T EVEN KNOW WHY WE'RE HAVING THIS VIGIL ANYWAYS.
IT'S OBVIOUS YOUR DYKE GIRLFRIEND KILLED HERSELF JUST TO GET AWAY FROM YOU!
PLOP

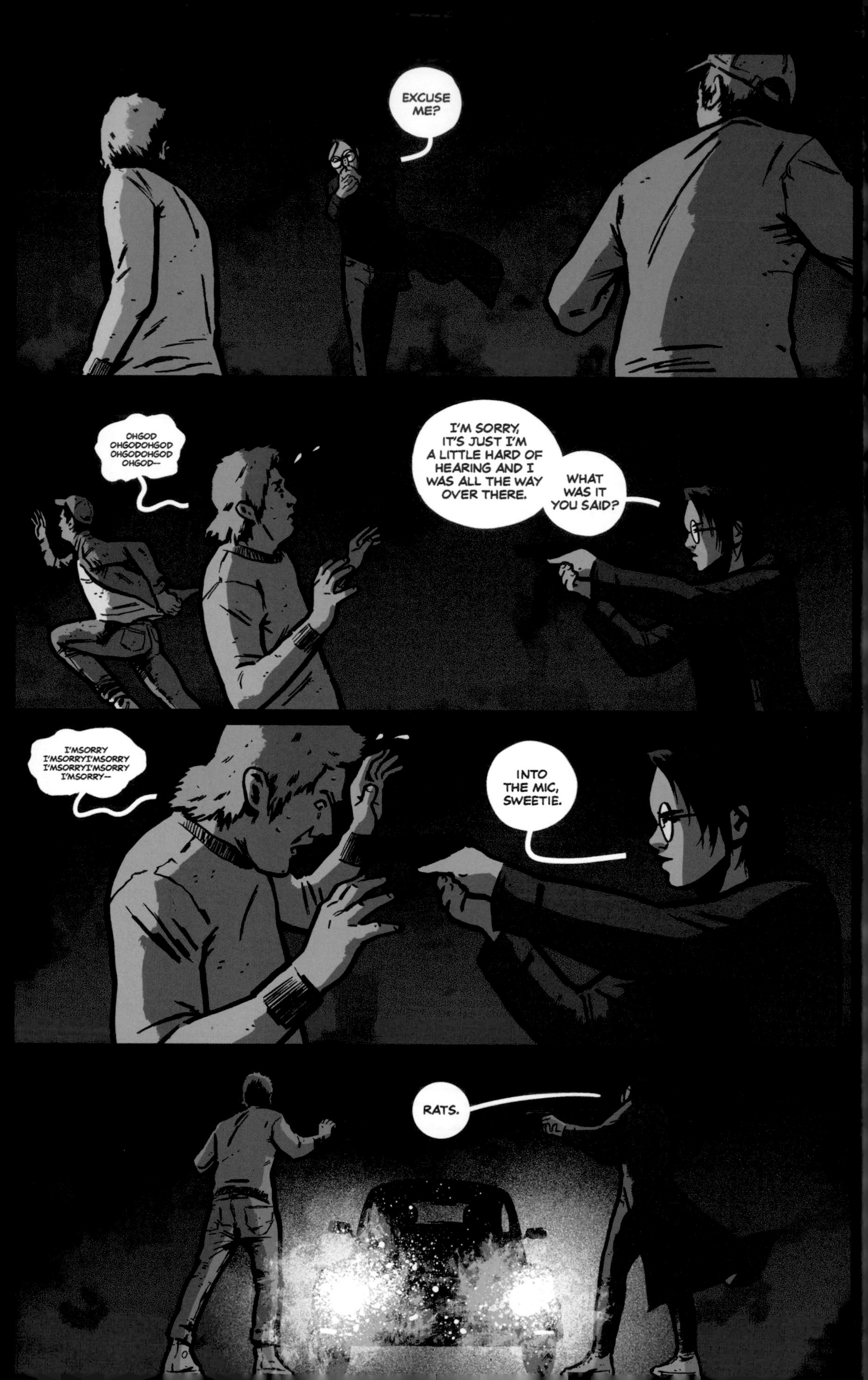
EXCUSE ME?
OHGOD OHGODOHGOD OHGODOHGOD OHGOD--
I'M SORRY, IT'S JUST I'M A LITTLE HARD OF HEARING AND I WAS ALL THE WAY OVER THERE.
WHAT WAS IT YOU SAID?
I'MSORRY I'MSORRYI'MSORRY I'MSORRYI'MSORRY I'MSORRY--
INTO THE MIC, SWEETIE.
RATS.

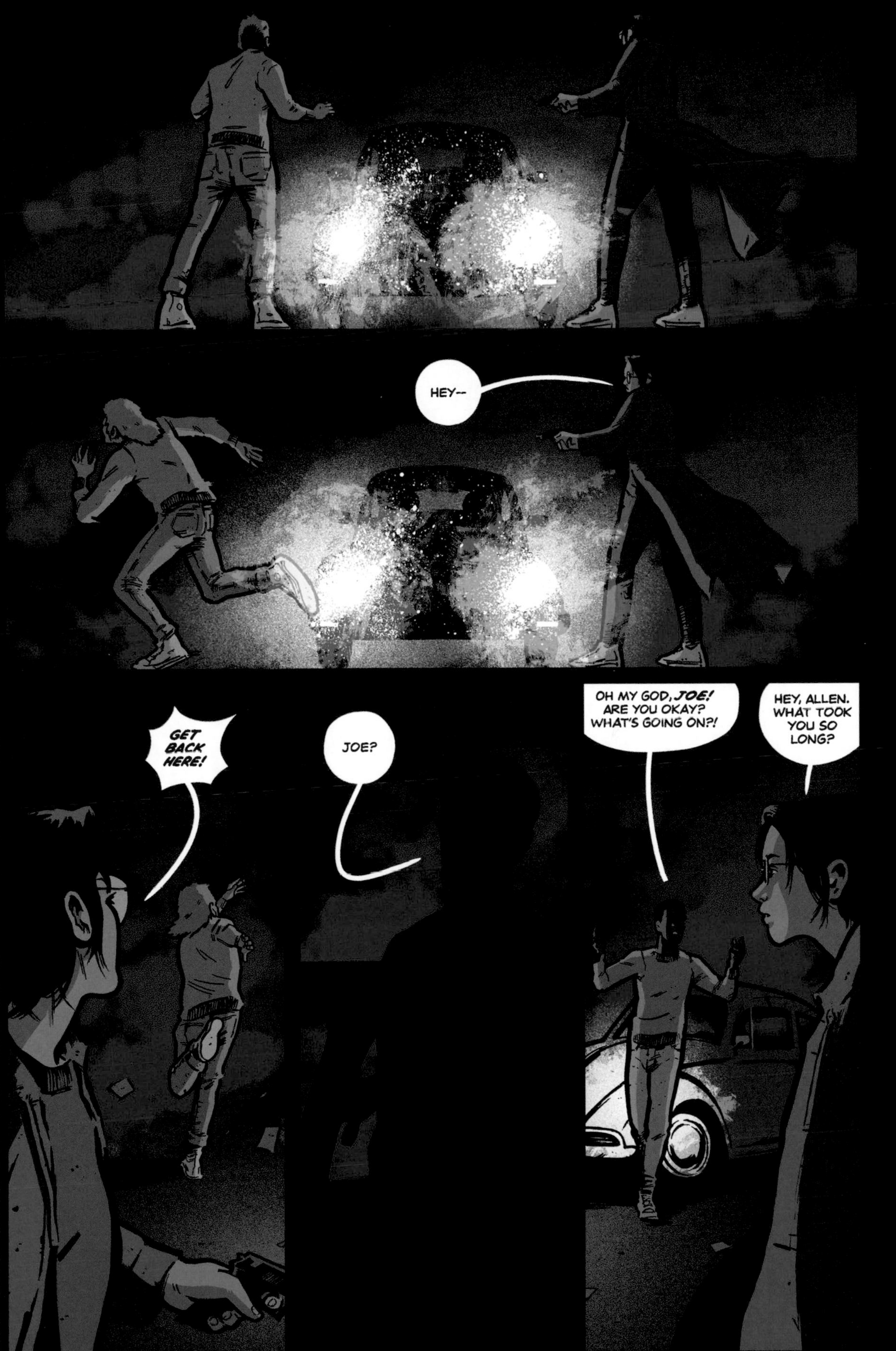
HEY--
GET BACK HERE!
JOE?
OH MY GOD, JOE! ARE YOU OKAY? WHAT'S GOING ON?!
HEY, ALLEN. WHAT TOOK YOU SO LONG?

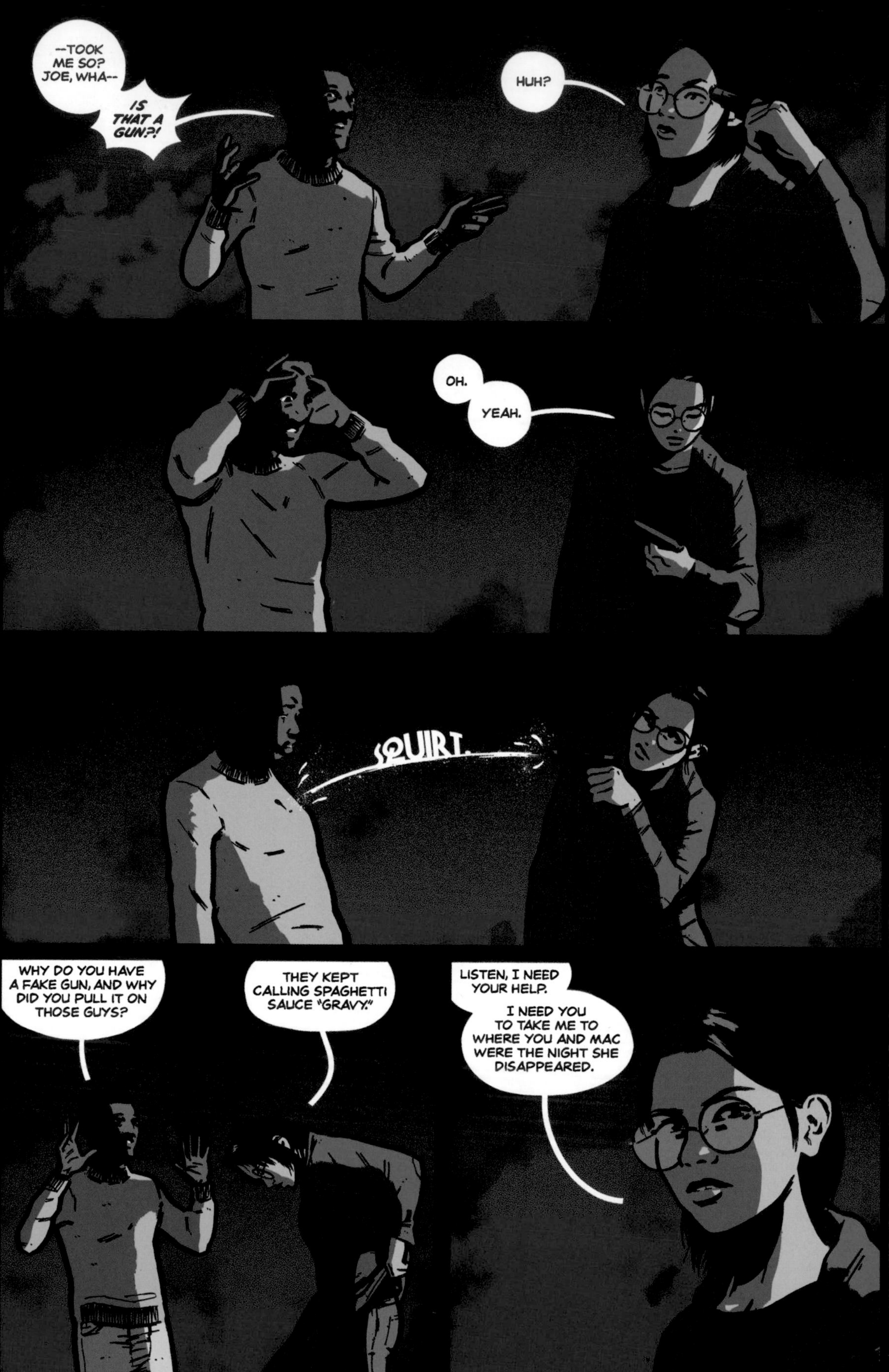
--TOOK ME SO? JOE, WHA--
IS THAT A GUN?!
HUH?
OH.
YEAH.
SQUIRT.
WHY DO YOU HAVE A FAKE GUN, AND WHY DID YOU PULL IT ON THOSE GUYS?
THEY KEPT CALLING SPAGHETTI SAUCE "GRAVY."
LISTEN, I NEED YOUR HELP.
I NEED YOU TO TAKE ME TO WHERE YOU AND MAC WERE THE NIGHT SHE DISAPPEARED.

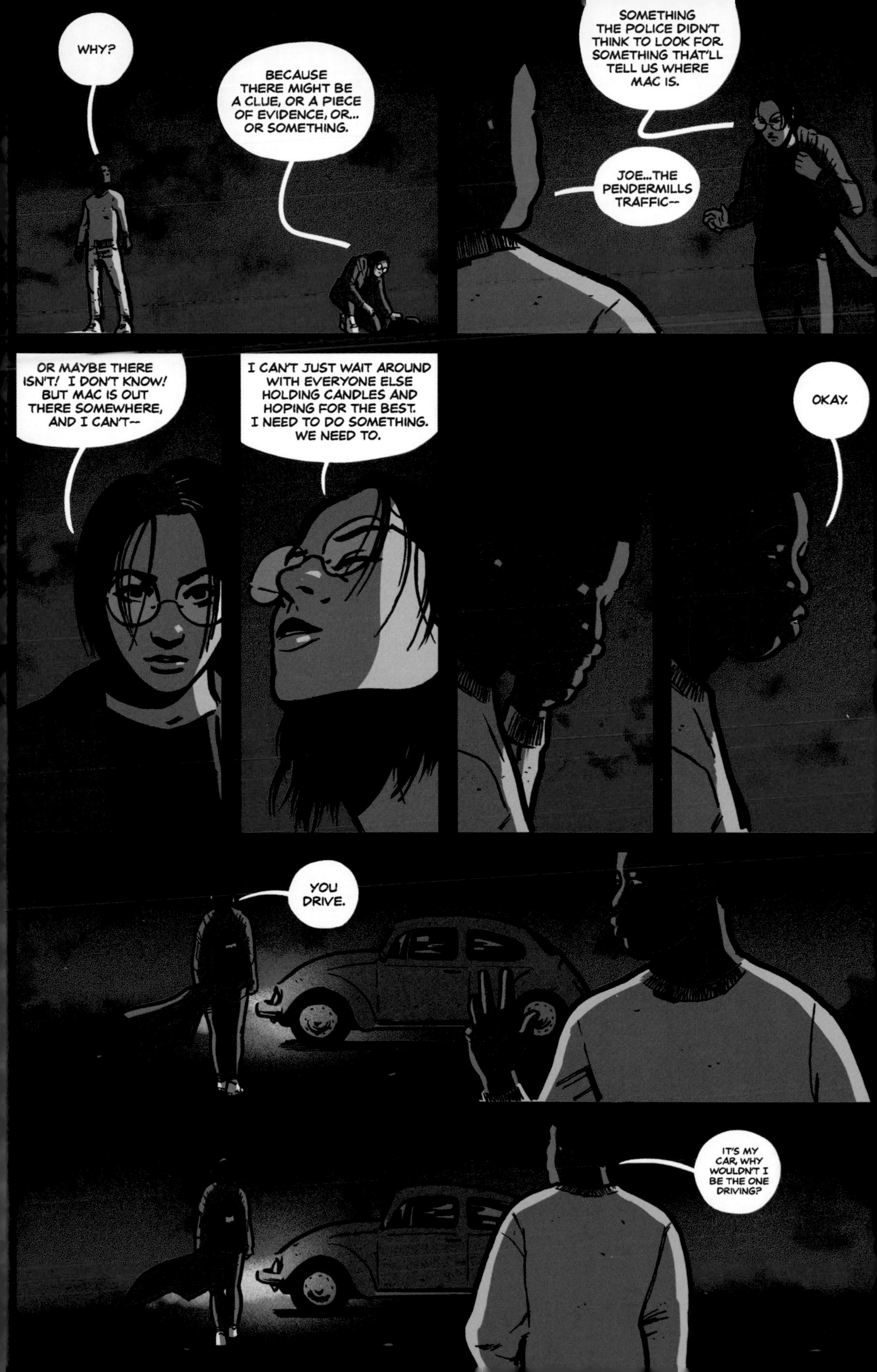
WHY?
BECAUSE THERE MIGHT BE A CLUE, OR A PIECE OF EVIDENCE, OR... OR SOMETHING.
SOMETHING THE POLICE DIDN'T THINK TO LOOK FOR. SOMETHING THAT'LL TELL US WHERE MAC IS.
JOE...THE PENDERMILLS TRAFFIC--
OR MAYBE THERE ISN'T! I DON'T KNOW! BUT MAC IS OUT THERE SOMEWHERE, AND I CAN'T--
I CAN'T JUST WAIT AROUND WITH EVERYONE ELSE HOLDING CANDLES AND HOPING FOR THE BEST. I NEED TO DO SOMETHING. WE NEED TO.
OKAY.
YOU DRIVE.
IT'S MY CAR, WHY WOULDN'T I BE THE ONE DRIVING?

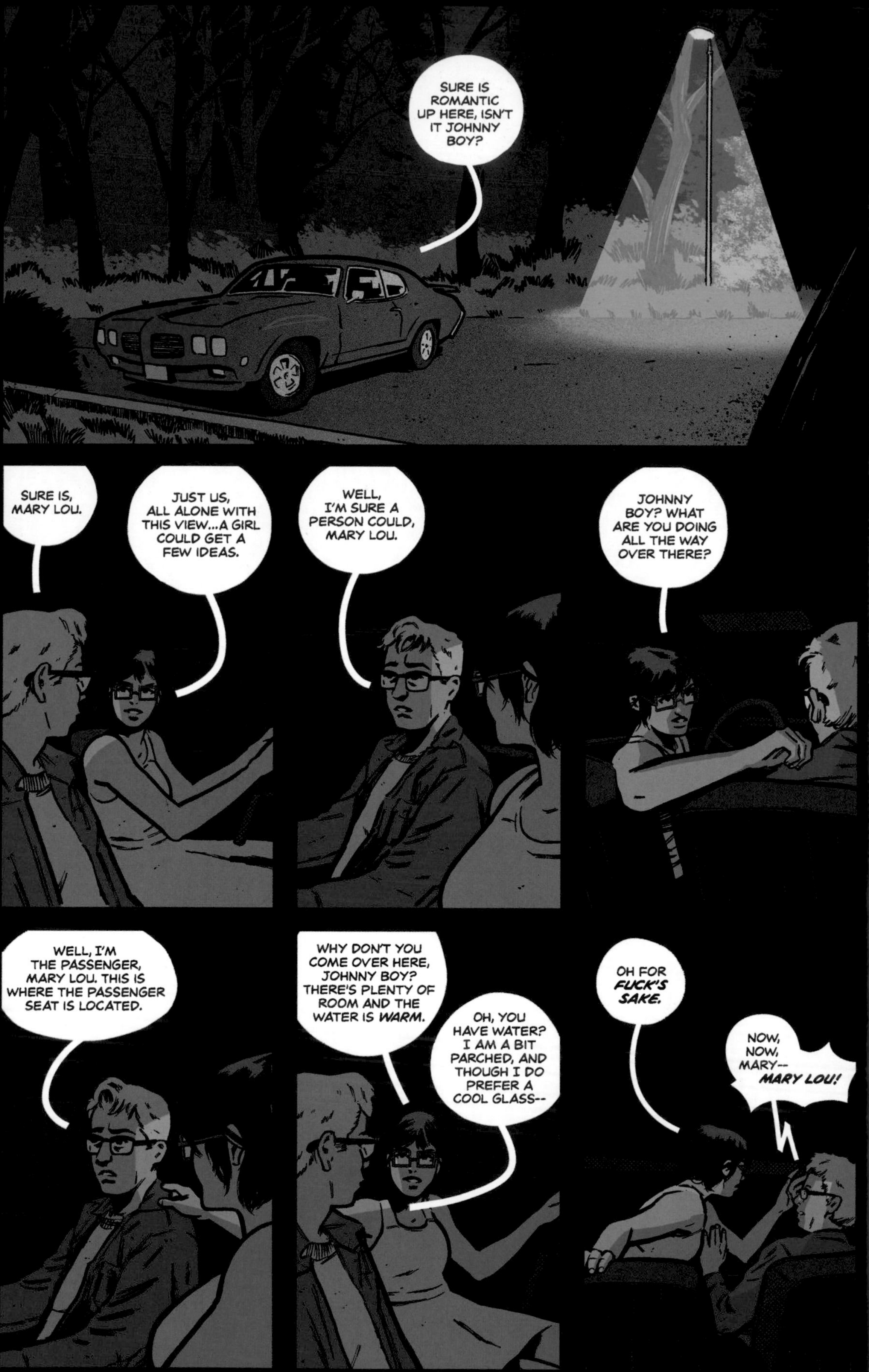
SURE IS ROMANTIC UP HERE, ISN'T IT JOHNNY BOY?
SURE IS, MARY LOU.
JUST US, ALL ALONE WITH THIS VIEW...A GIRL COULD GET A FEW IDEAS.
WELL, I'M SURE A PERSON COULD, MARY LOU.
JOHNNY BOY? WHAT ARE YOU DOING ALL THE WAY OVER THERE?
WELL, I'M THE PASSENGER, MARY LOU. THIS IS WHERE THE PASSENGER SEAT IS LOCATED.
WHY DON'T YOU COME OVER HERE, JOHNNY BOY? THERE'S PLENTY OF ROOM AND THE WATER IS *WARM*.
OH, YOU HAVE WATER? I AM A BIT PARCHED, AND THOUGH I DO PREFER A COOL GLASS--
OH FOR ***FUCK'S SAKE.***
NOW, NOW, MARY-- ***MARY LOU!***

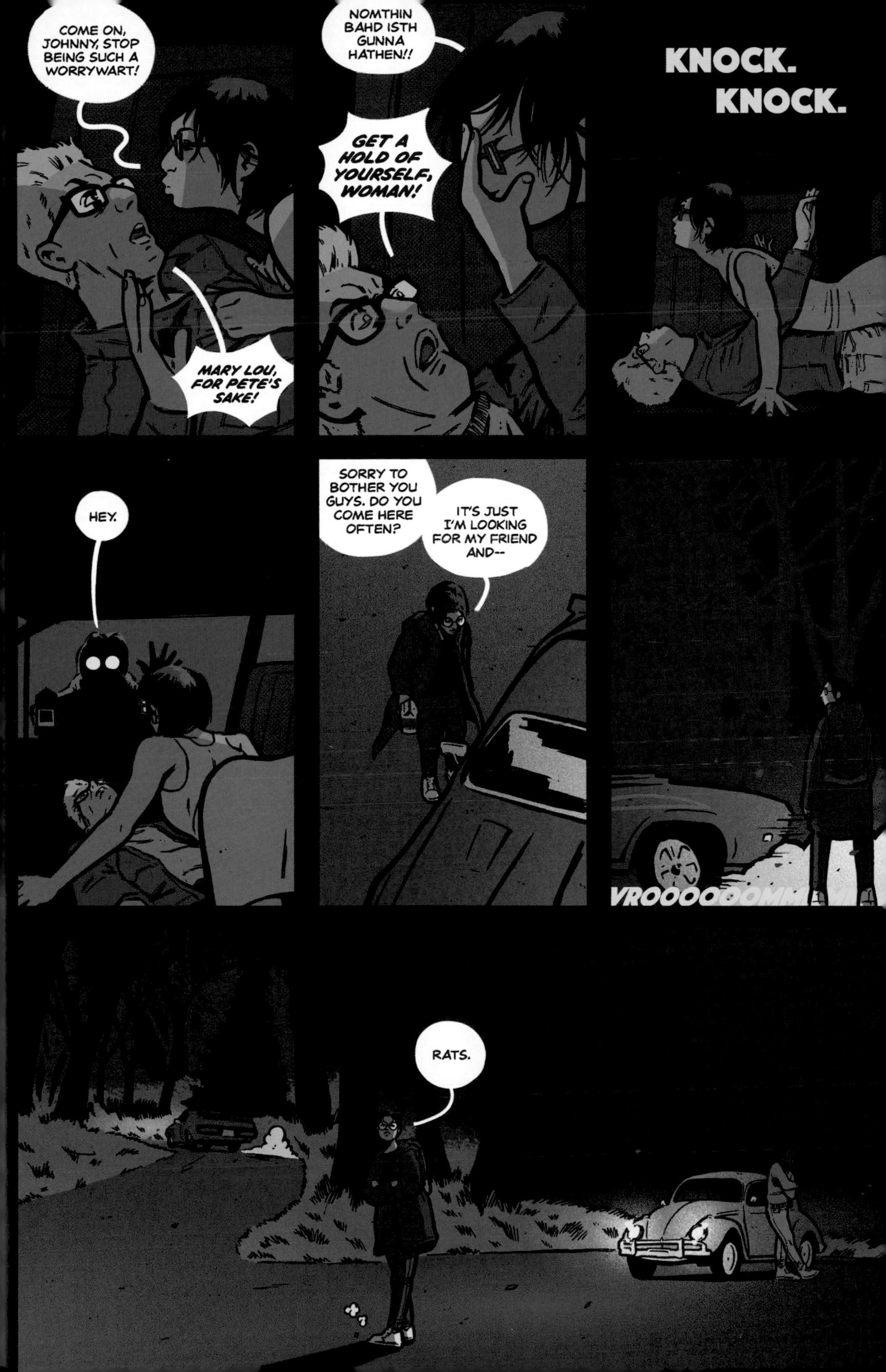
COME ON, JOHNNY, STOP BEING SUCH A WORRYWART!
MARY LOU, FOR PETE'S SAKE!
NOMTHIN BAHD ISTH GUNNA HATHEN!!
GET A HOLD OF YOURSELF, WOMAN!
KNOCK.
KNOCK.
HEY.
SORRY TO BOTHER YOU GUYS. DO YOU COME HERE OFTEN?
IT'S JUST I'M LOOKING FOR MY FRIEND AND--
VROOOOOOMM
RATS.

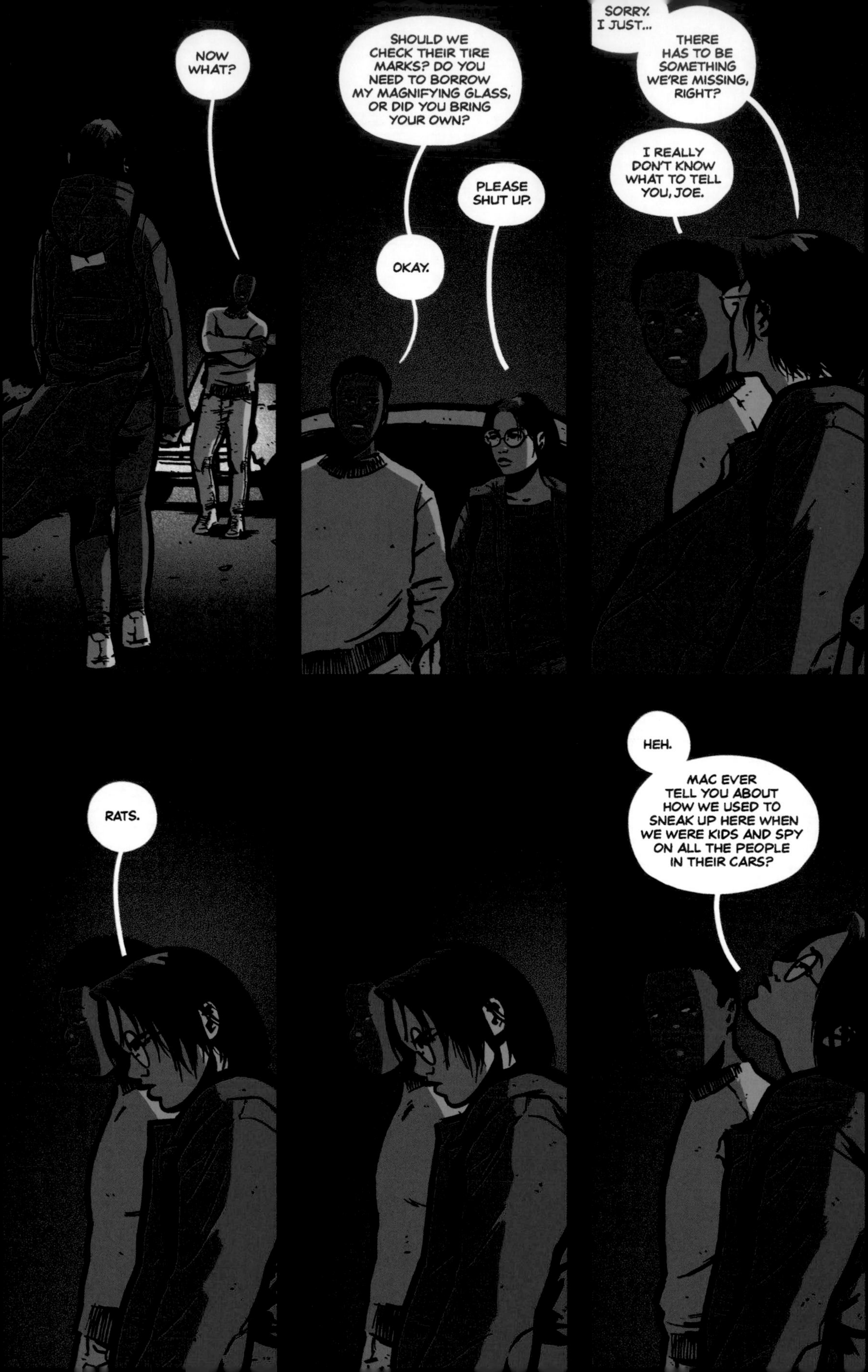
NOW WHAT?
SHOULD WE CHECK THEIR TIRE MARKS? DO YOU NEED TO BORROW MY MAGNIFYING GLASS, OR DID YOU BRING YOUR OWN?
OKAY.
PLEASE SHUT UP.
SORRY. I JUST...
THERE HAS TO BE SOMETHING WE'RE MISSING, RIGHT?
I REALLY DON'T KNOW WHAT TO TELL YOU, JOE.
RATS.
HEH.
MAC EVER TELL YOU ABOUT HOW WE USED TO SNEAK UP HERE WHEN WE WERE KIDS AND SPY ON ALL THE PEOPLE IN THEIR CARS?

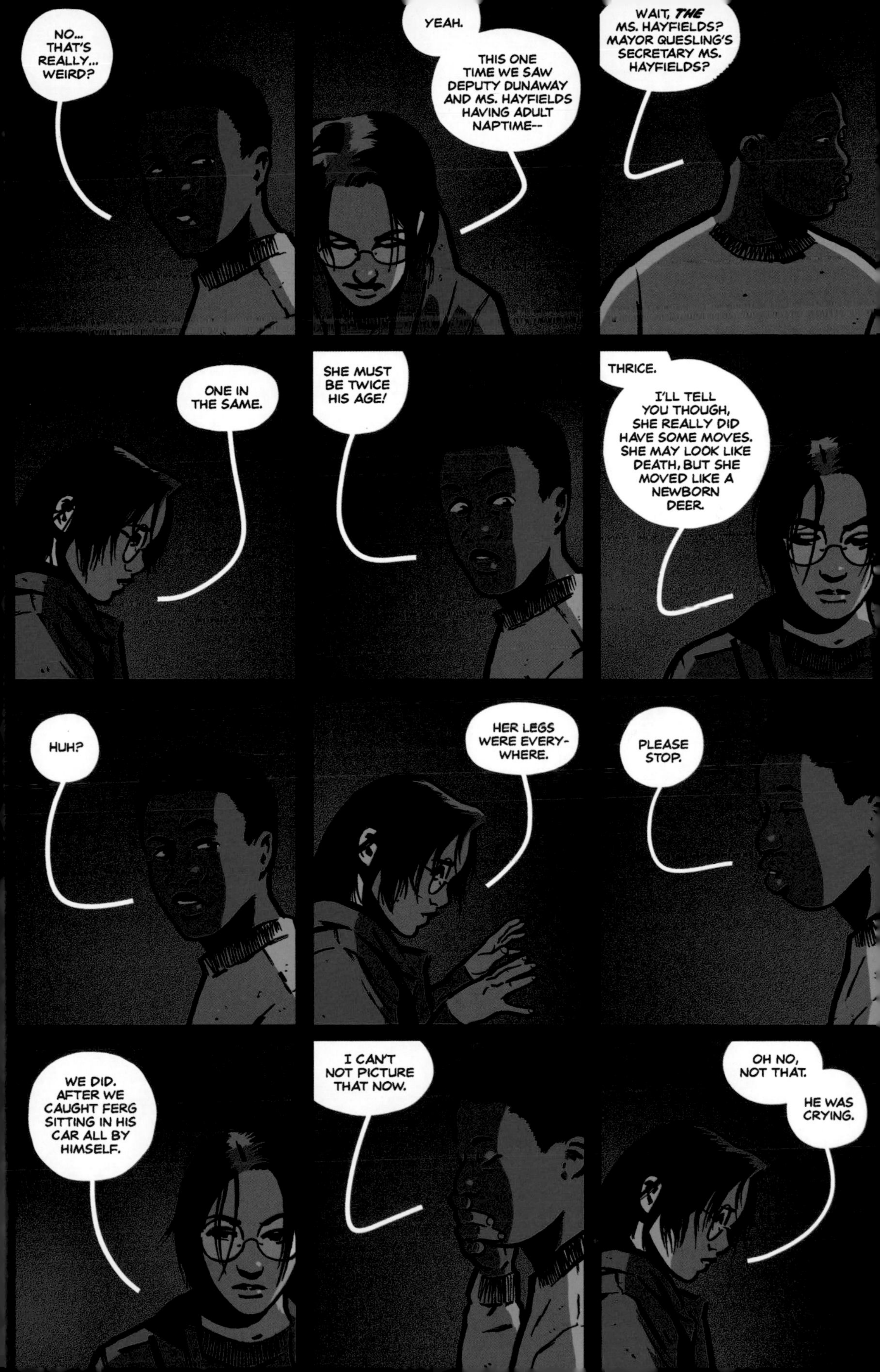
NO... THAT'S REALLY... WEIRD?
YEAH.
THIS ONE TIME WE SAW DEPUTY DUNAWAY AND MS. HAYFIELDS HAVING ADULT NAPTIME--
WAIT, THE MS. HAYFIELDS? MAYOR QUESLING'S SECRETARY MS. HAYFIELDS?
ONE IN THE SAME.
SHE MUST BE TWICE HIS AGE!
THRICE.
I'LL TELL YOU THOUGH, SHE REALLY DID HAVE SOME MOVES. SHE MAY LOOK LIKE DEATH, BUT SHE MOVED LIKE A NEWBORN DEER.
HUH?
HER LEGS WERE EVERY-WHERE.
PLEASE STOP.
WE DID. AFTER WE CAUGHT FERG SITTING IN HIS CAR ALL BY HIMSELF.
I CAN'T NOT PICTURE THAT NOW.
OH NO, NOT THAT.
HE WAS CRYING.

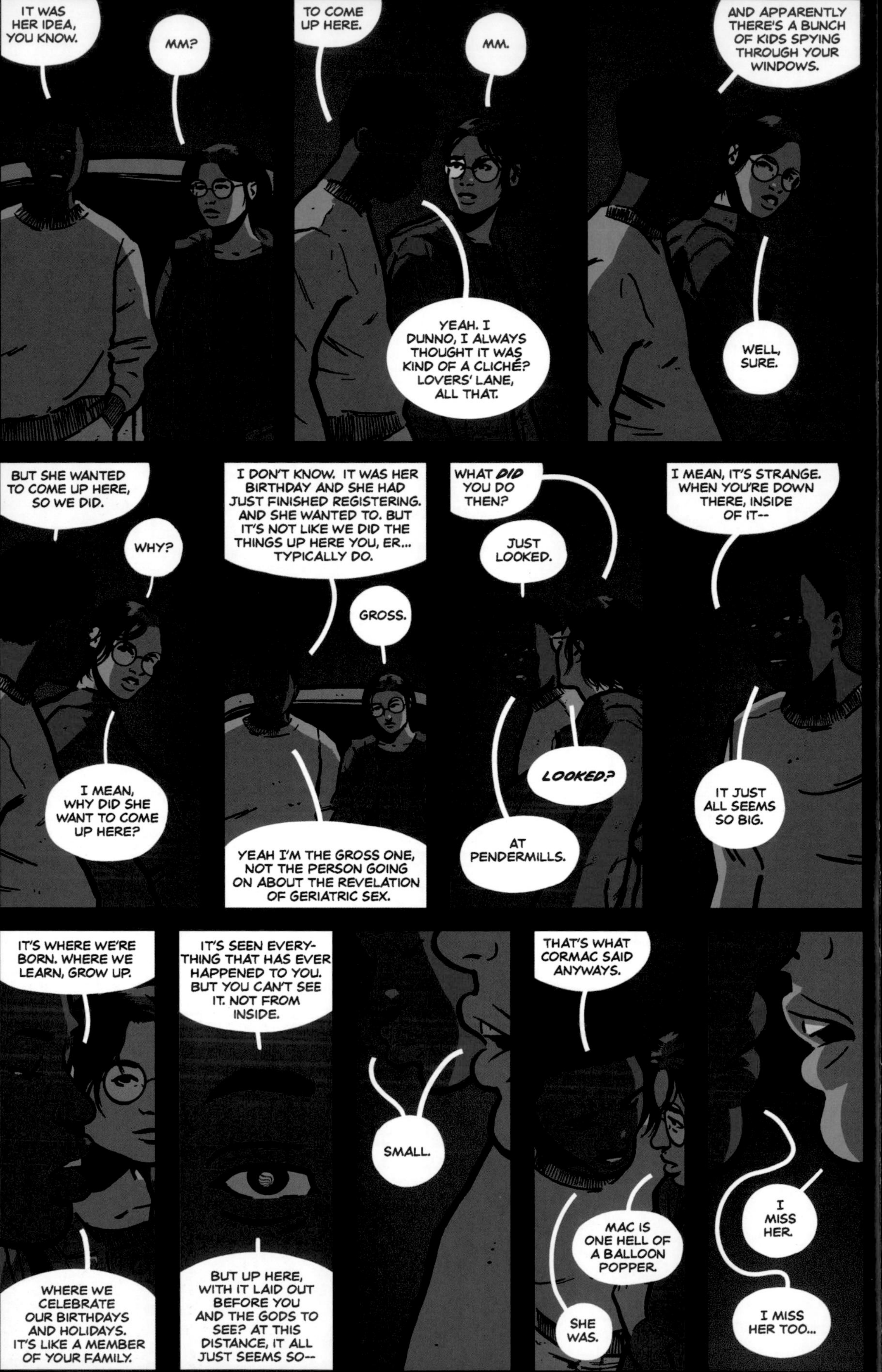

IT WAS HER IDEA, YOU KNOW.
MM?
TO COME UP HERE.
MM.
YEAH. I DUNNO, I ALWAYS THOUGHT IT WAS KIND OF A CLICHÉ? LOVERS' LANE, ALL THAT.
AND APPARENTLY THERE'S A BUNCH OF KIDS SPYING THROUGH YOUR WINDOWS.
WELL, SURE.
BUT SHE WANTED TO COME UP HERE, SO WE DID.
WHY?
I MEAN, WHY DID SHE WANT TO COME UP HERE?
I DON'T KNOW. IT WAS HER BIRTHDAY AND SHE HAD JUST FINISHED REGISTERING. AND SHE WANTED TO. BUT IT'S NOT LIKE WE DID THE THINGS UP HERE YOU, ER... TYPICALLY DO.
GROSS.
YEAH I'M THE GROSS ONE, NOT THE PERSON GOING ON ABOUT THE REVELATION OF GERIATRIC SEX.
WHAT *DID* YOU DO THEN?
JUST LOOKED.
LOOKED?
AT PENDERMILLS.
I MEAN, IT'S STRANGE. WHEN YOU'RE DOWN THERE, INSIDE OF IT--
IT JUST ALL SEEMS SO BIG.
IT'S WHERE WE'RE BORN. WHERE WE LEARN, GROW UP.
WHERE WE CELEBRATE OUR BIRTHDAYS AND HOLIDAYS. IT'S LIKE A MEMBER OF YOUR FAMILY.
IT'S SEEN EVERY-THING THAT HAS EVER HAPPENED TO YOU. BUT YOU CAN'T SEE IT. NOT FROM INSIDE.
BUT UP HERE, WITH IT LAID OUT BEFORE YOU AND THE GODS TO SEE? AT THIS DISTANCE, IT ALL JUST SEEMS SO--
SMALL.
THAT'S WHAT CORMAC SAID ANYWAYS.
MAC IS ONE HELL OF A BALLOON POPPER.
SHE WAS.
I MISS HER.
I MISS HER TOO...

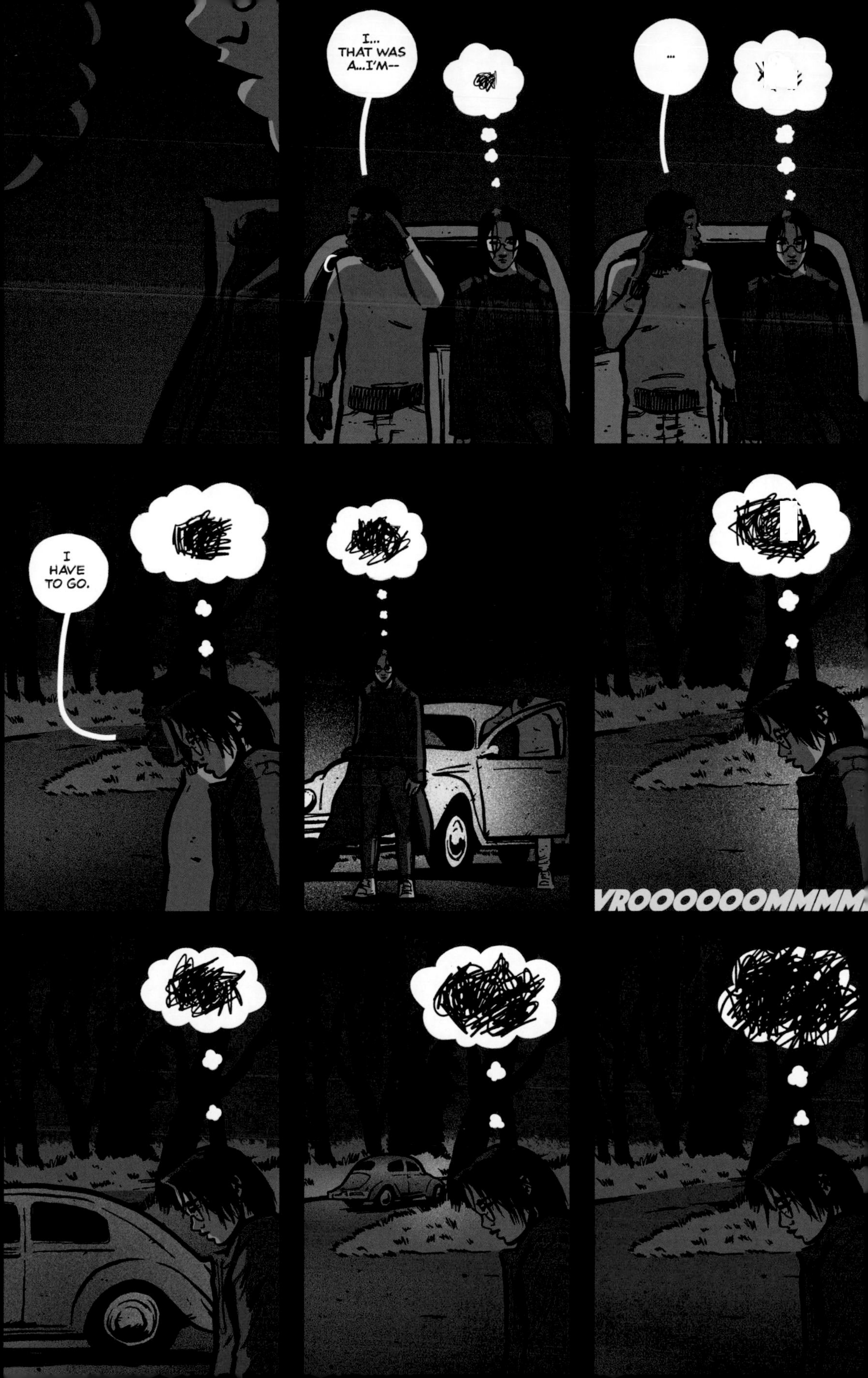
I... THAT WAS A...I'M--
...
I HAVE TO GO.
VROOOOOOMMMM

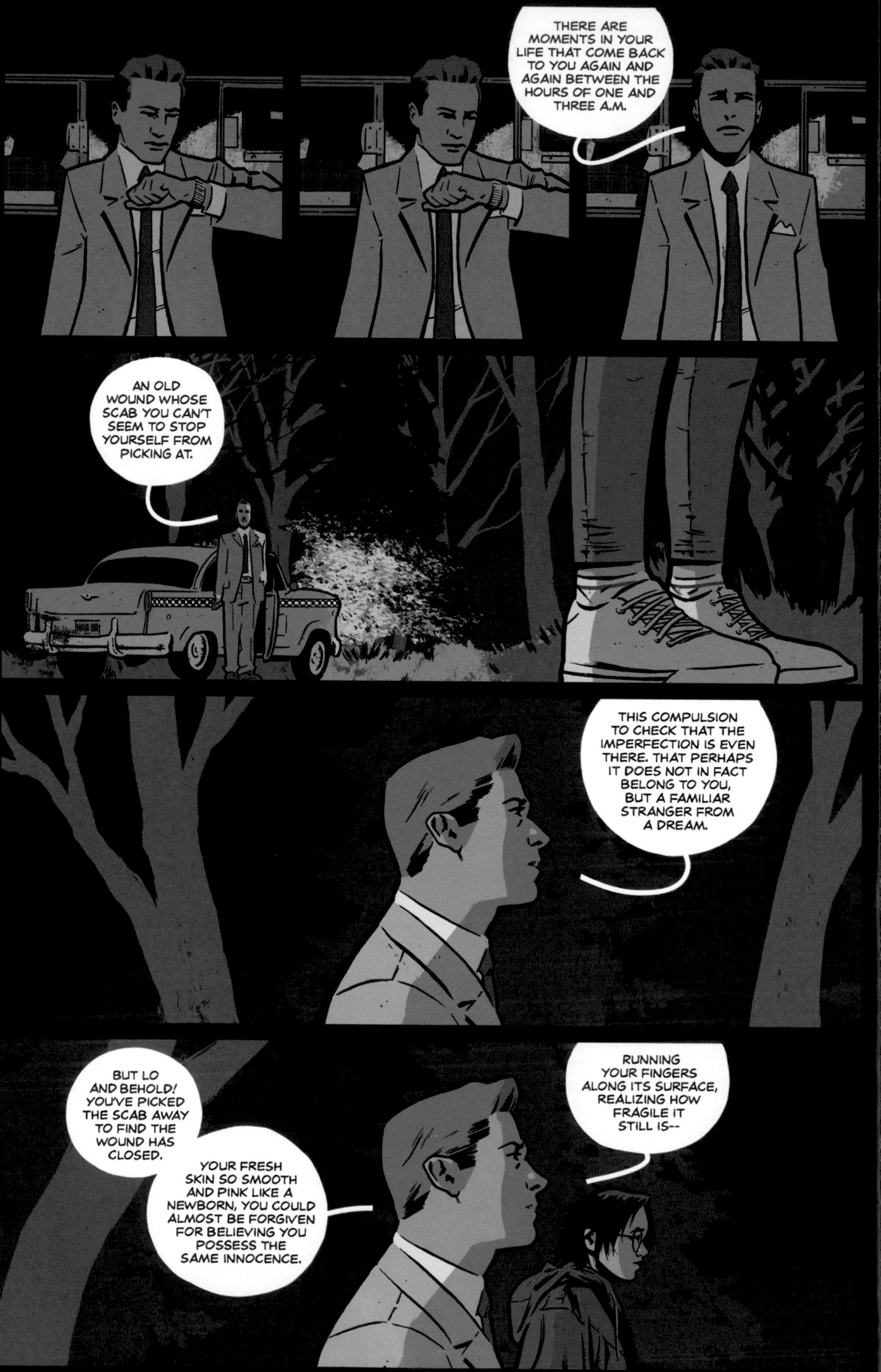
THERE ARE MOMENTS IN YOUR LIFE THAT COME BACK TO YOU AGAIN AND AGAIN BETWEEN THE HOURS OF ONE AND THREE A.M.
AN OLD WOUND WHOSE SCAB YOU CAN'T SEEM TO STOP YOURSELF FROM PICKING AT.
THIS COMPULSION TO CHECK THAT THE IMPERFECTION IS EVEN THERE. THAT PERHAPS IT DOES NOT IN FACT BELONG TO YOU, BUT A FAMILIAR STRANGER FROM A DREAM.
RUNNING YOUR FINGERS ALONG ITS SURFACE, REALIZING HOW FRAGILE IT STILL IS--
BUT LO AND BEHOLD! YOU'VE PICKED THE SCAB AWAY TO FIND THE WOUND HAS CLOSED.
YOUR FRESH SKIN SO SMOOTH AND PINK LIKE A NEWBORN, YOU COULD ALMOST BE FORGIVEN FOR BELIEVING YOU POSSESS THE SAME INNOCENCE.

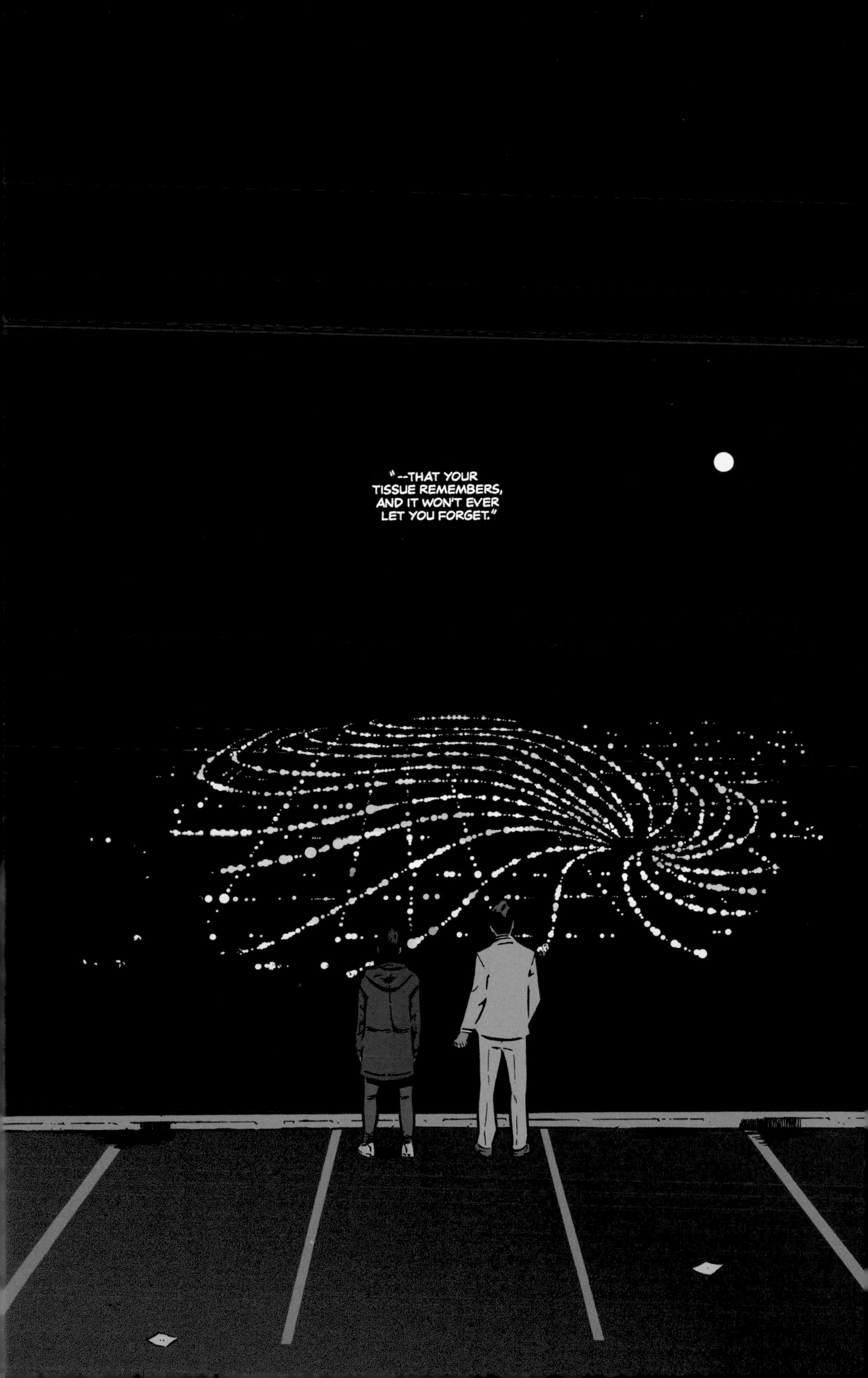
"--THAT YOUR TISSUE REMEMBERS, AND IT WON'T EVER LET YOU FORGET."

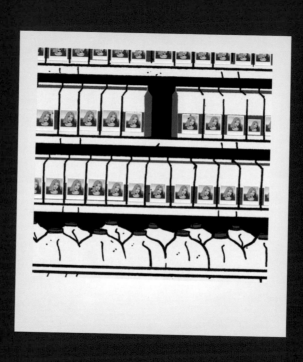

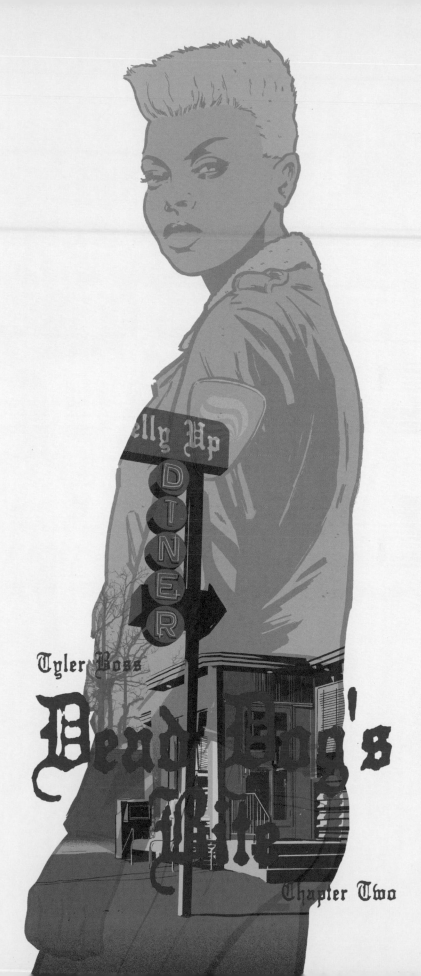

Tyler Boss

Dead Dog's Bite

Chapter Two

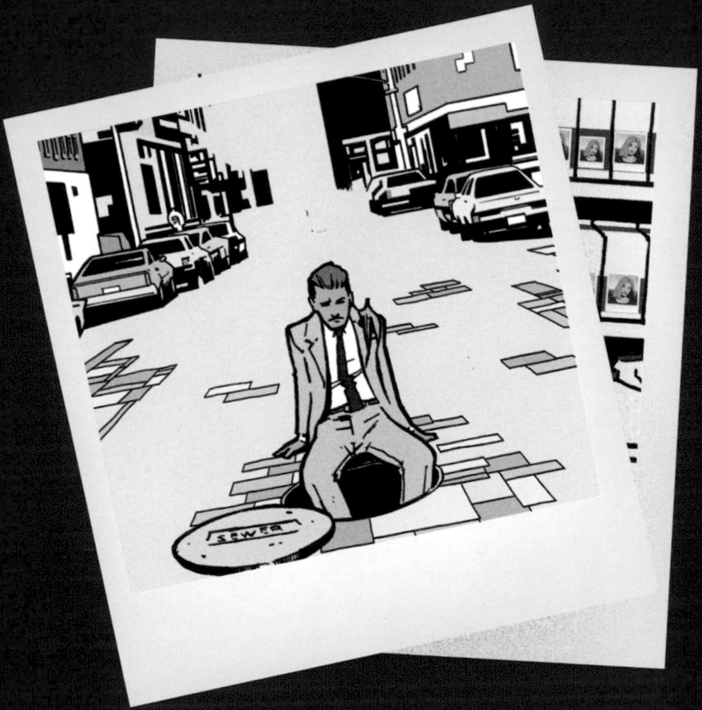
SEWER

"Questions arose.
Like, what in the fuck
was going on here, basically."
--T.P.

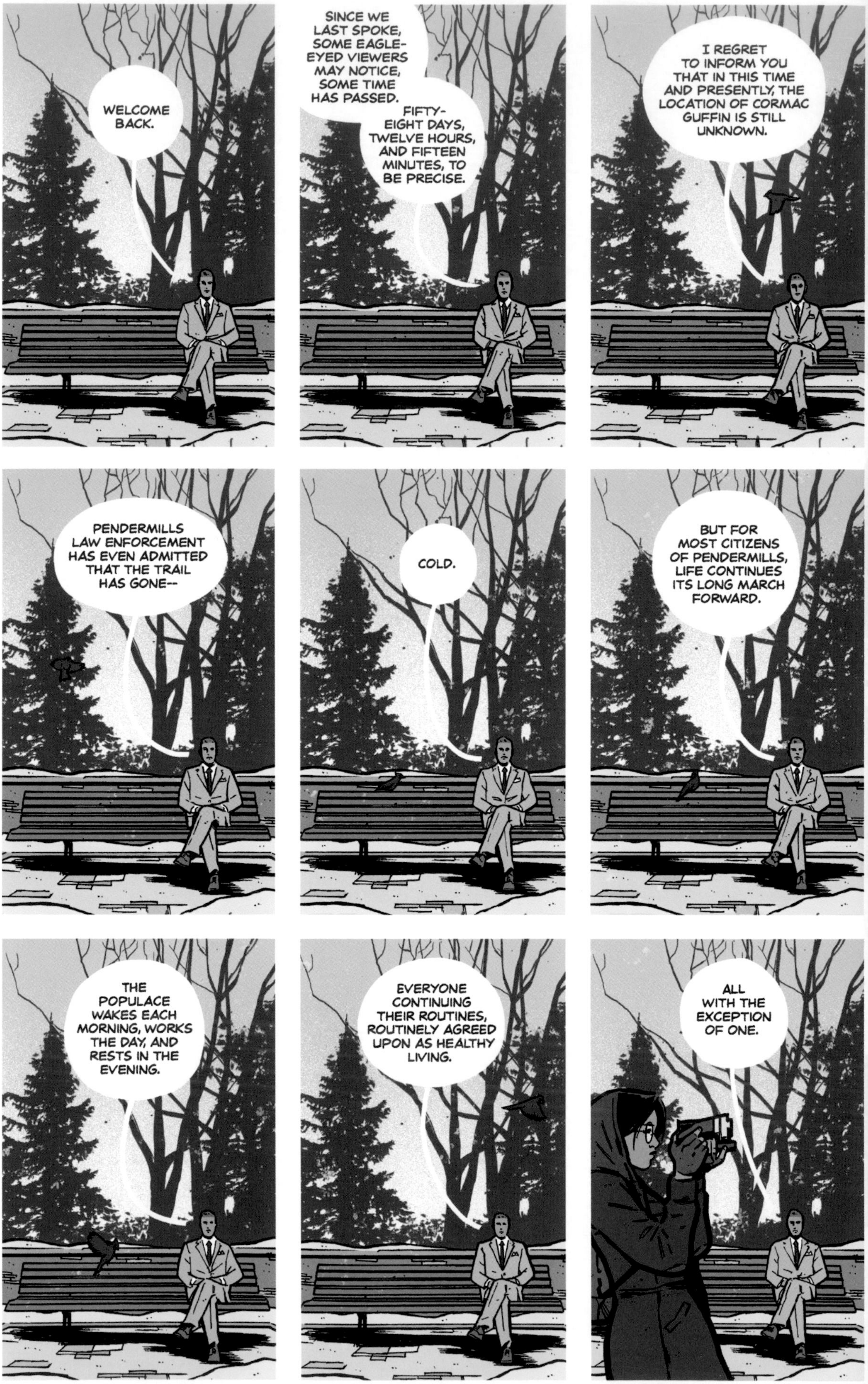
WELCOME BACK.
SINCE WE LAST SPOKE, SOME EAGLE-EYED VIEWERS MAY NOTICE, SOME TIME HAS PASSED.
FIFTY-EIGHT DAYS, TWELVE HOURS, AND FIFTEEN MINUTES, TO BE PRECISE.
I REGRET TO INFORM YOU THAT IN THIS TIME AND PRESENTLY, THE LOCATION OF CORMAC GUFFIN IS STILL UNKNOWN.
PENDERMILLS LAW ENFORCEMENT HAS EVEN ADMITTED THAT THE TRAIL HAS GONE--
COLD.
BUT FOR MOST CITIZENS OF PENDERMILLS, LIFE CONTINUES ITS LONG MARCH FORWARD.
THE POPULACE WAKES EACH MORNING, WORKS THE DAY, AND RESTS IN THE EVENING.
EVERYONE CONTINUING THEIR ROUTINES, ROUTINELY AGREED UPON AS HEALTHY LIVING.
ALL WITH THE EXCEPTION OF ONE.

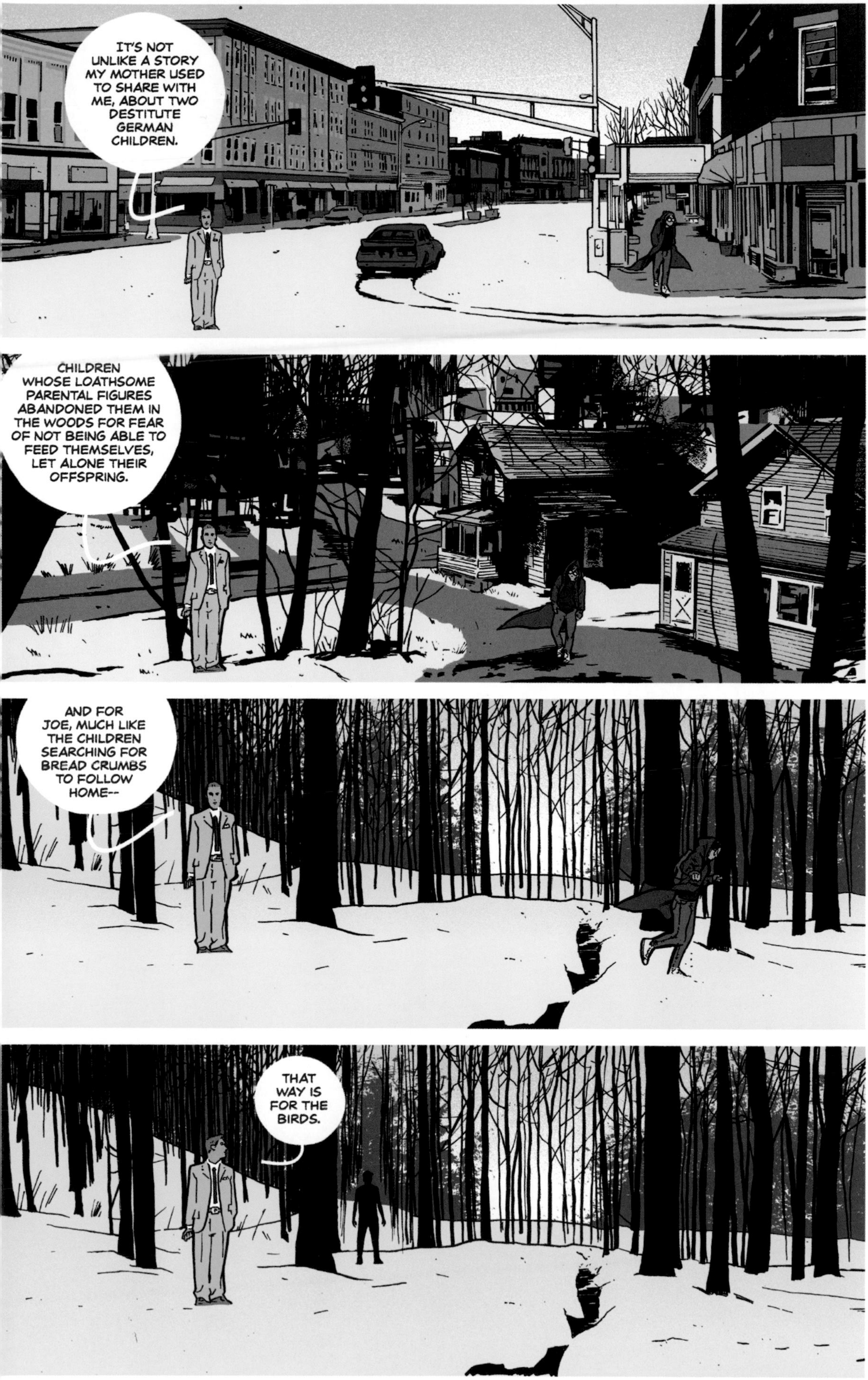
IT'S NOT UNLIKE A STORY MY MOTHER USED TO SHARE WITH ME, ABOUT TWO DESTITUTE GERMAN CHILDREN.
CHILDREN WHOSE LOATHSOME PARENTAL FIGURES ABANDONED THEM IN THE WOODS FOR FEAR OF NOT BEING ABLE TO FEED THEMSELVES, LET ALONE THEIR OFFSPRING.
AND FOR JOE, MUCH LIKE THE CHILDREN SEARCHING FOR BREAD CRUMBS TO FOLLOW HOME--
THAT WAY IS FOR THE BIRDS.

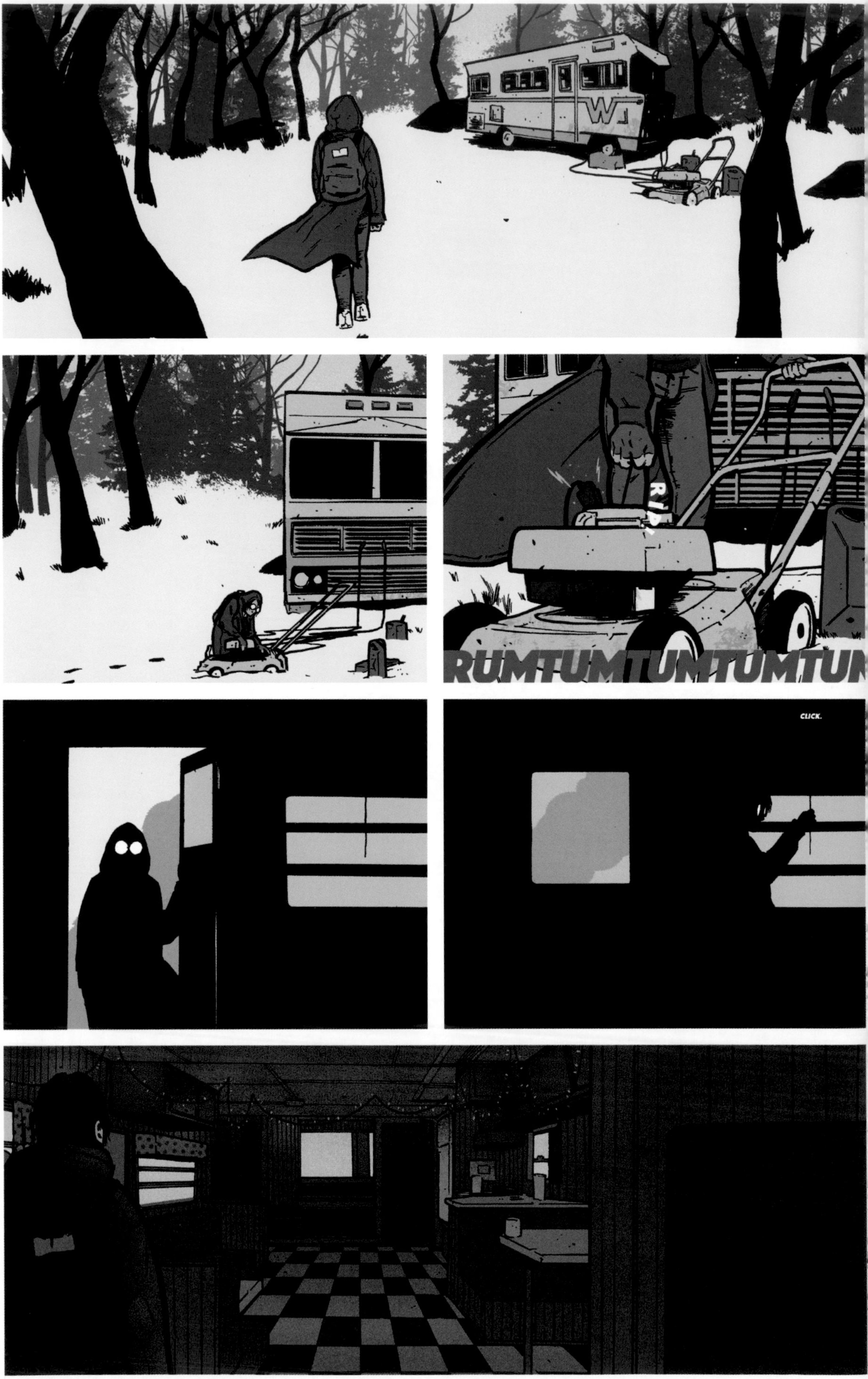
RIP
RUMTUMTUMTUMTU
CLICK.

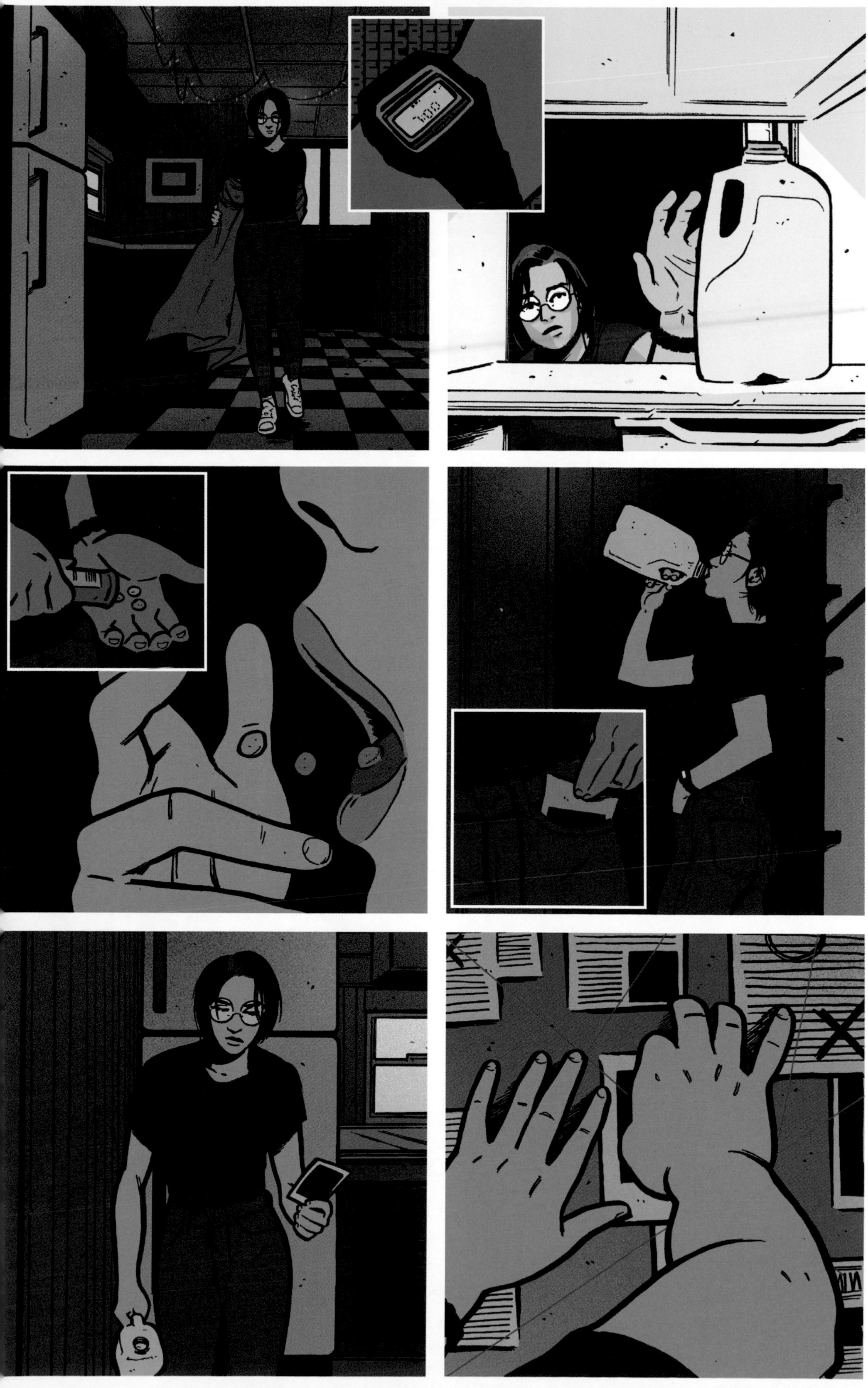

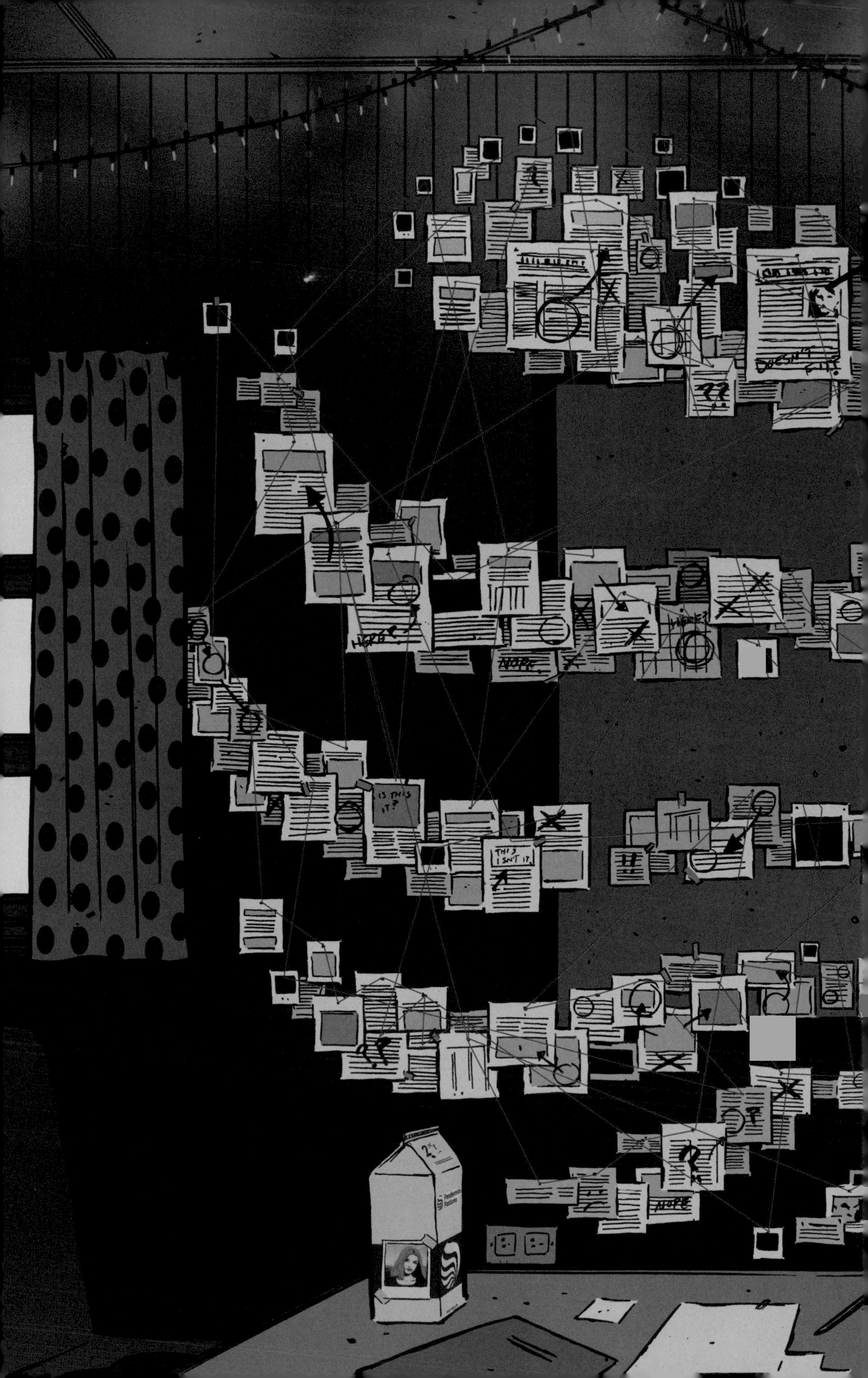
DOESN'T FIT?
??
HERE?
NOPE
HERE?
IS THIS IT?
THIS ISN'T IT.
!!
NOPE

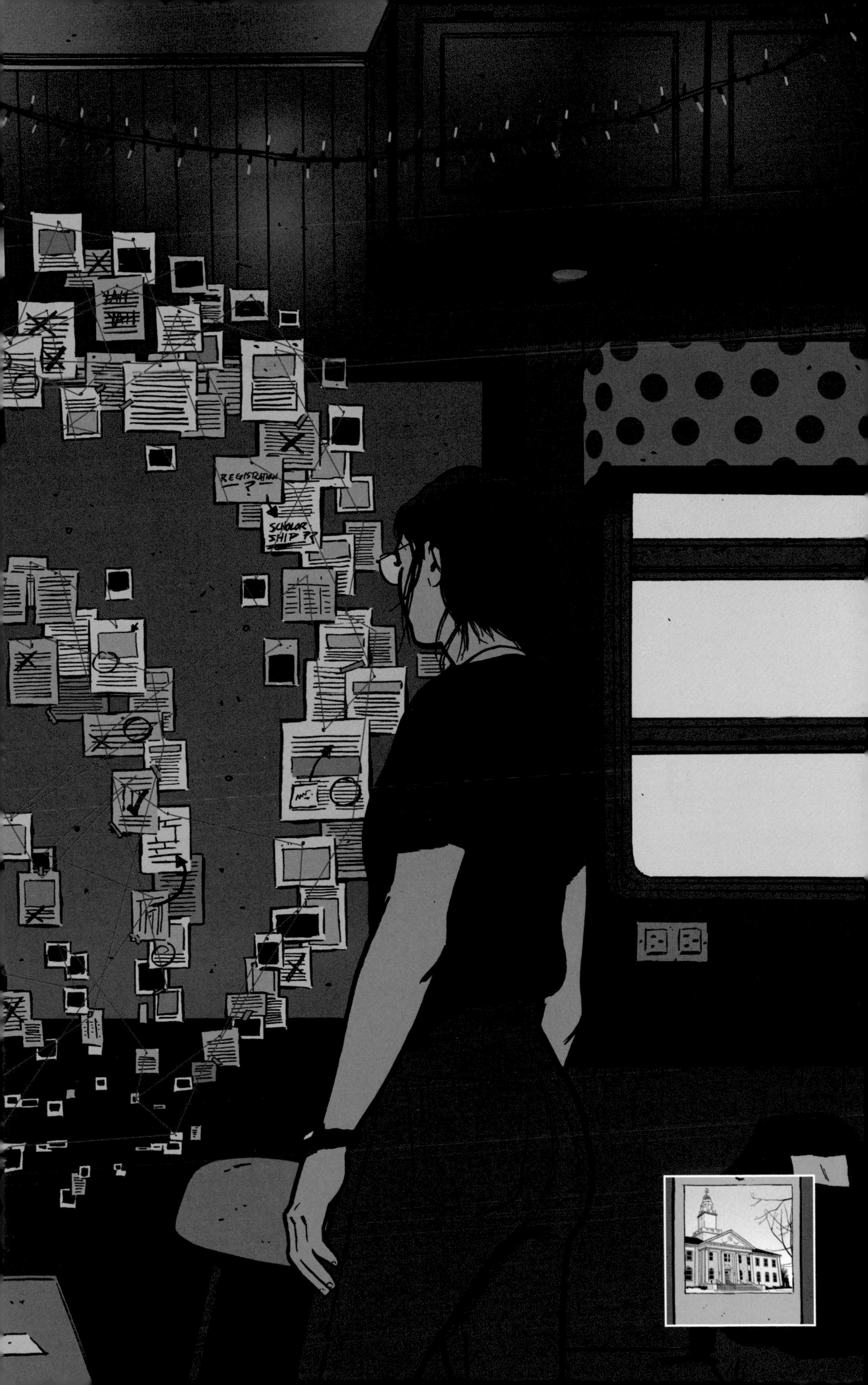
REGISTRATION ?
SCHOLOR SHIP ??

NO, NO, NO, NO, NO, NO, I DON'T THINK SO.

NO.

WHAT DO YOU MEAN, "NO"?

I'M SORRY, YOUNG LADY, BUT THE MAYOR HAS MANY IMPORTANT MATTERS TO ATTEND TO AND THIS DOES NOT CONSTITUTE AN IMPORTANT MATTER.

NOW, MS. HAYFIELDS, BE REASONABLE. THIS IS THE CAMPAIGN TO REELECT MAYOR QUESLING CAMPAIGN WE'RE TALKING ABOUT. SURELY *NOTHING* COULD BE MORE IMPORTANT A MATTER.

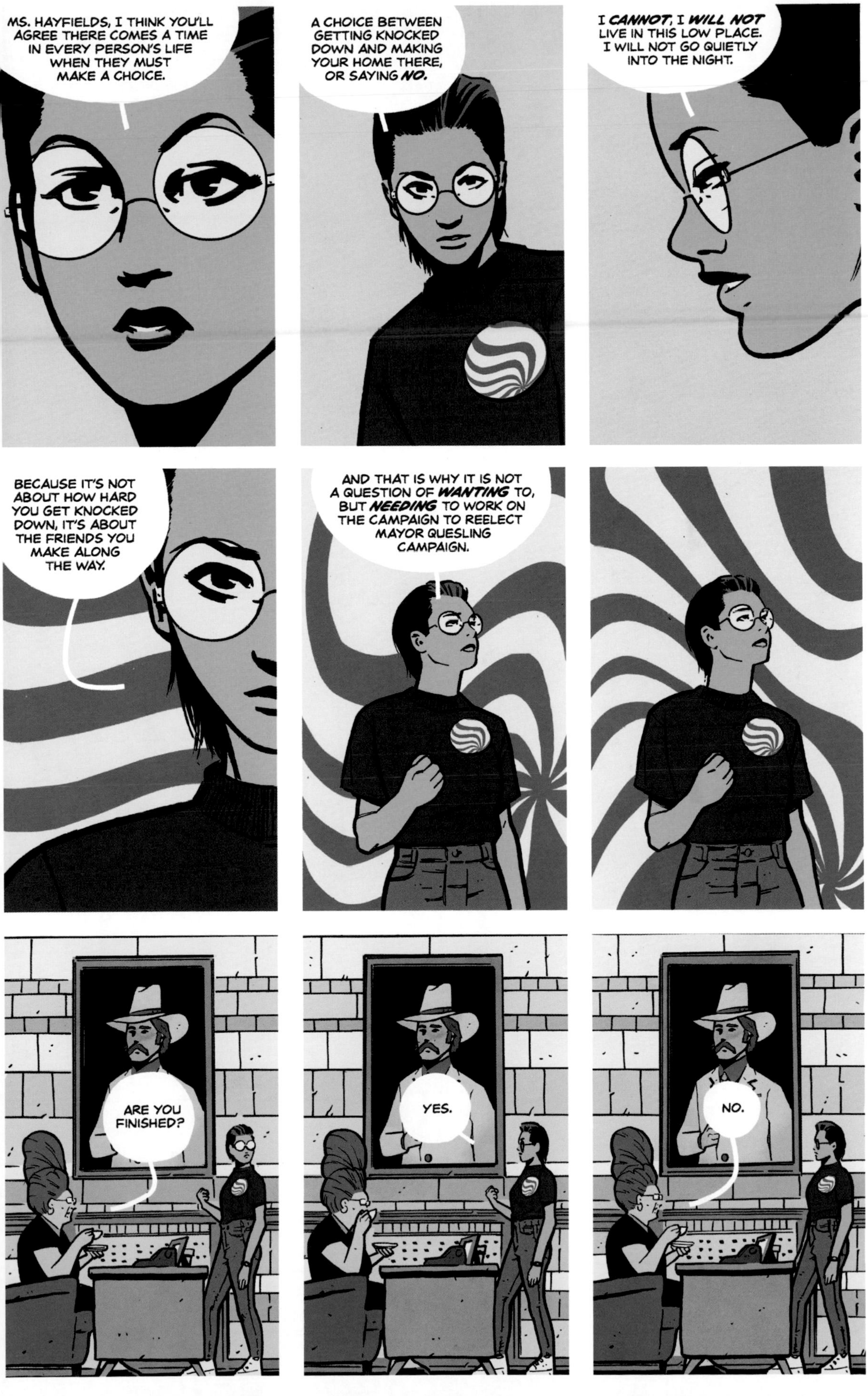
MS. HAYFIELDS, I THINK YOU'LL AGREE THERE COMES A TIME IN EVERY PERSON'S LIFE WHEN THEY MUST MAKE A CHOICE.
A CHOICE BETWEEN GETTING KNOCKED DOWN AND MAKING YOUR HOME THERE, OR SAYING *NO.*
I *CANNOT*, I *WILL NOT* LIVE IN THIS LOW PLACE. I WILL NOT GO QUIETLY INTO THE NIGHT.
BECAUSE IT'S NOT ABOUT HOW HARD YOU GET KNOCKED DOWN, IT'S ABOUT THE FRIENDS YOU MAKE ALONG THE WAY.
AND THAT IS WHY IT IS NOT A QUESTION OF *WANTING* TO, BUT *NEEDING* TO WORK ON THE CAMPAIGN TO REELECT MAYOR QUESLING CAMPAIGN.
ARE YOU FINISHED?
YES.
NO.

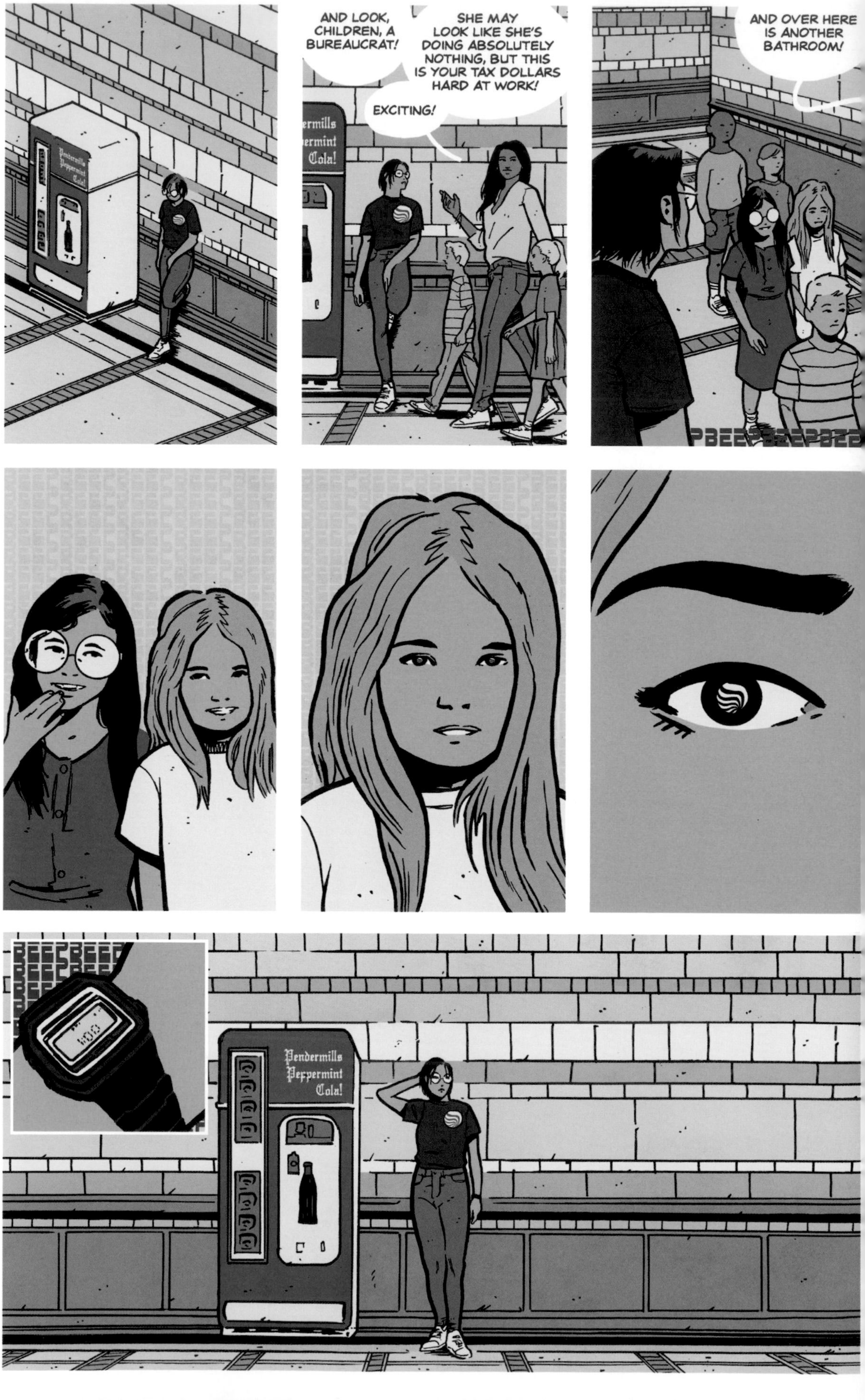

Pendermills Peppermint Cola!
AND LOOK, CHILDREN, A BUREAUCRAT!
SHE MAY LOOK LIKE SHE'S DOING ABSOLUTELY NOTHING, BUT THIS IS YOUR TAX DOLLARS HARD AT WORK!
EXCITING!
AND OVER HERE IS ANOTHER BATHROOM!
BEEP BEEP BEEP
Pendermills Peppermint Cola!

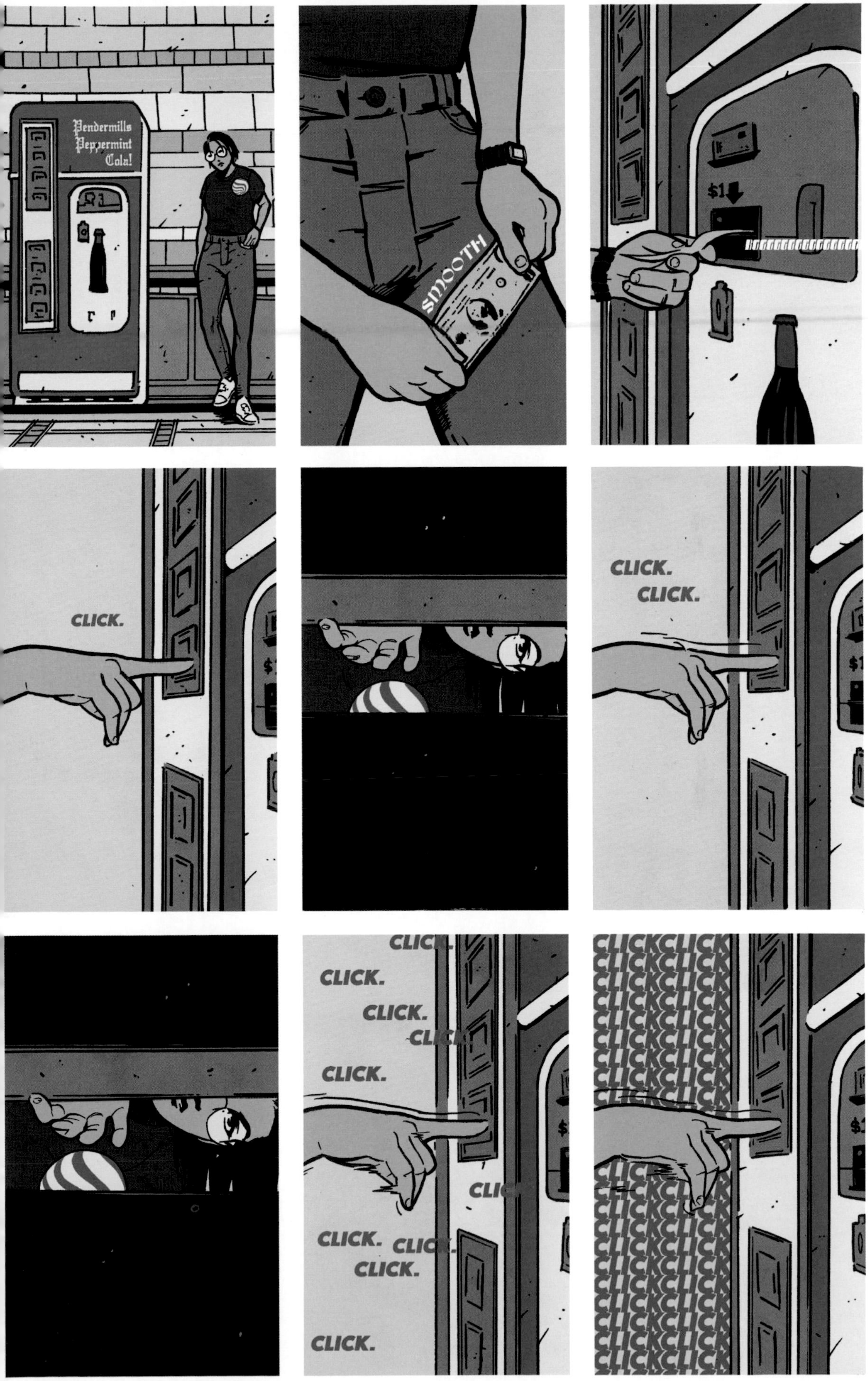
Pendermills
Peppermint
Cola!
SMOOTH
$1
CLICK.
CLICK.
CLICK.
CLICK.
CLICK.
CLICK.
CLICK.
CLICK.
CLICK.
CLICKCLICK

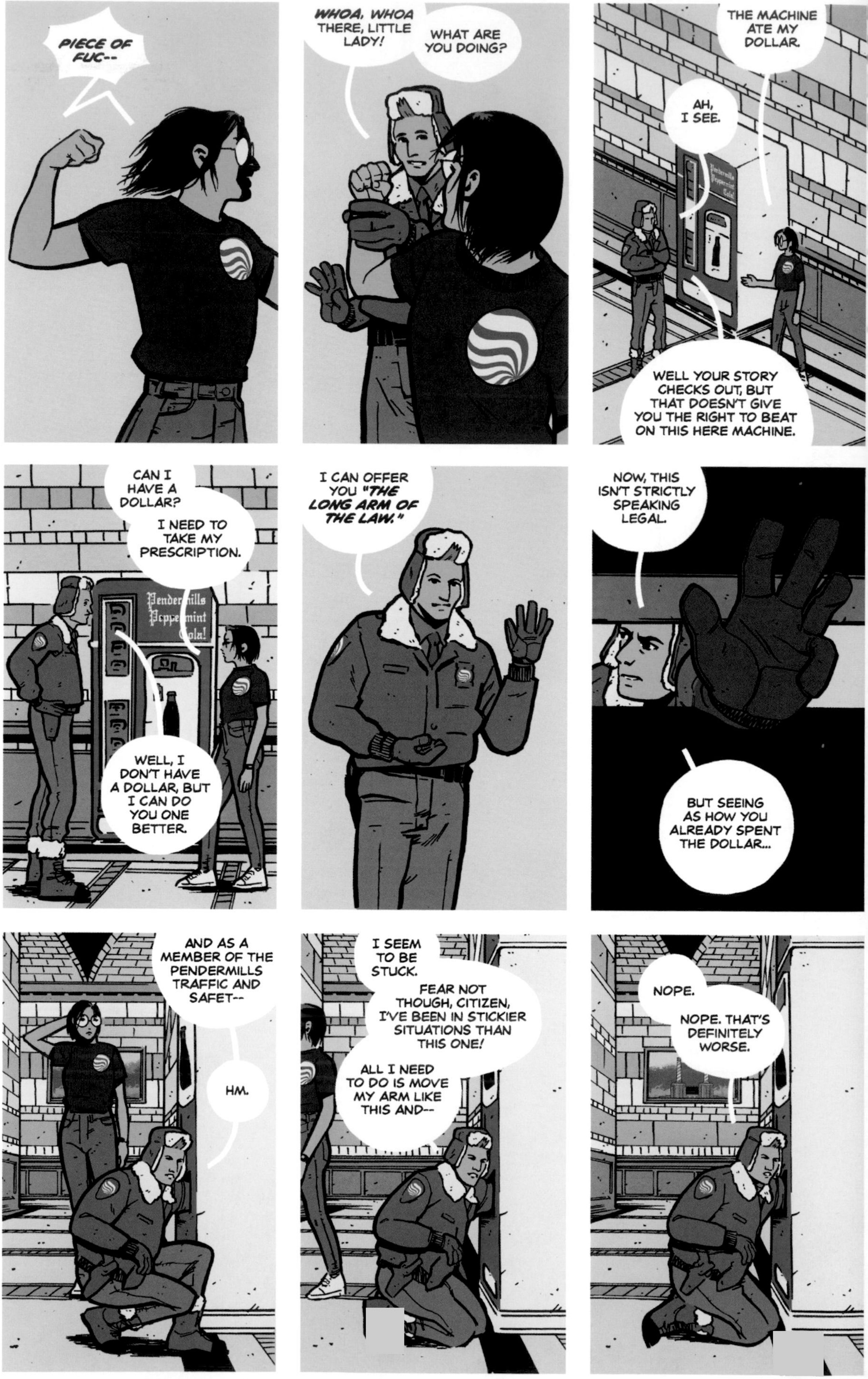
PIECE OF FUC--
WHOA, WHOA THERE, LITTLE LADY!
WHAT ARE YOU DOING?
THE MACHINE ATE MY DOLLAR.
AH, I SEE.
Pendermills Peppermint Cola!
WELL YOUR STORY CHECKS OUT, BUT THAT DOESN'T GIVE YOU THE RIGHT TO BEAT ON THIS HERE MACHINE.
CAN I HAVE A DOLLAR?
I NEED TO TAKE MY PRESCRIPTION.
Pendermills Peppermint Cola!
WELL, I DON'T HAVE A DOLLAR, BUT I CAN DO YOU ONE BETTER.
I CAN OFFER YOU "THE LONG ARM OF THE LAW."
NOW, THIS ISN'T STRICTLY SPEAKING LEGAL.
BUT SEEING AS HOW YOU ALREADY SPENT THE DOLLAR...
AND AS A MEMBER OF THE PENDERMILLS TRAFFIC AND SAFET--
HM.
I SEEM TO BE STUCK.
FEAR NOT THOUGH, CITIZEN, I'VE BEEN IN STICKIER SITUATIONS THAN THIS ONE!
ALL I NEED TO DO IS MOVE MY ARM LIKE THIS AND--
NOPE.
NOPE. THAT'S DEFINITELY WORSE.

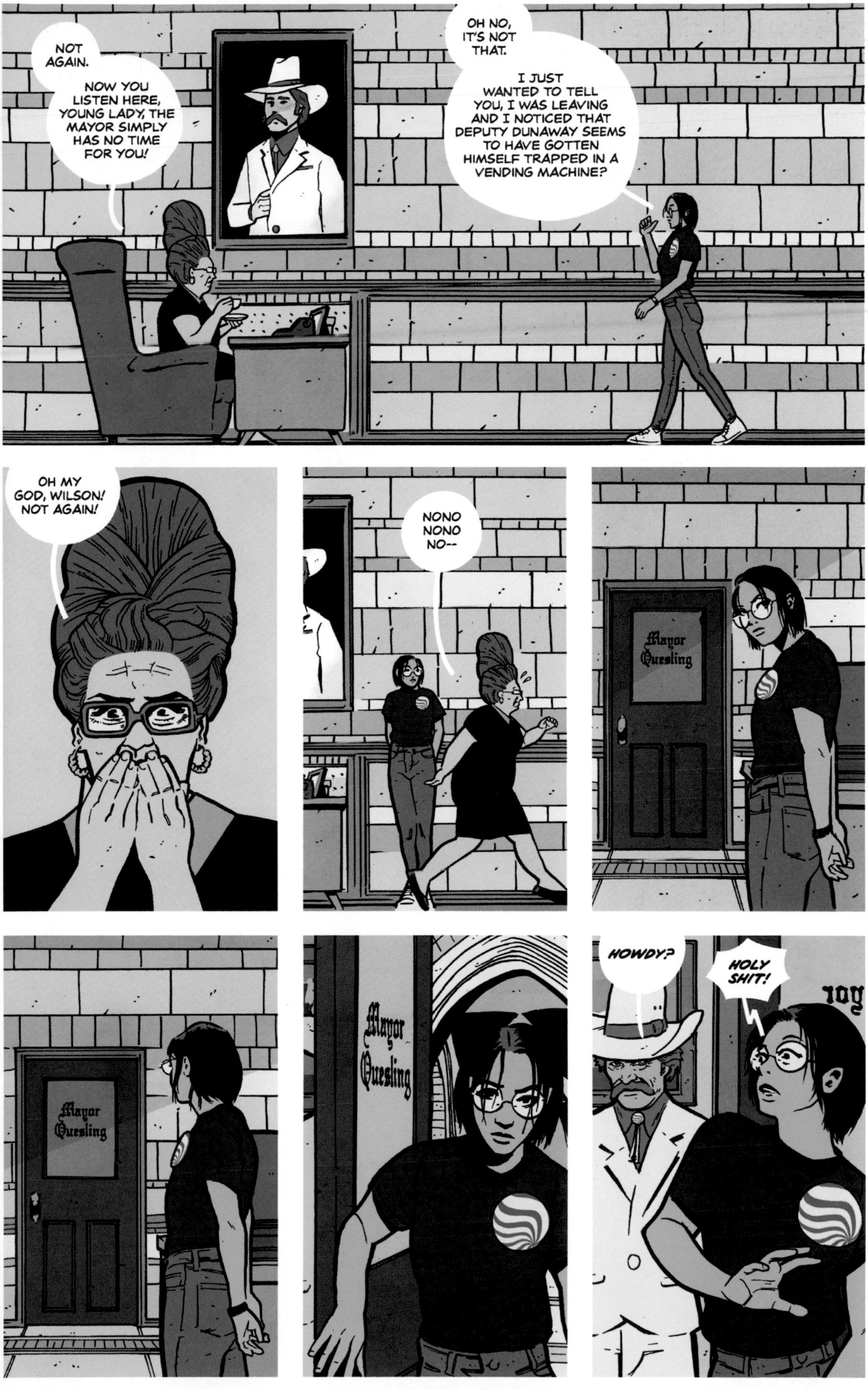
NOT AGAIN.
NOW YOU LISTEN HERE, YOUNG LADY, THE MAYOR SIMPLY HAS NO TIME FOR YOU!
OH NO, IT'S NOT THAT.
I JUST WANTED TO TELL YOU, I WAS LEAVING AND I NOTICED THAT DEPUTY DUNAWAY SEEMS TO HAVE GOTTEN HIMSELF TRAPPED IN A VENDING MACHINE?
OH MY GOD, WILSON! NOT AGAIN!
NONO NONO NO--
Mayor Quesling
Mayor Quesling
Mayor Quesling
HOWDY?
HOLY SHIT!

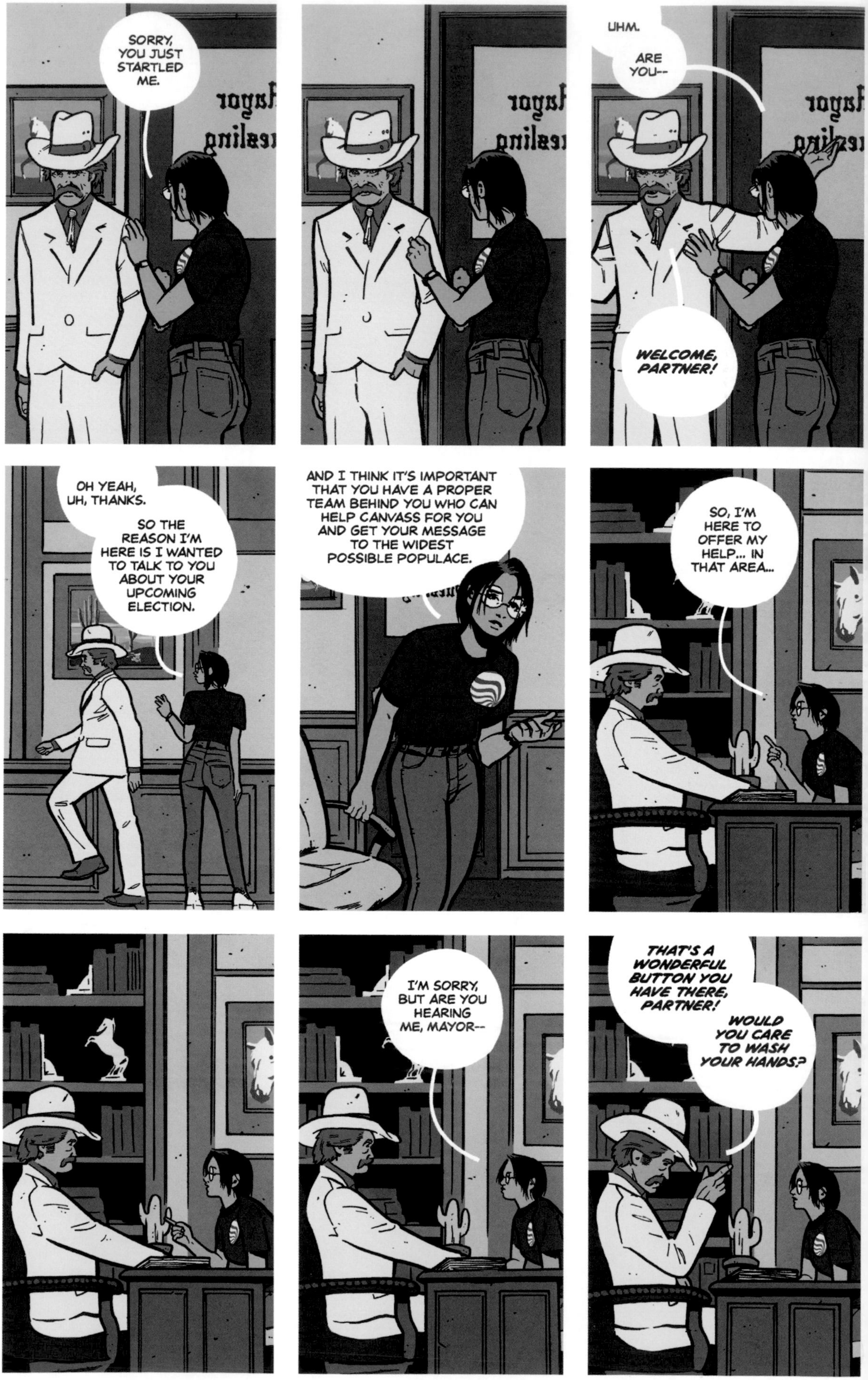
SORRY, YOU JUST STARTLED ME.
UHM.
ARE YOU--
WELCOME, PARTNER!
OH YEAH, UH, THANKS.
SO THE REASON I'M HERE IS I WANTED TO TALK TO YOU ABOUT YOUR UPCOMING ELECTION.
AND I THINK IT'S IMPORTANT THAT YOU HAVE A PROPER TEAM BEHIND YOU WHO CAN HELP CANVASS FOR YOU AND GET YOUR MESSAGE TO THE WIDEST POSSIBLE POPULACE.
SO, I'M HERE TO OFFER MY HELP... IN THAT AREA...
I'M SORRY, BUT ARE YOU HEARING ME, MAYOR--
THAT'S A WONDERFUL BUTTON YOU HAVE THERE, PARTNER!
WOULD YOU CARE TO WASH YOUR HANDS?

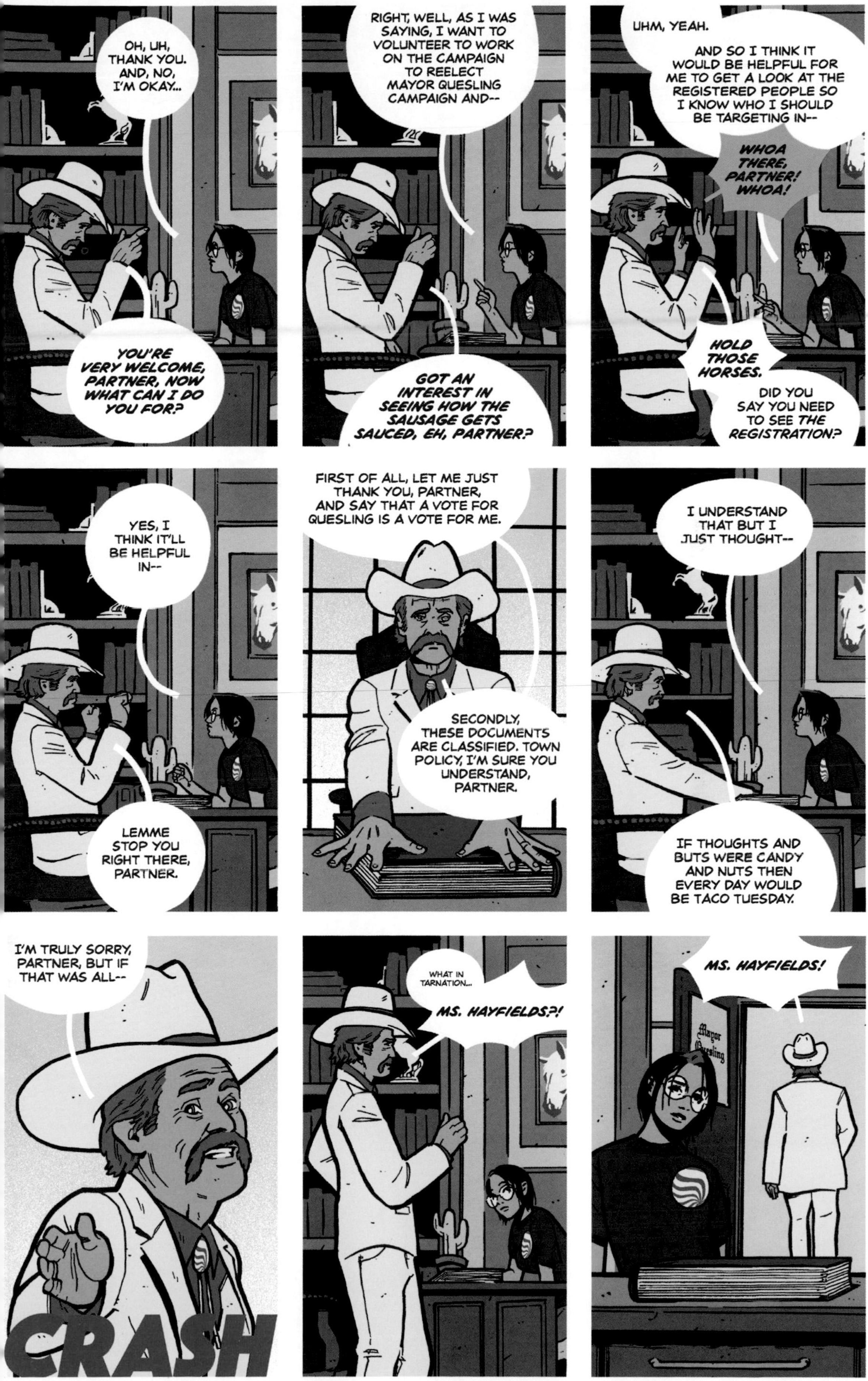
OH, UH, THANK YOU. AND, NO, I'M OKAY...
YOU'RE VERY WELCOME, PARTNER, NOW WHAT CAN I DO YOU FOR?
RIGHT, WELL, AS I WAS SAYING, I WANT TO VOLUNTEER TO WORK ON THE CAMPAIGN TO REELECT MAYOR QUESLING CAMPAIGN AND--
GOT AN INTEREST IN SEEING HOW THE SAUSAGE GETS SAUCED, EH, PARTNER?
UHM, YEAH.
AND SO I THINK IT WOULD BE HELPFUL FOR ME TO GET A LOOK AT THE REGISTERED PEOPLE SO I KNOW WHO I SHOULD BE TARGETING IN--
WHOA THERE, PARTNER! WHOA!
HOLD THOSE HORSES.
DID YOU SAY YOU NEED TO SEE THE REGISTRATION?
YES, I THINK IT'LL BE HELPFUL IN--
LEMME STOP YOU RIGHT THERE, PARTNER.
FIRST OF ALL, LET ME JUST THANK YOU, PARTNER, AND SAY THAT A VOTE FOR QUESLING IS A VOTE FOR ME.
SECONDLY, THESE DOCUMENTS ARE CLASSIFIED. TOWN POLICY, I'M SURE YOU UNDERSTAND, PARTNER.
I UNDERSTAND THAT BUT I JUST THOUGHT--
IF THOUGHTS AND BUTS WERE CANDY AND NUTS THEN EVERY DAY WOULD BE TACO TUESDAY.
I'M TRULY SORRY, PARTNER, BUT IF THAT WAS ALL--
CRASH
WHAT IN TARNATION...
MS. HAYFIELDS?!
MS. HAYFIELDS!
Mayor Quesling

Registration Ledger Volume XIII
HEY, MAC.
BINGO.

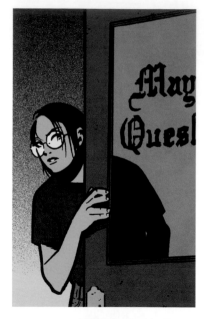

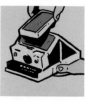

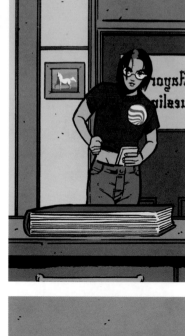

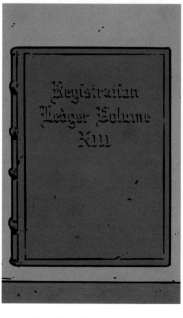

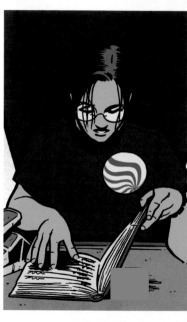

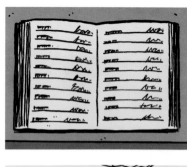

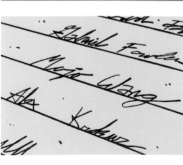

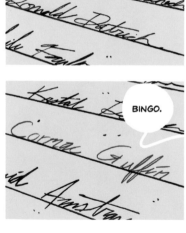

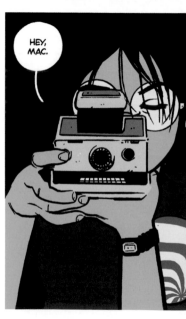

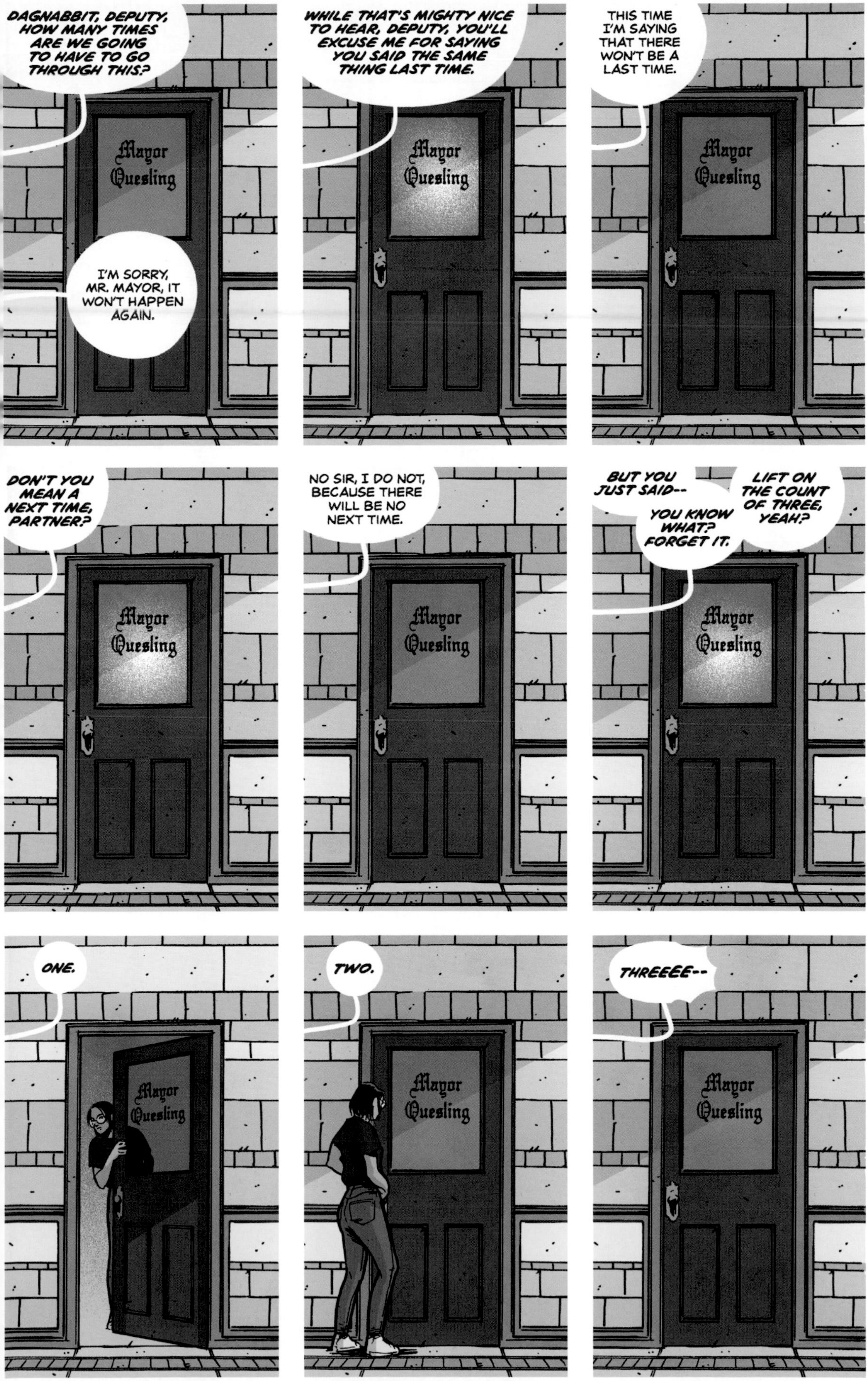
DAGNABBIT, DEPUTY, HOW MANY TIMES ARE WE GOING TO HAVE TO GO THROUGH THIS?
Mayor Quesling
I'M SORRY, MR. MAYOR, IT WON'T HAPPEN AGAIN.
WHILE THAT'S MIGHTY NICE TO HEAR, DEPUTY, YOU'LL EXCUSE ME FOR SAYING YOU SAID THE SAME THING LAST TIME.
THIS TIME I'M SAYING THAT THERE WON'T BE A LAST TIME.
DON'T YOU MEAN A NEXT TIME, PARTNER?
NO SIR, I DO NOT, BECAUSE THERE WILL BE NO NEXT TIME.
BUT YOU JUST SAID--
YOU KNOW WHAT? FORGET IT.
LIFT ON THE COUNT OF THREE, YEAH?
ONE.
TWO.
THREEEE--

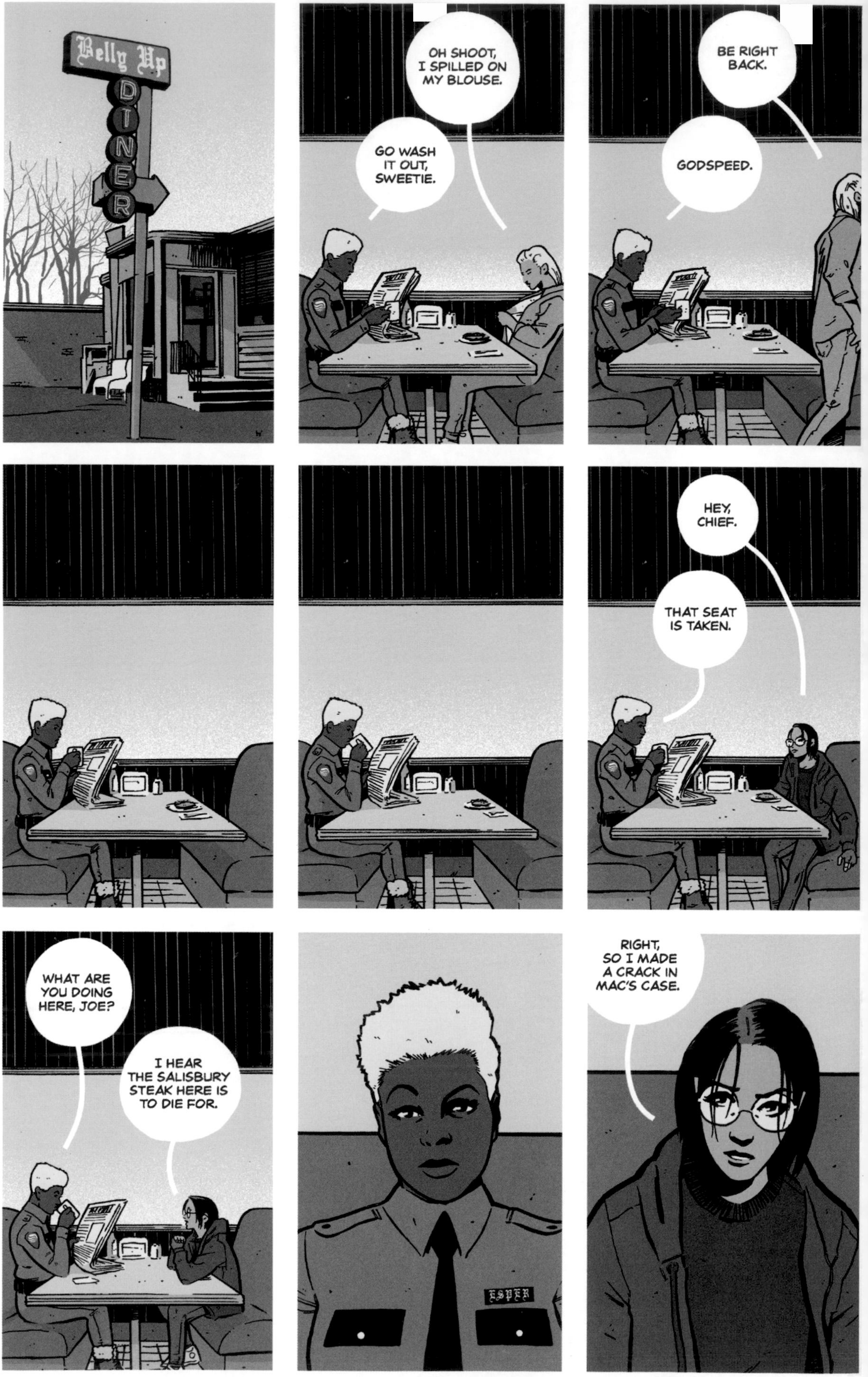
Belly Up
DINER
OH SHOOT, I SPILLED ON MY BLOUSE.
GO WASH IT OUT, SWEETIE.
BE RIGHT BACK.
GODSPEED.
HEY, CHIEF.
THAT SEAT IS TAKEN.
WHAT ARE YOU DOING HERE, JOE?
I HEAR THE SALISBURY STEAK HERE IS TO DIE FOR.
ESPER
RIGHT, SO I MADE A CRACK IN MAC'S CASE.

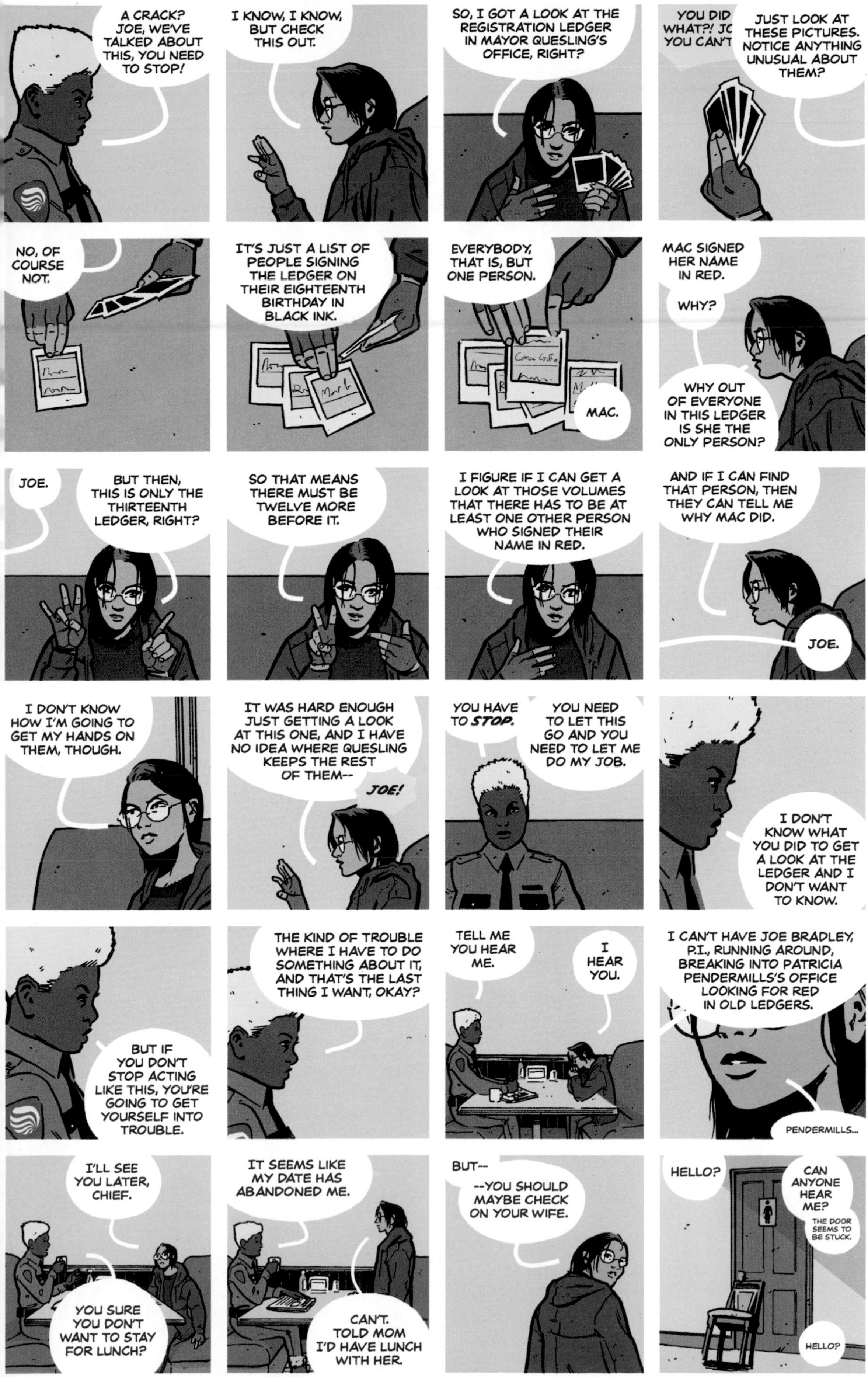

A CRACK? JOE, WE'VE TALKED ABOUT THIS, YOU NEED TO STOP!
I KNOW, I KNOW, BUT CHECK THIS OUT.
SO, I GOT A LOOK AT THE REGISTRATION LEDGER IN MAYOR QUESLING'S OFFICE, RIGHT?
YOU DID WHAT?! JO YOU CAN'T
JUST LOOK AT THESE PICTURES. NOTICE ANYTHING UNUSUAL ABOUT THEM?
NO, OF COURSE NOT.
IT'S JUST A LIST OF PEOPLE SIGNING THE LEDGER ON THEIR EIGHTEENTH BIRTHDAY IN BLACK INK.
EVERYBODY, THAT IS, BUT ONE PERSON.
MAC.
MAC SIGNED HER NAME IN RED.
WHY?
WHY OUT OF EVERYONE IN THIS LEDGER IS SHE THE ONLY PERSON?
JOE.
BUT THEN, THIS IS ONLY THE THIRTEENTH LEDGER, RIGHT?
SO THAT MEANS THERE MUST BE TWELVE MORE BEFORE IT.
I FIGURE IF I CAN GET A LOOK AT THOSE VOLUMES THAT THERE HAS TO BE AT LEAST ONE OTHER PERSON WHO SIGNED THEIR NAME IN RED.
AND IF I CAN FIND THAT PERSON, THEN THEY CAN TELL ME WHY MAC DID.
JOE.
I DON'T KNOW HOW I'M GOING TO GET MY HANDS ON THEM, THOUGH.
IT WAS HARD ENOUGH JUST GETTING A LOOK AT THIS ONE, AND I HAVE NO IDEA WHERE QUESLING KEEPS THE REST OF THEM--
JOE!
YOU HAVE TO STOP.
YOU NEED TO LET THIS GO AND YOU NEED TO LET ME DO MY JOB.
I DON'T KNOW WHAT YOU DID TO GET A LOOK AT THE LEDGER AND I DON'T WANT TO KNOW.
BUT IF YOU DON'T STOP ACTING LIKE THIS, YOU'RE GOING TO GET YOURSELF INTO TROUBLE.
THE KIND OF TROUBLE WHERE I HAVE TO DO SOMETHING ABOUT IT, AND THAT'S THE LAST THING I WANT, OKAY?
TELL ME YOU HEAR ME.
I HEAR YOU.
I CAN'T HAVE JOE BRADLEY, P.I., RUNNING AROUND, BREAKING INTO PATRICIA PENDERMILLS'S OFFICE LOOKING FOR RED IN OLD LEDGERS.
PENDERMILLS...
I'LL SEE YOU LATER, CHIEF.
YOU SURE YOU DON'T WANT TO STAY FOR LUNCH?
IT SEEMS LIKE MY DATE HAS ABANDONED ME.
CAN'T. TOLD MOM I'D HAVE LUNCH WITH HER.
BUT--
--YOU SHOULD MAYBE CHECK ON YOUR WIFE.
HELLO?
CAN ANYONE HEAR ME?
THE DOOR SEEMS TO BE STUCK.
HELLO?

Bendermills Peppermints

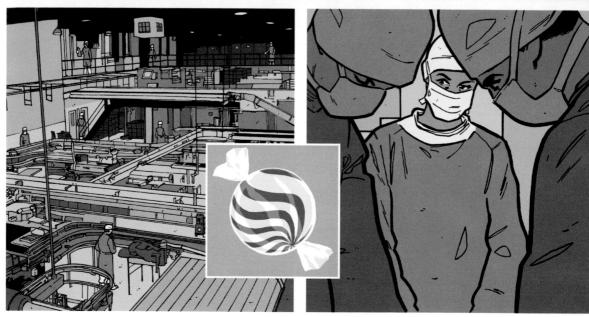

REEEEEEEEEEE

HEY, MOM.

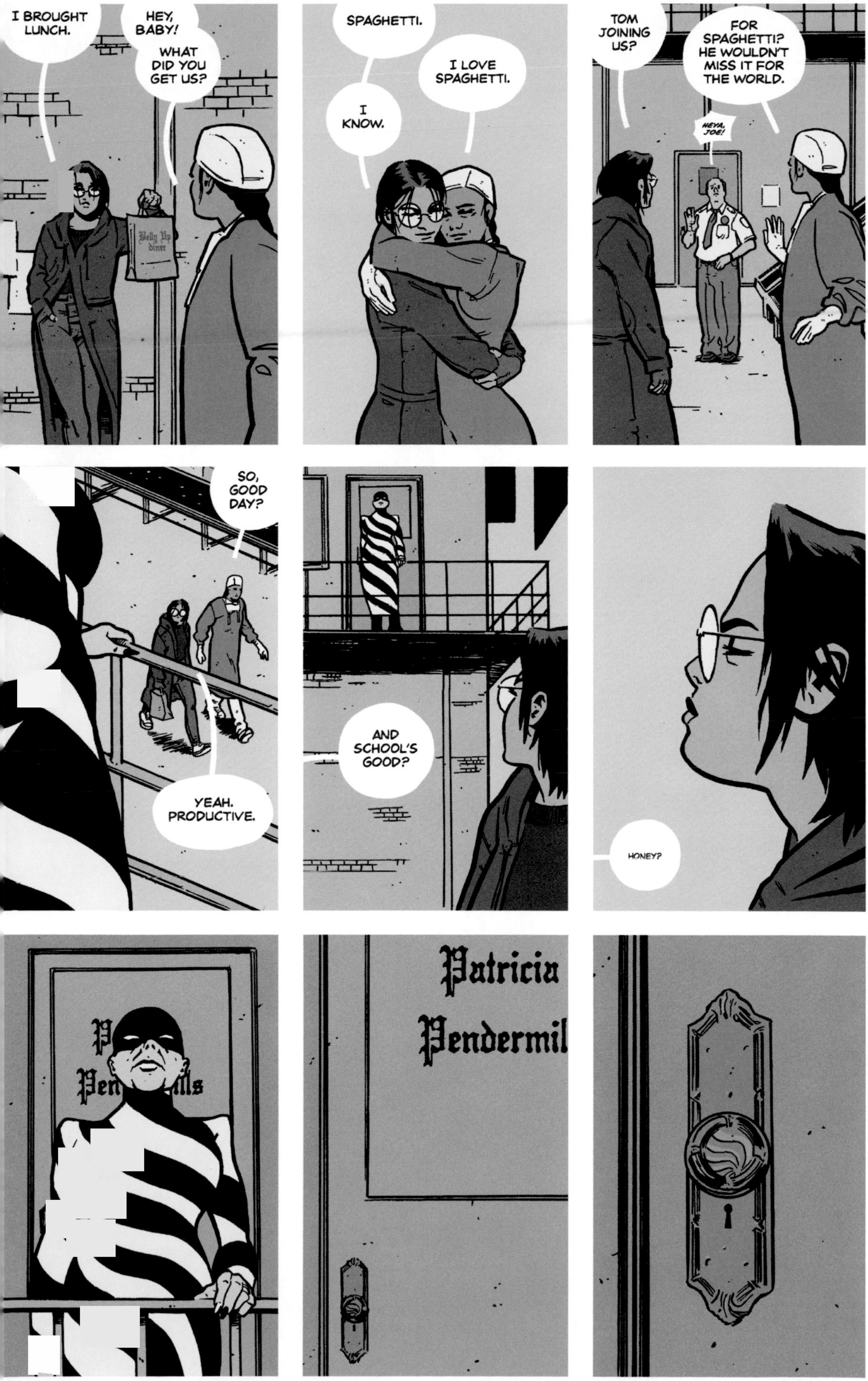
I BROUGHT LUNCH.
HEY, BABY!
WHAT DID YOU GET US?
Belly Up diner
SPAGHETTI.
I LOVE SPAGHETTI.
I KNOW.
TOM JOINING US?
FOR SPAGHETTI? HE WOULDN'T MISS IT FOR THE WORLD.
HEYA, JOE!
SO, GOOD DAY?
YEAH. PRODUCTIVE.
AND SCHOOL'S GOOD?
HONEY?
Patricia
Pendermil

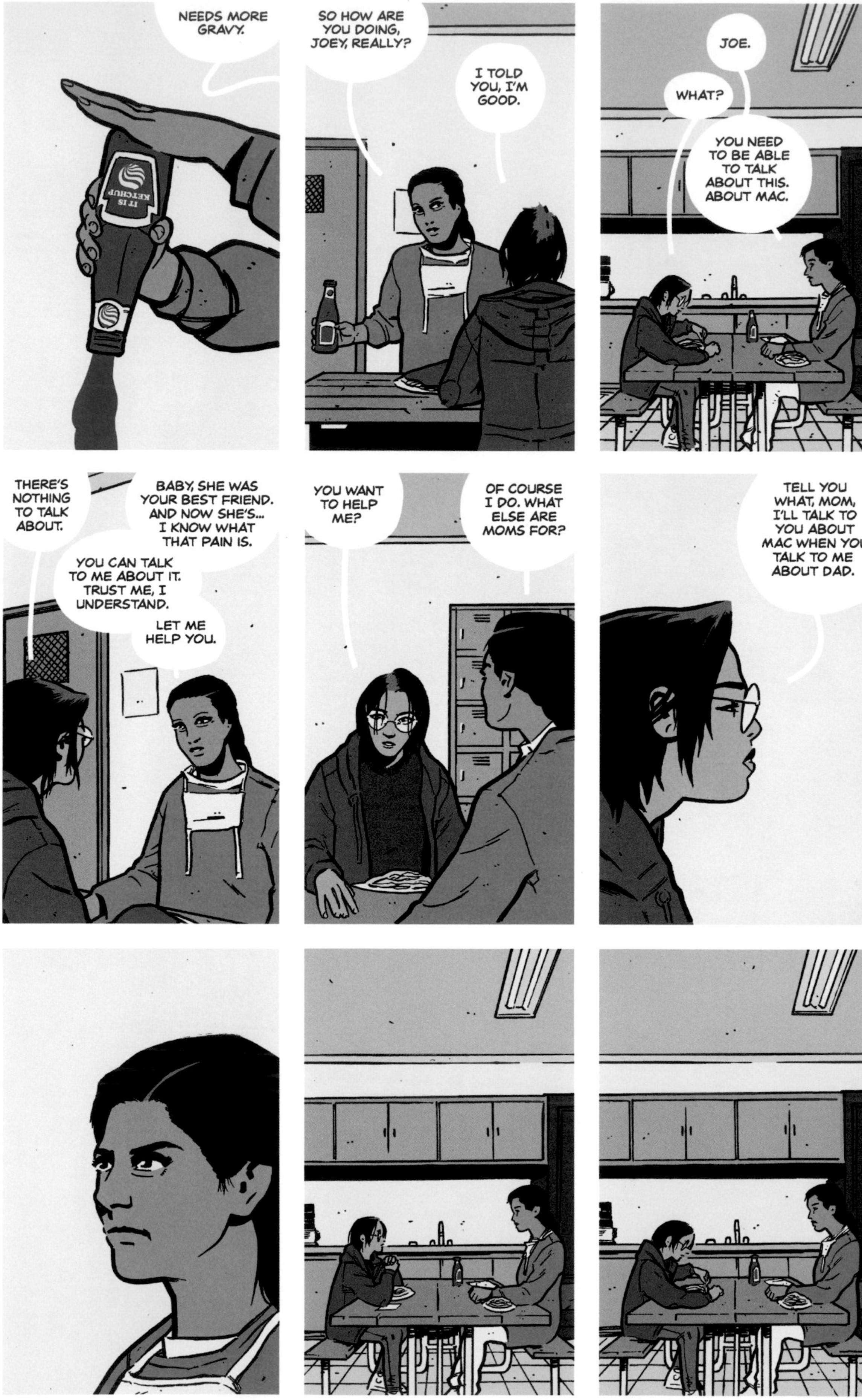
NEEDS MORE GRAVY.
IT IS KETCHUP
SO HOW ARE YOU DOING, JOEY, REALLY?
I TOLD YOU, I'M GOOD.
JOE.
WHAT?
YOU NEED TO BE ABLE TO TALK ABOUT THIS. ABOUT MAC.
THERE'S NOTHING TO TALK ABOUT.
BABY, SHE WAS YOUR BEST FRIEND. AND NOW SHE'S... I KNOW WHAT THAT PAIN IS.
YOU CAN TALK TO ME ABOUT IT. TRUST ME, I UNDERSTAND.
LET ME HELP YOU.
YOU WANT TO HELP ME?
OF COURSE I DO. WHAT ELSE ARE MOMS FOR?
TELL YOU WHAT, MOM, I'LL TALK TO YOU ABOUT MAC WHEN YOU TALK TO ME ABOUT DAD.

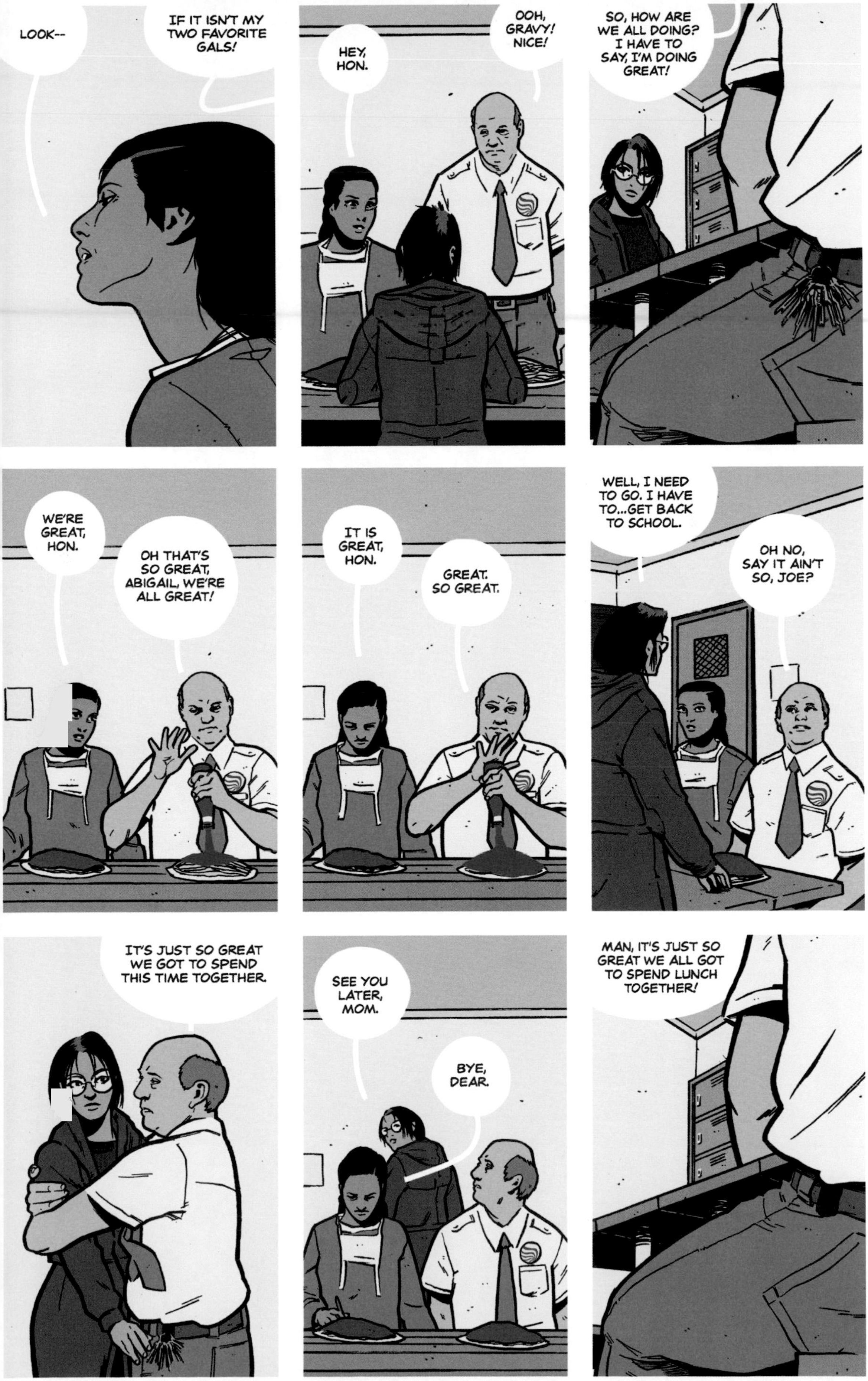
LOOK--
IF IT ISN'T MY TWO FAVORITE GALS!
HEY, HON.
OOH, GRAVY! NICE!
SO, HOW ARE WE ALL DOING? I HAVE TO SAY, I'M DOING GREAT!
WE'RE GREAT, HON.
OH THAT'S SO GREAT, ABIGAIL, WE'RE ALL GREAT!
IT IS GREAT, HON.
GREAT. SO GREAT.
WELL, I NEED TO GO. I HAVE TO...GET BACK TO SCHOOL.
OH NO, SAY IT AIN'T SO, JOE?
IT'S JUST SO GREAT WE GOT TO SPEND THIS TIME TOGETHER.
SEE YOU LATER, MOM.
BYE, DEAR.
MAN, IT'S JUST SO GREAT WE ALL GOT TO SPEND LUNCH TOGETHER!

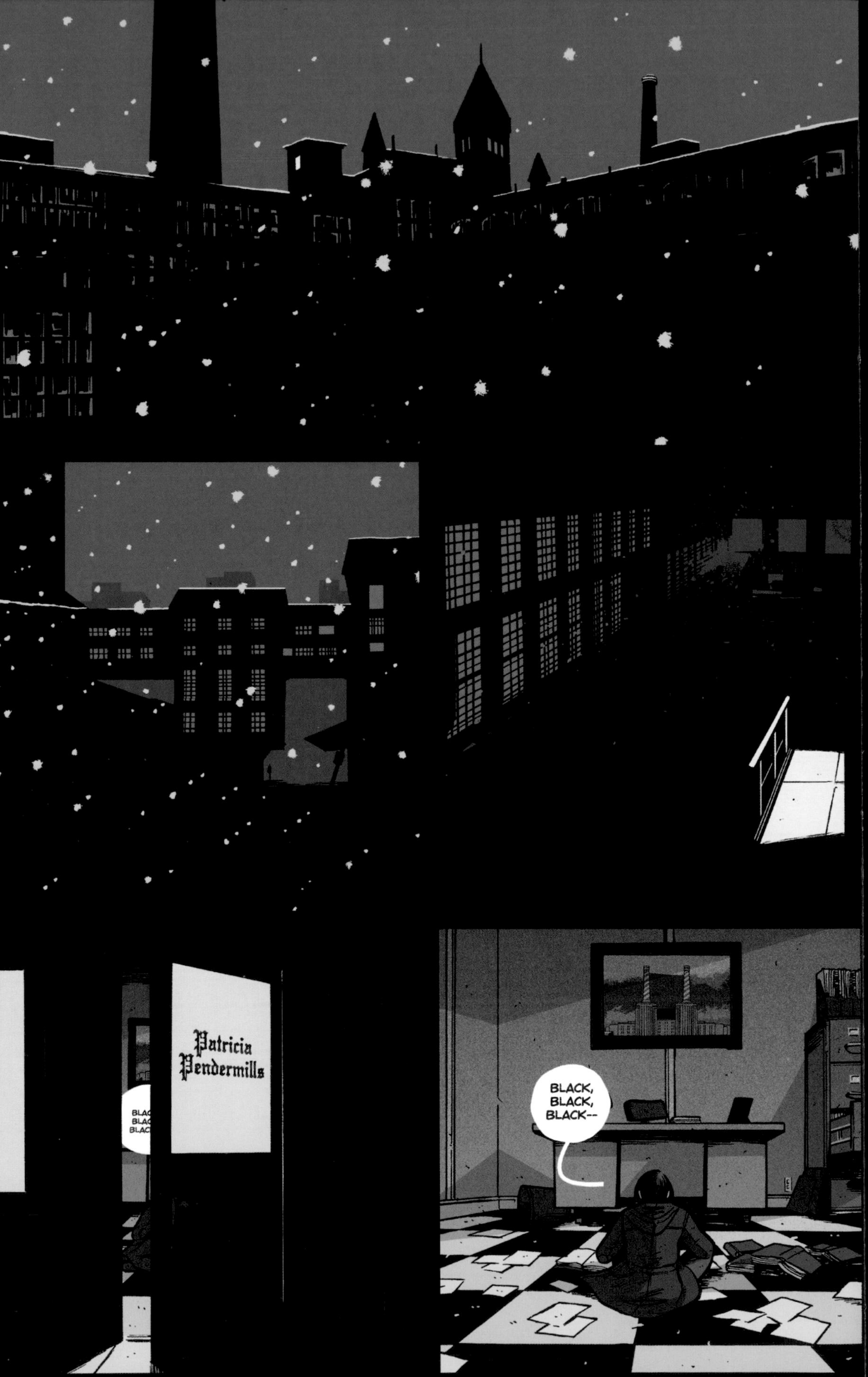
Patricia Pendermills
BLACK, BLACK, BLACK--

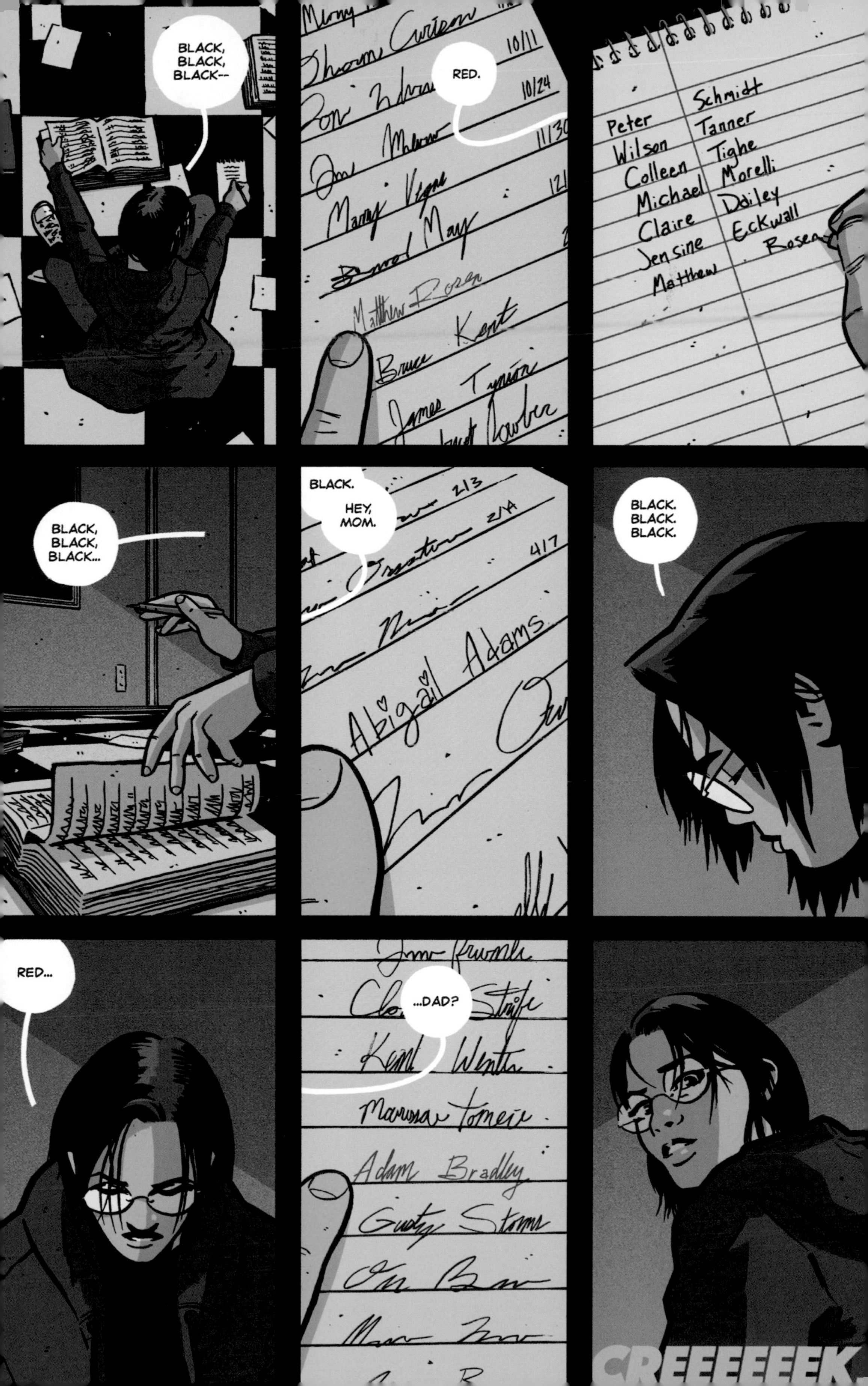
BLACK, BLACK, BLACK--
RED.
BLACK, BLACK, BLACK...
BLACK.
HEY, MOM.
BLACK. BLACK. BLACK.
RED...
...DAD?
CREEEEEEK.

HEY--

HEY!

FLAP
FLAP
FLAP

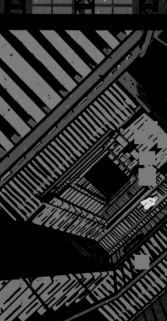

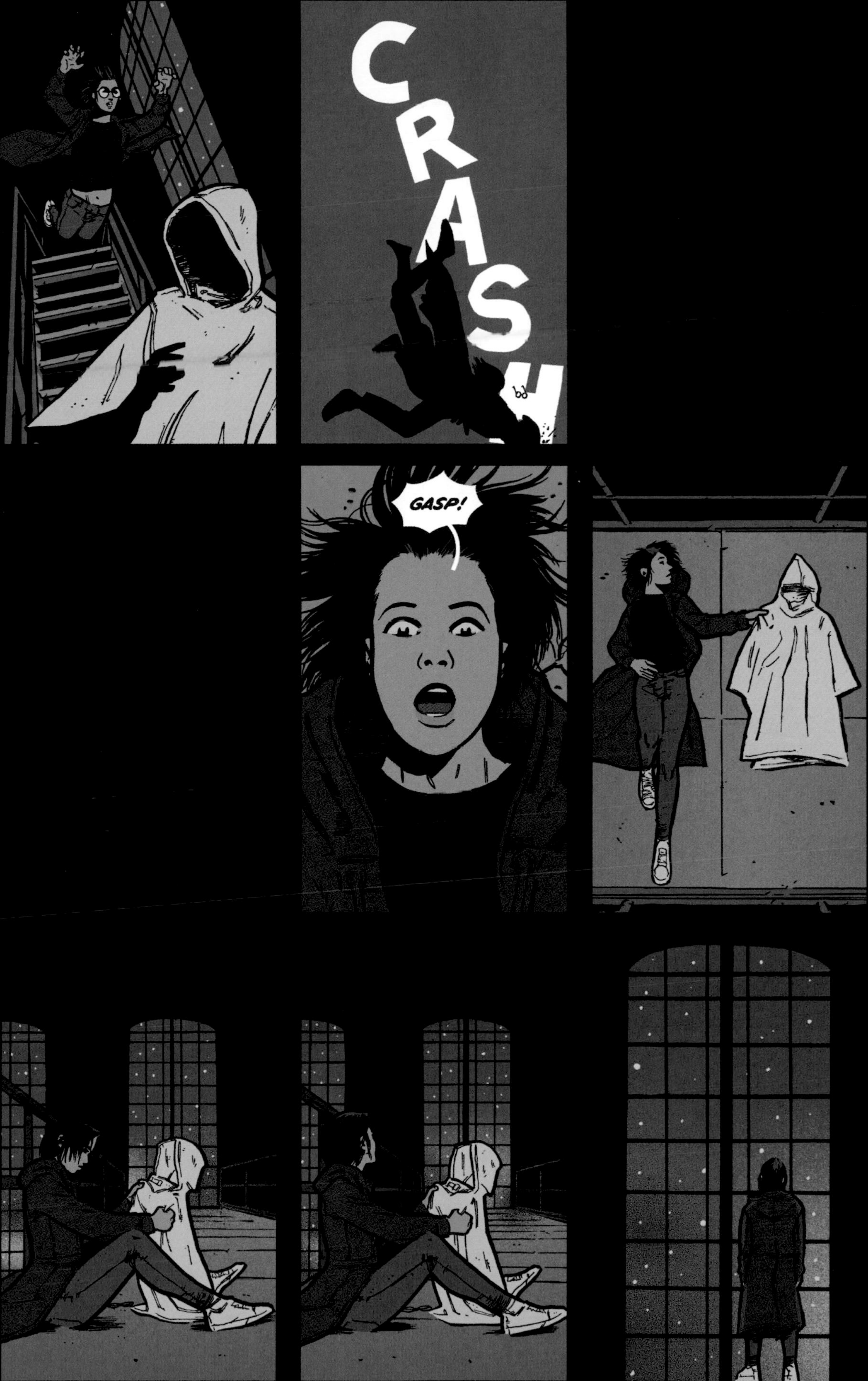
CRASH
GASP!

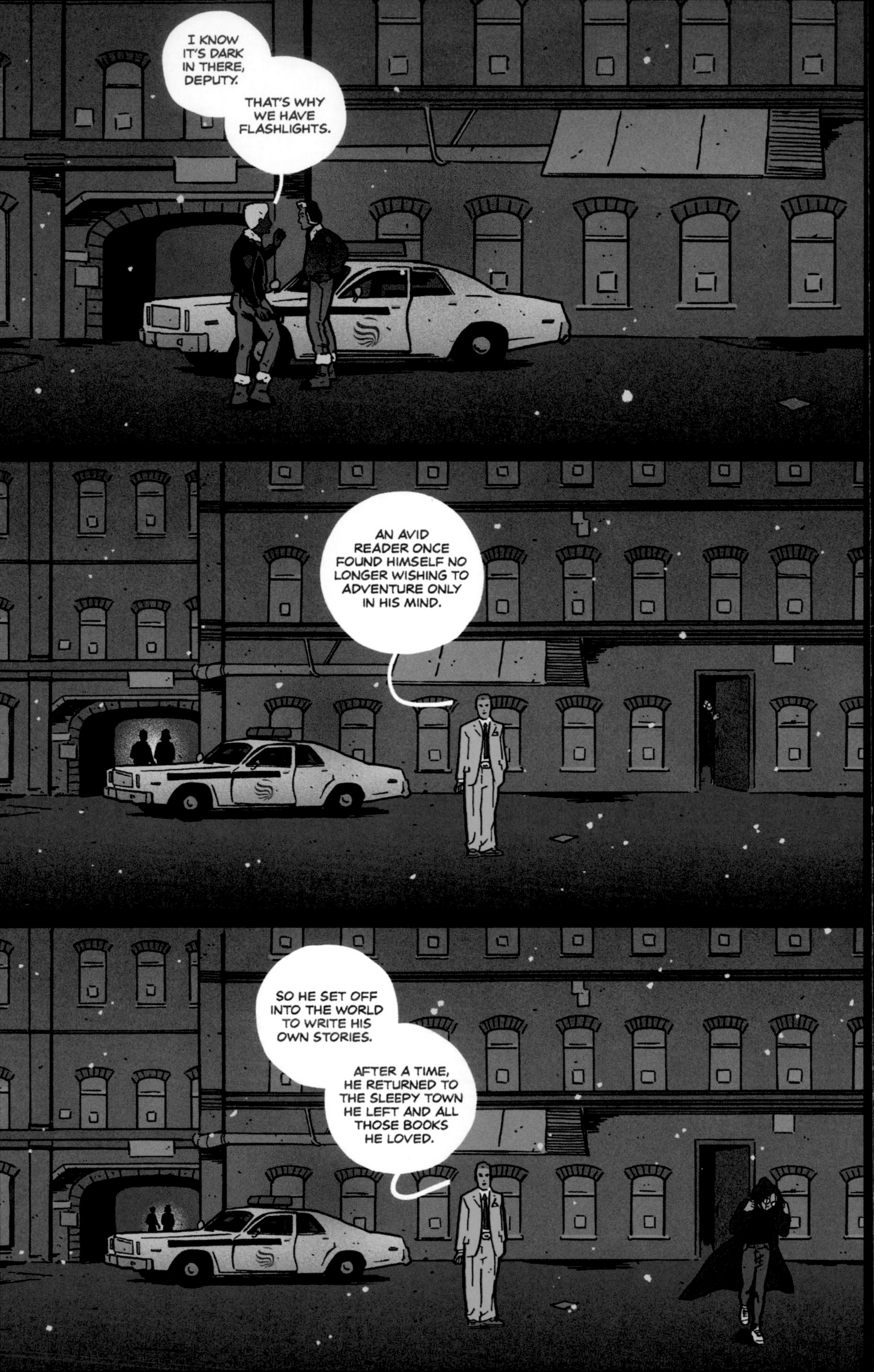
I KNOW IT'S DARK IN THERE, DEPUTY.
THAT'S WHY WE HAVE FLASHLIGHTS.
AN AVID READER ONCE FOUND HIMSELF NO LONGER WISHING TO ADVENTURE ONLY IN HIS MIND.
SO HE SET OFF INTO THE WORLD TO WRITE HIS OWN STORIES.
AFTER A TIME, HE RETURNED TO THE SLEEPY TOWN HE LEFT AND ALL THOSE BOOKS HE LOVED.

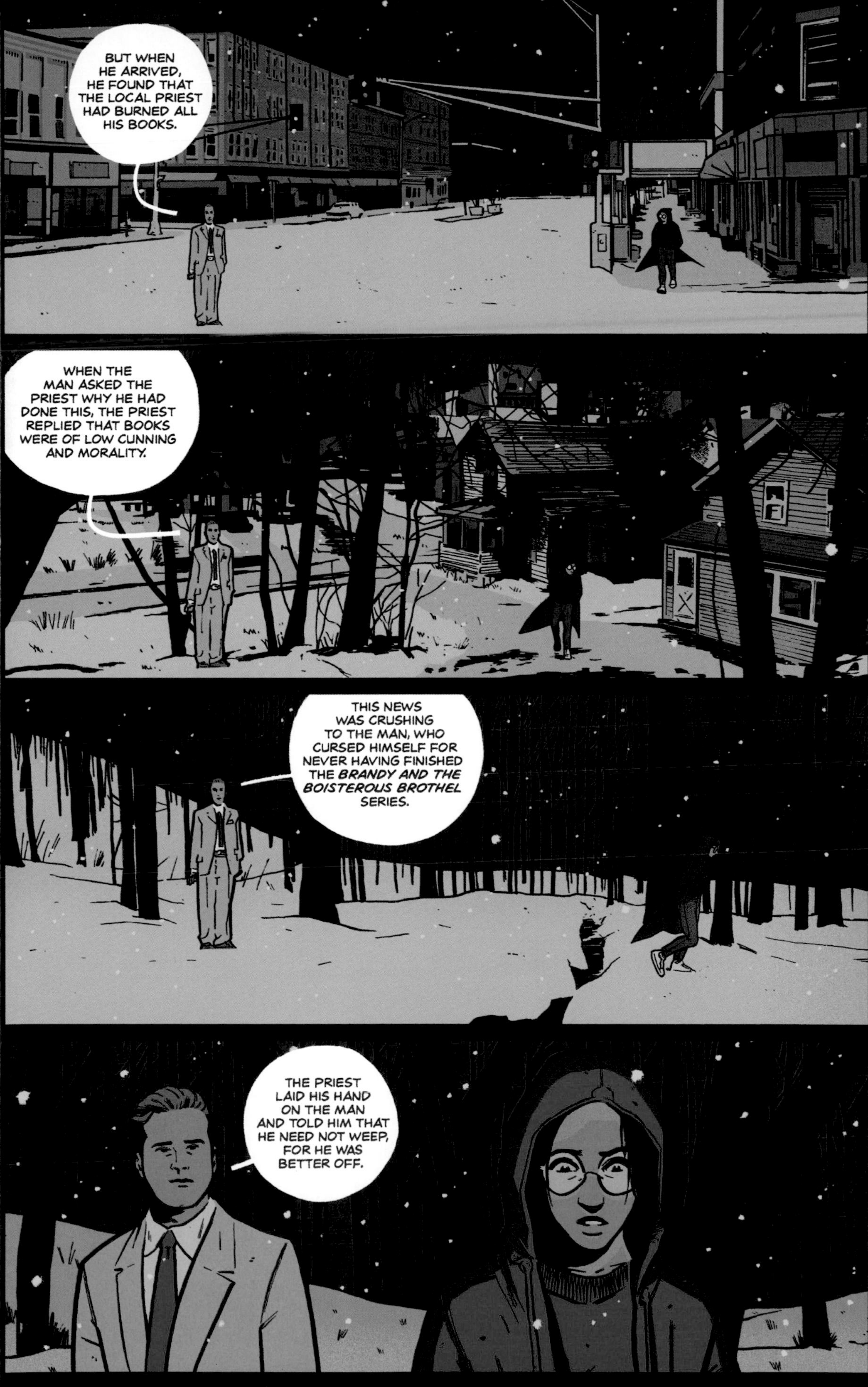
BUT WHEN HE ARRIVED, HE FOUND THAT THE LOCAL PRIEST HAD BURNED ALL HIS BOOKS.
WHEN THE MAN ASKED THE PRIEST WHY HE HAD DONE THIS, THE PRIEST REPLIED THAT BOOKS WERE OF LOW CUNNING AND MORALITY.
THIS NEWS WAS CRUSHING TO THE MAN, WHO CURSED HIMSELF FOR NEVER HAVING FINISHED THE *BRANDY AND THE BOISTEROUS BROTHEL* SERIES.
THE PRIEST LAID HIS HAND ON THE MAN AND TOLD HIM THAT HE NEED NOT WEEP, FOR HE WAS BETTER OFF.

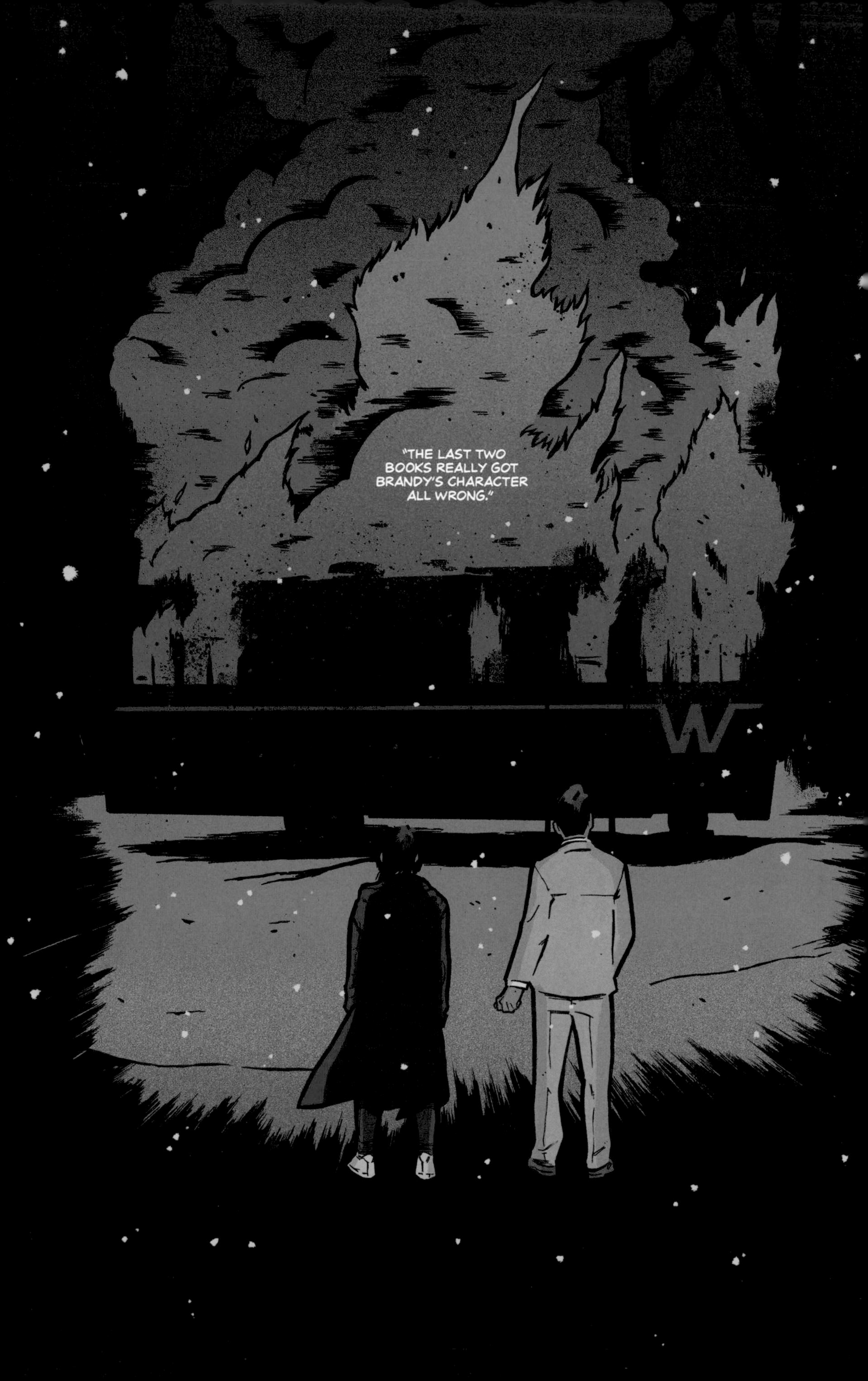
"THE LAST TWO BOOKS REALLY GOT BRANDY'S CHARACTER ALL WRONG."

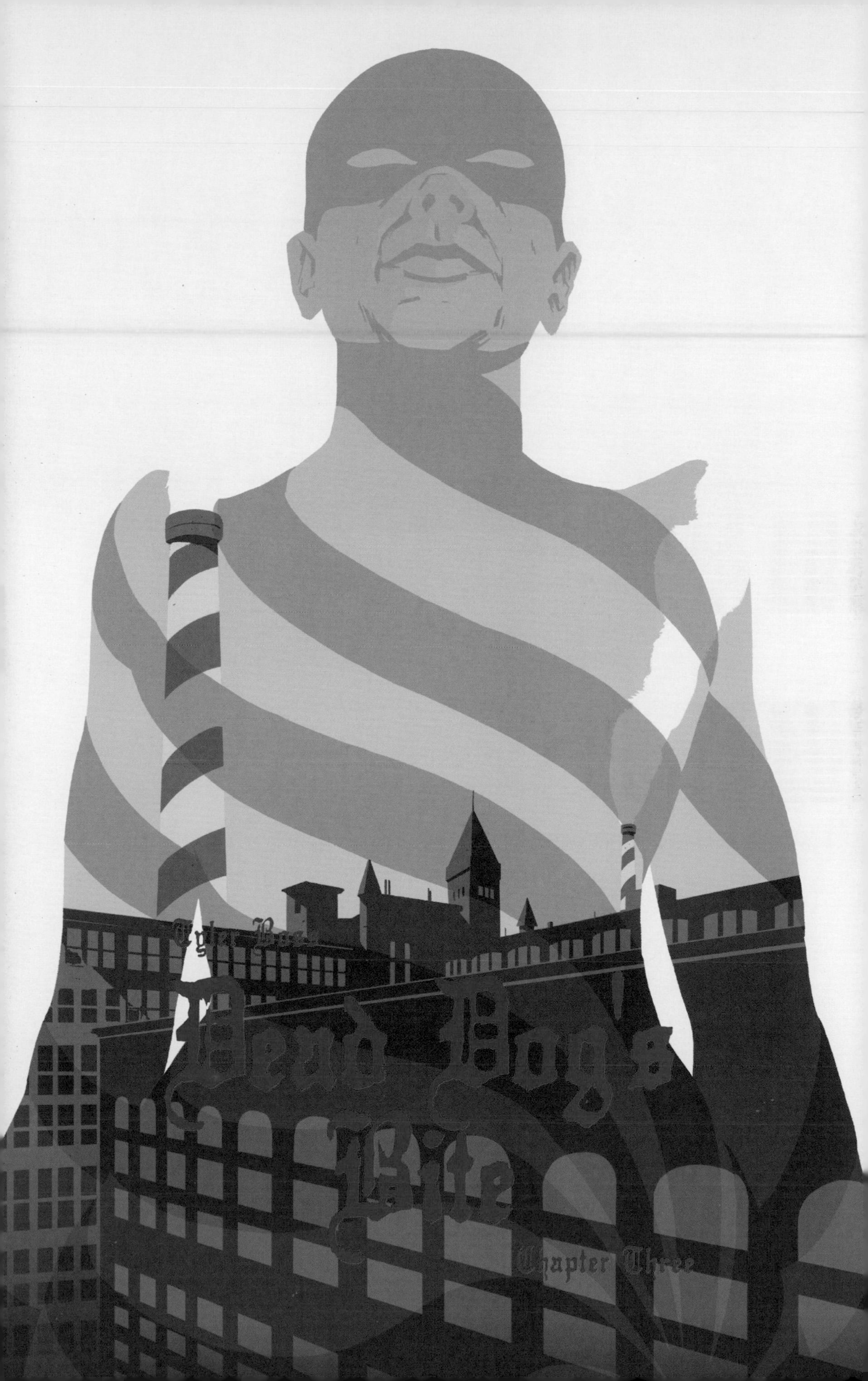
Tyler Boss
Dead Dog's Bite
Chapter Three

"It's weird to feel like you
miss someone you're not even
sure you know."
--D.F.W.

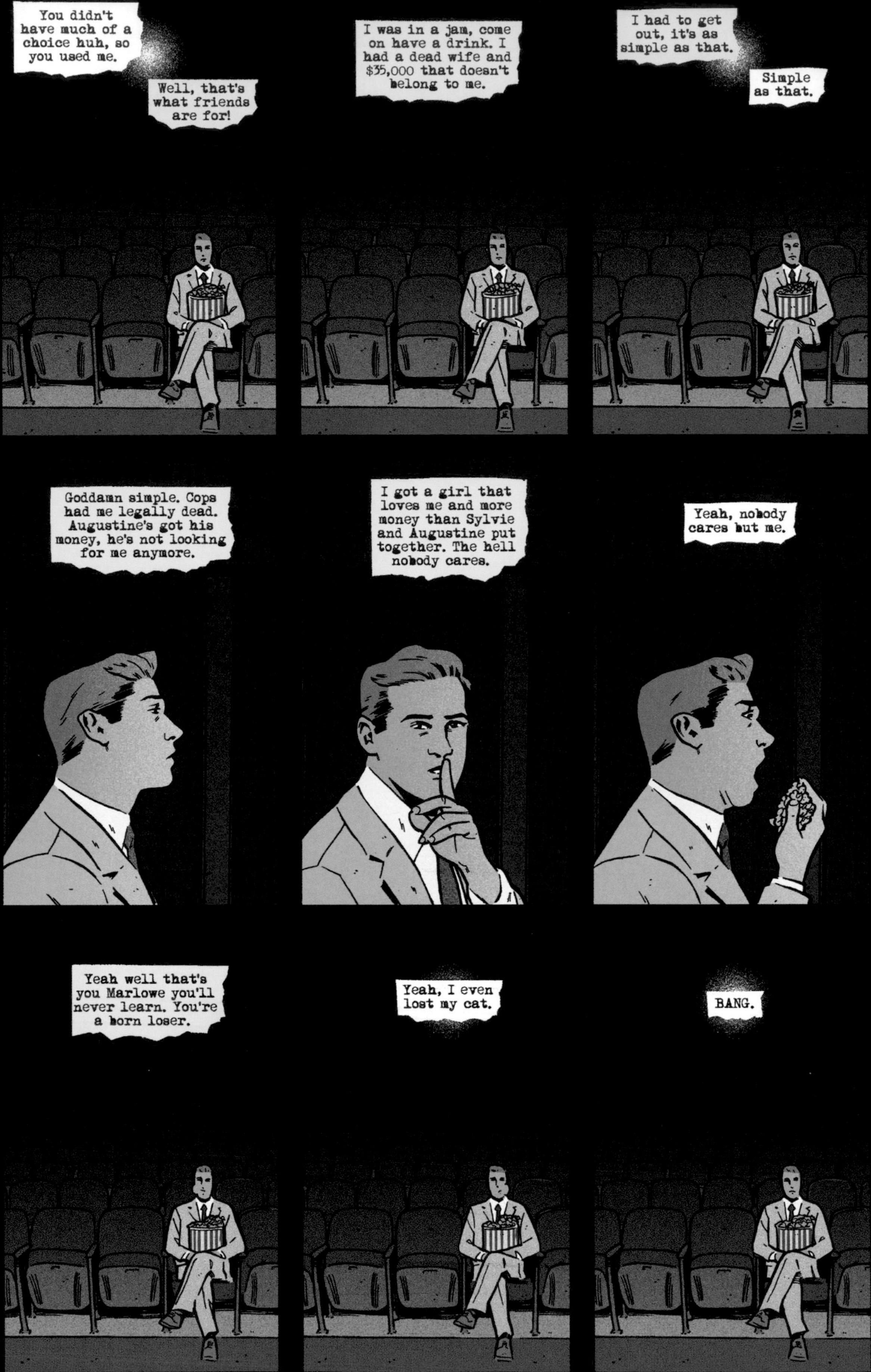
You didn't have much of a choice huh, so you used me.
Well, that's what friends are for!
I was in a jam, come on have a drink. I had a dead wife and $35,000 that doesn't belong to me.
I had to get out, it's as simple as that.
Simple as that.
Goddamn simple. Cops had me legally dead. Augustine's got his money, he's not looking for me anymore.
I got a girl that loves me and more money than Sylvie and Augustine put together. The hell nobody cares.
Yeah, nobody cares but me.
Yeah well that's you Marlowe you'll never learn. You're a born loser.
Yeah, I even lost my cat.
BANG.

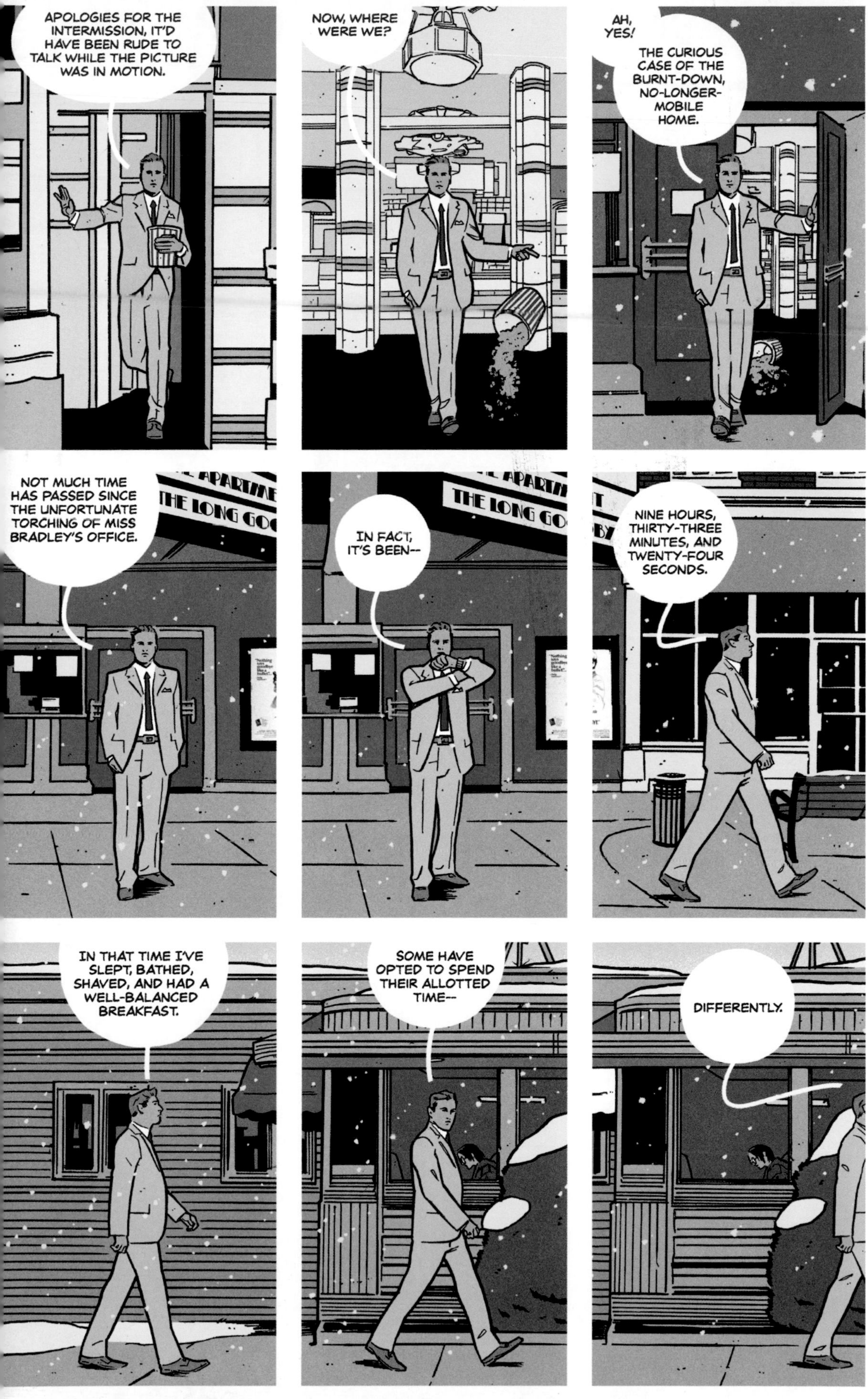
APOLOGIES FOR THE INTERMISSION, IT'D HAVE BEEN RUDE TO TALK WHILE THE PICTURE WAS IN MOTION.
NOW, WHERE WERE WE?
AH, YES!
THE CURIOUS CASE OF THE BURNT-DOWN, NO-LONGER-MOBILE HOME.
NOT MUCH TIME HAS PASSED SINCE THE UNFORTUNATE TORCHING OF MISS BRADLEY'S OFFICE.
IN FACT, IT'S BEEN--
NINE HOURS, THIRTY-THREE MINUTES, AND TWENTY-FOUR SECONDS.
IN THAT TIME I'VE SLEPT, BATHED, SHAVED, AND HAD A WELL-BALANCED BREAKFAST.
SOME HAVE OPTED TO SPEND THEIR ALLOTTED TIME--
DIFFERENTLY.

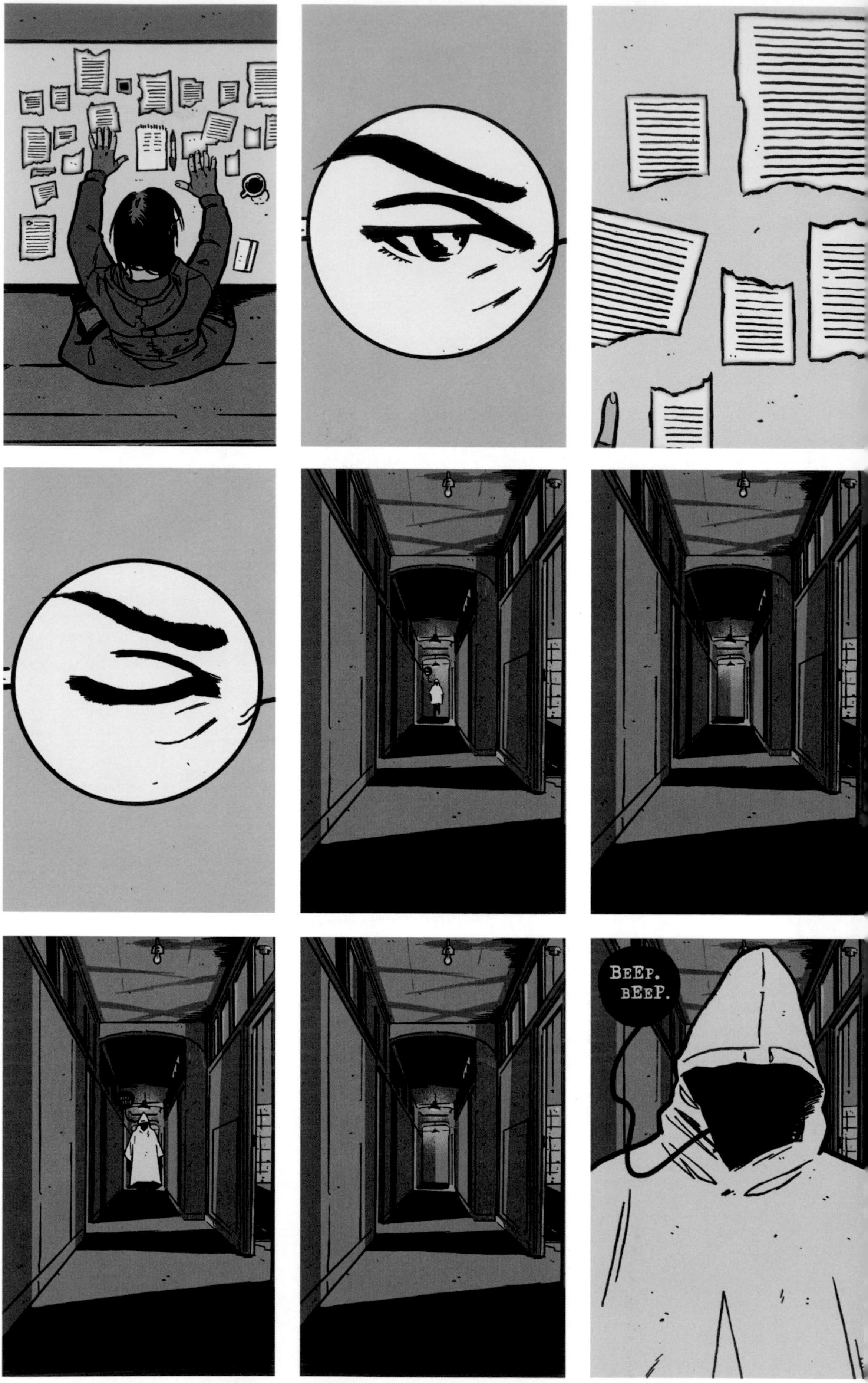
BEEP. BEEP.

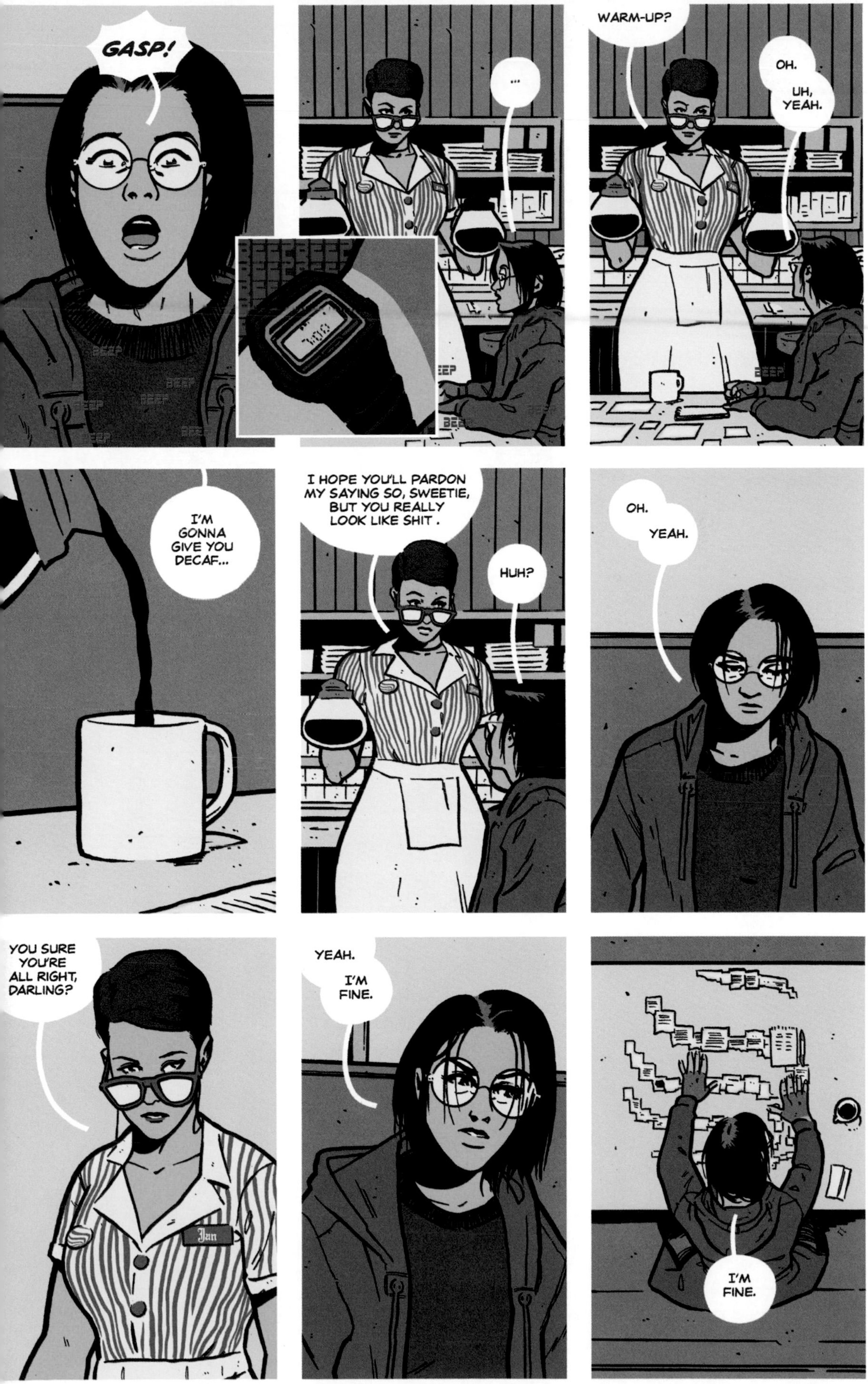
GASP!
...
WARM-UP?
OH.
UH, YEAH.
I'M GONNA GIVE YOU DECAF...
I HOPE YOU'LL PARDON MY SAYING SO, SWEETIE, BUT YOU REALLY LOOK LIKE SHIT .
HUH?
OH.
YEAH.
YOU SURE YOU'RE ALL RIGHT, DARLING?
Jan
YEAH.
I'M FINE.
I'M FINE.

Peter Schmidt
Wilson Tanner
Colleen Tighe
Michael Morelli
Claire Dailey
Jensine Eckwall
Matthew Rosen
Adam Bradley
Pendermills Periodical
Pendermills Periodical
Pendermills Periodical
Pendermills Periodical
The Pendermills Periodical
No News Is Still News
Pendermills Public Library
Josephine Bradley
123450000042069
EXPIRES APR.
The Pendermills Periodical
Vigil Tonight promptly at sundown
The Pendermills Periodical
Vigil Tonight promptly at sundown
The Pendermills Periodical
MISSING!
Local boy Peter Schmidt has been unaccounted for
Ferg's Gives Away Free Milk?
The Pendermills Periodical
MISSING!
Ferg's Gives Away Free Milk?
Peter Schmidt
Wilson Tanner
Colleen Tighe
Michael Morelli
Claire Dailey
Jensine Eckwall
Matthew Rosen
Adam Bradley
idt
MISSING!
Local boy Peter Schmidt has been unaccounted for

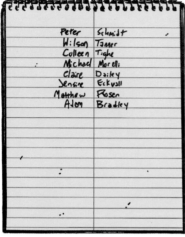

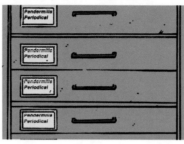

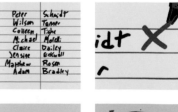

Celebrations
The Pendermills Periodical
Remembering our Semicentennial Celebrations
Print
Celebrations
The Pendermills Periodical
Have you seen me?
Missing son, Wilson Tanner
Is Bigger Better?
The Mothman: an Erotic Journey
Have yo
Missing
Permanent
Peter Schmidt
Wilson Tanner
Colleen Tighe
Michael Morelli
Claire Dailey
Jensine Eckvall
Matthew Rosen
Adam Bradley

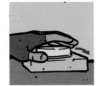

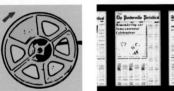

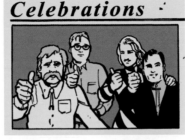

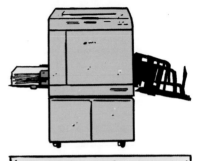

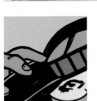

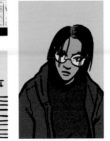

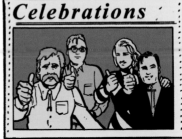

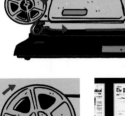

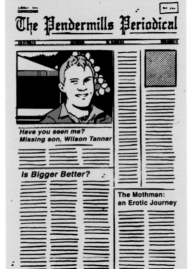

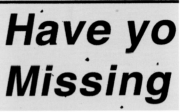

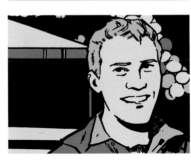

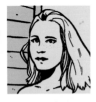

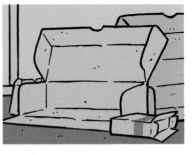

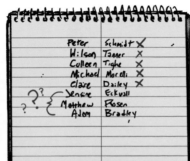

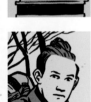

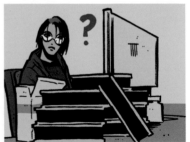

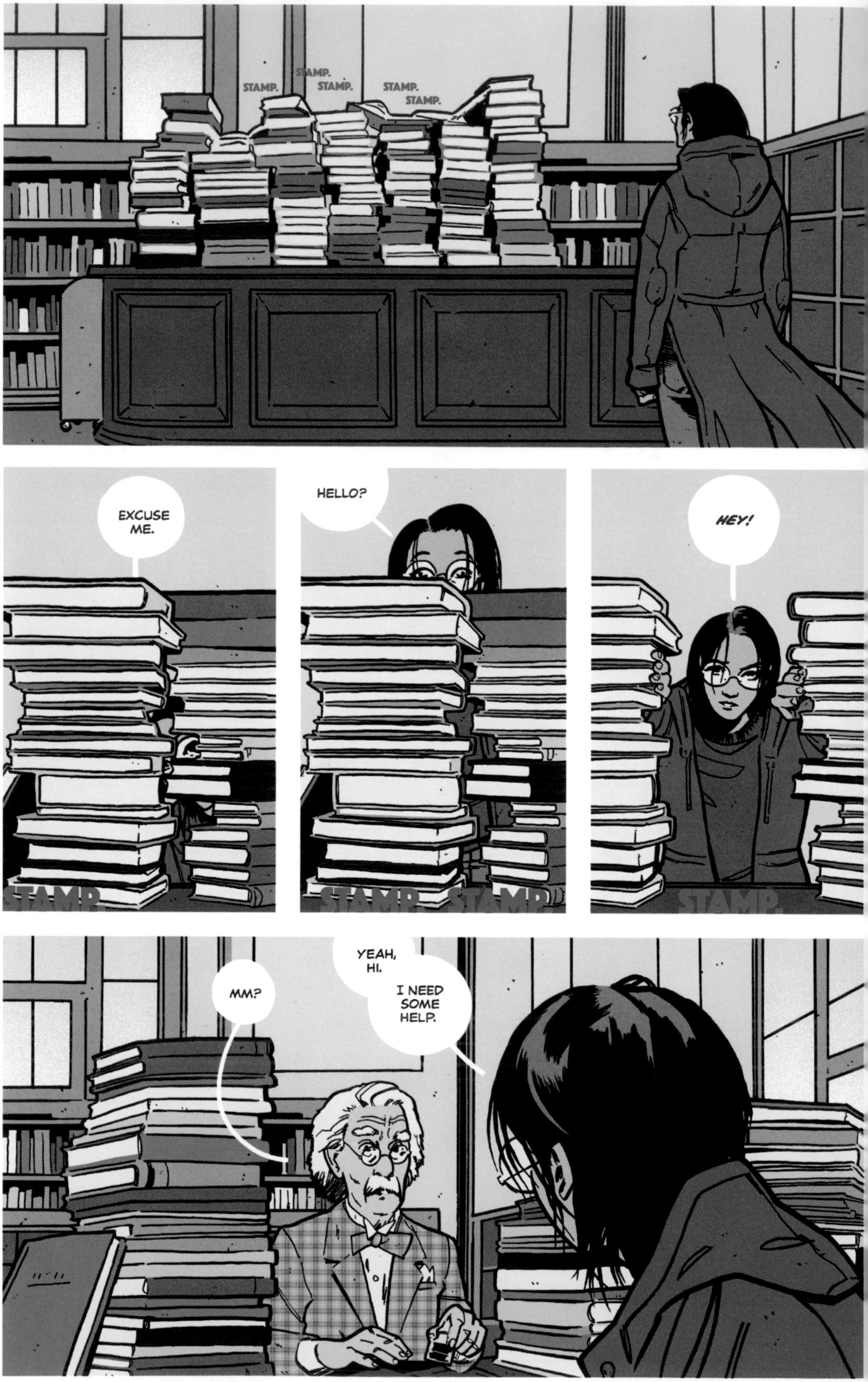
STAMP.
STAMP.
STAMP.
STAMP.
STAMP.
EXCUSE ME.
STAMP
HELLO?
STAMP STAMP
HEY!
STAMP
MM?
YEAH, HI.
I NEED SOME HELP.

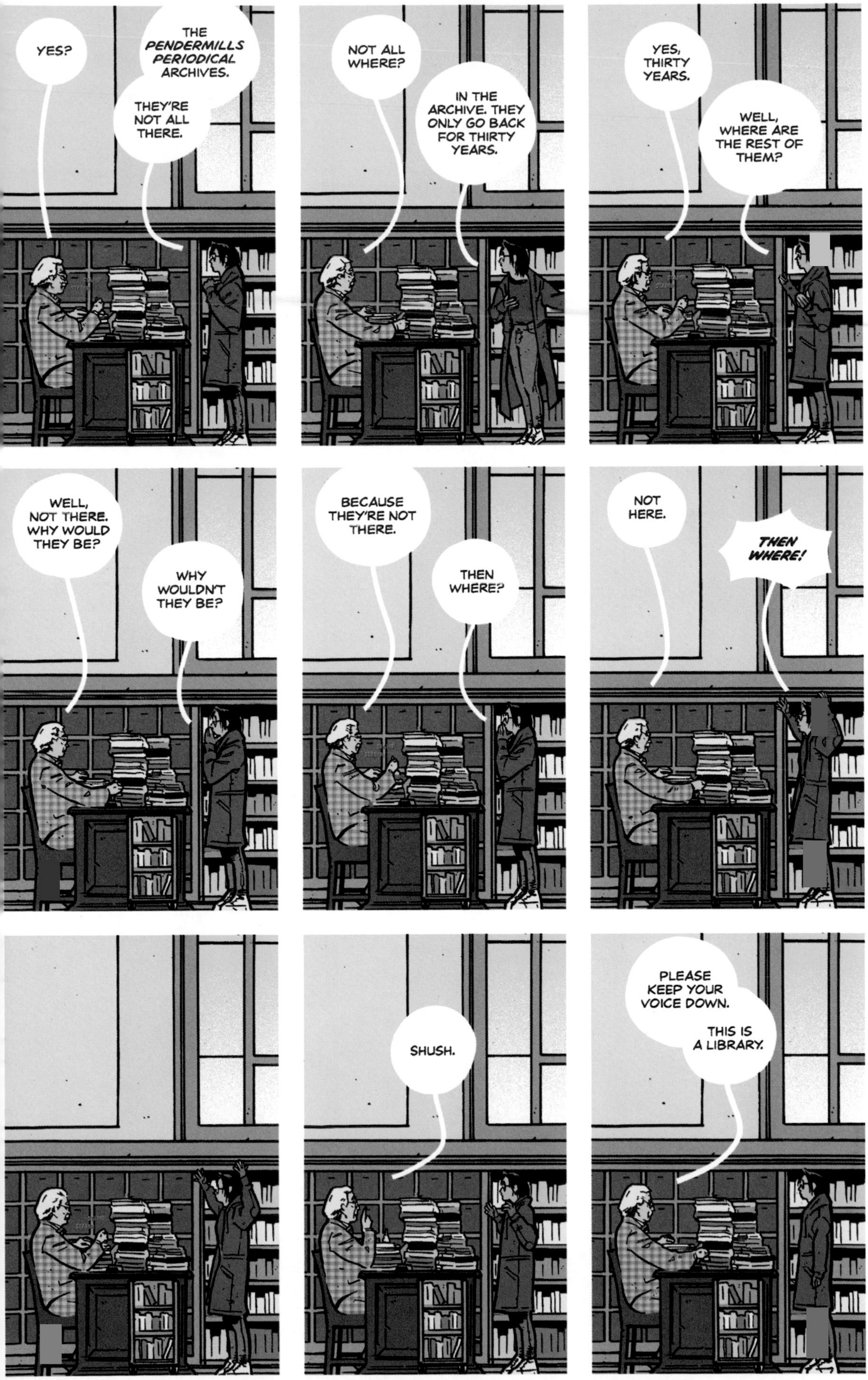
YES?
THE *PENDERMILLS PERIODICAL* ARCHIVES.
THEY'RE NOT ALL THERE.
NOT ALL WHERE?
IN THE ARCHIVE. THEY ONLY GO BACK FOR THIRTY YEARS.
YES, THIRTY YEARS.
WELL, WHERE ARE THE REST OF THEM?
WELL, NOT THERE. WHY WOULD THEY BE?
WHY WOULDN'T THEY BE?
BECAUSE THEY'RE NOT THERE.
THEN WHERE?
NOT HERE.
THEN WHERE!
SHUSH.
PLEASE KEEP YOUR VOICE DOWN.
THIS IS A LIBRARY.

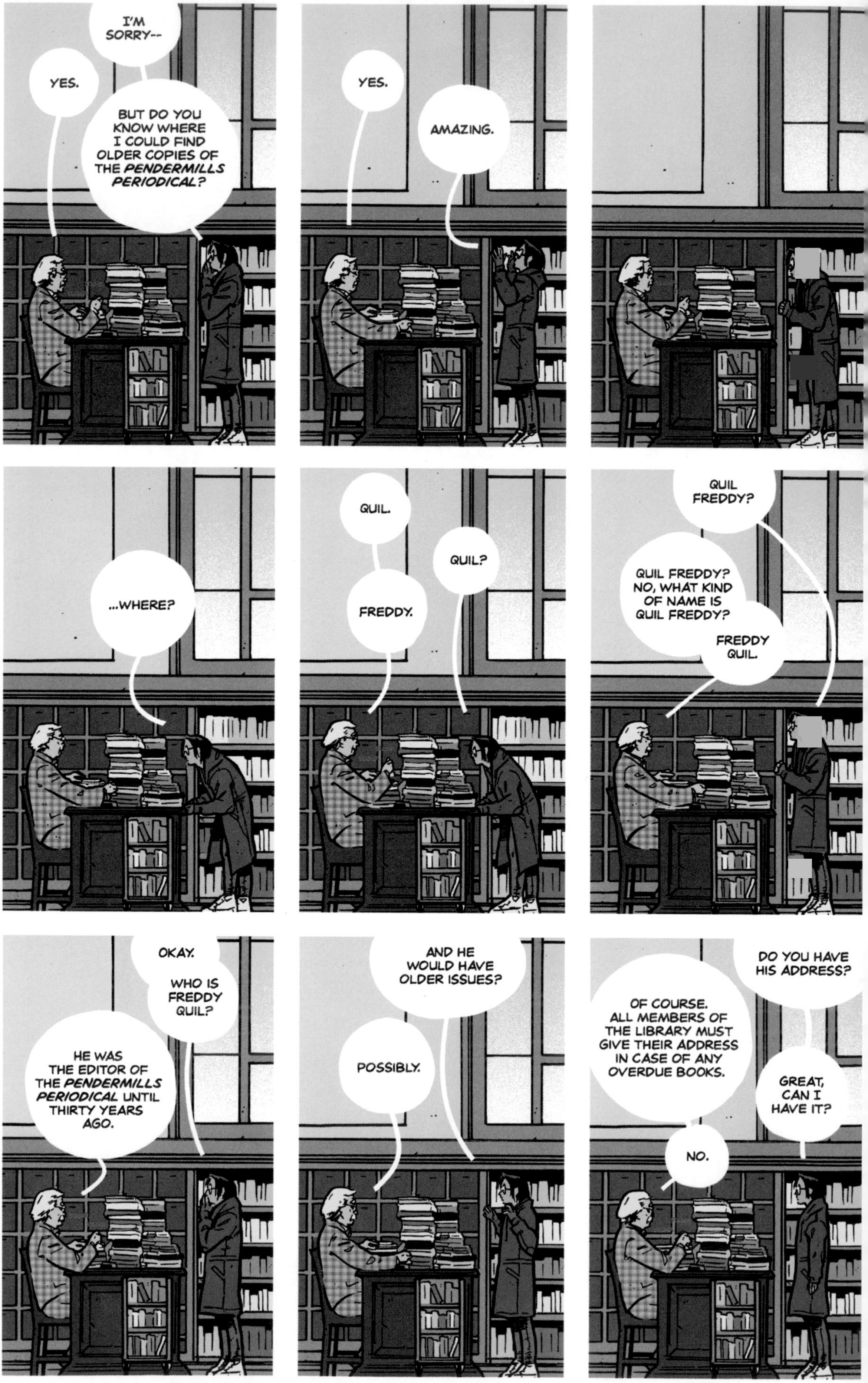
YES.
I'M SORRY--
BUT DO YOU KNOW WHERE I COULD FIND OLDER COPIES OF THE *PENDERMILLS PERIODICAL*?
YES.
AMAZING.
...WHERE?
QUIL.
FREDDY.
QUIL?
QUIL FREDDY?
QUIL FREDDY? NO, WHAT KIND OF NAME IS QUIL FREDDY?
FREDDY QUIL.
OKAY.
WHO IS FREDDY QUIL?
HE WAS THE EDITOR OF THE *PENDERMILLS PERIODICAL* UNTIL THIRTY YEARS AGO.
AND HE WOULD HAVE OLDER ISSUES?
POSSIBLY.
DO YOU HAVE HIS ADDRESS?
OF COURSE. ALL MEMBERS OF THE LIBRARY MUST GIVE THEIR ADDRESS IN CASE OF ANY OVERDUE BOOKS.
GREAT, CAN I HAVE IT?
NO.

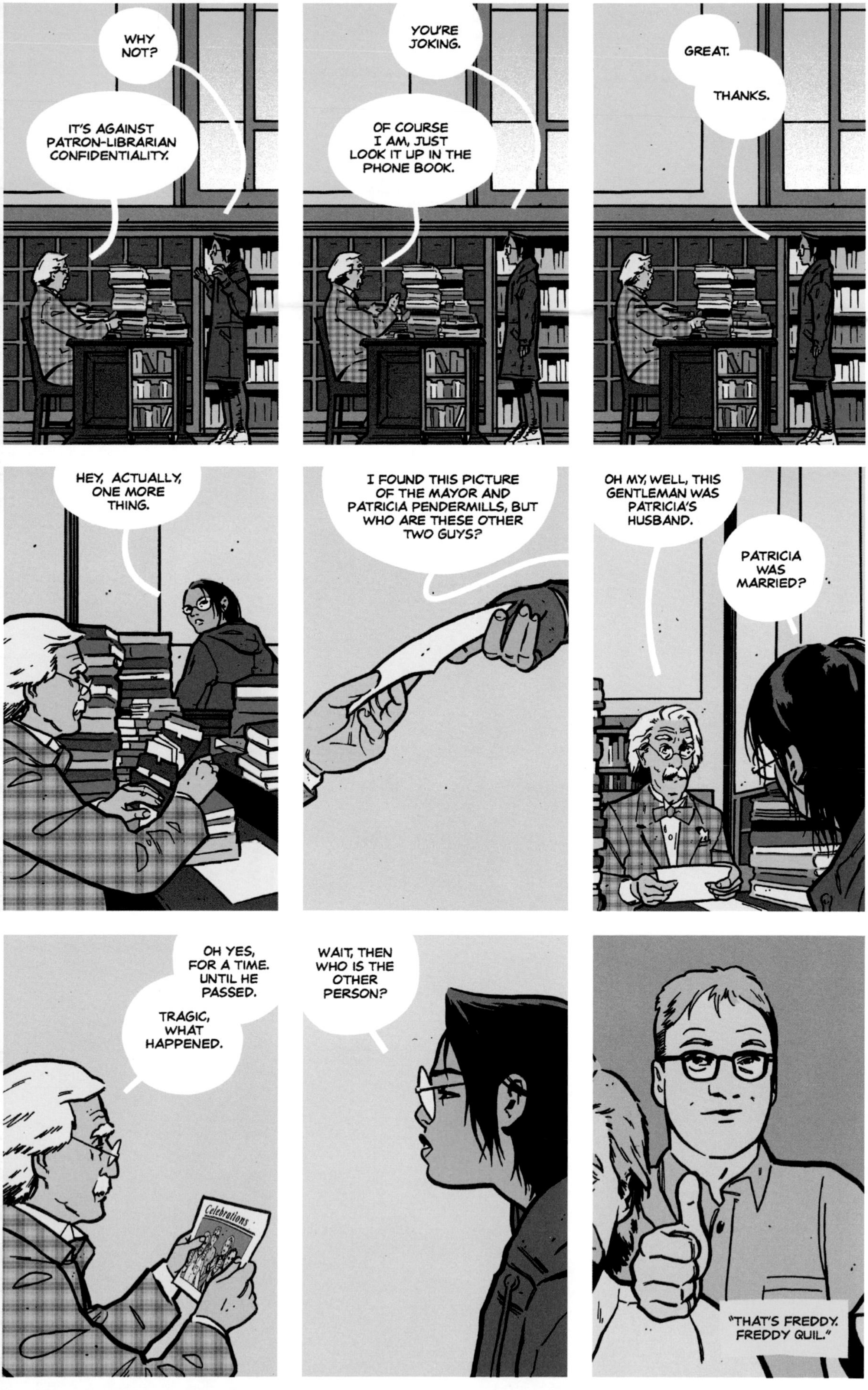
WHY NOT?
IT'S AGAINST PATRON-LIBRARIAN CONFIDENTIALITY.
YOU'RE JOKING.
OF COURSE I AM, JUST LOOK IT UP IN THE PHONE BOOK.
GREAT.
THANKS.
HEY, ACTUALLY, ONE MORE THING.
I FOUND THIS PICTURE OF THE MAYOR AND PATRICIA PENDERMILLS, BUT WHO ARE THESE OTHER TWO GUYS?
OH MY, WELL, THIS GENTLEMAN WAS PATRICIA'S HUSBAND.
PATRICIA WAS MARRIED?
OH YES, FOR A TIME. UNTIL HE PASSED.
TRAGIC, WHAT HAPPENED.
Celebrations
WAIT, THEN WHO IS THE OTHER PERSON?
"THAT'S FREDDY. FREDDY QUIL."

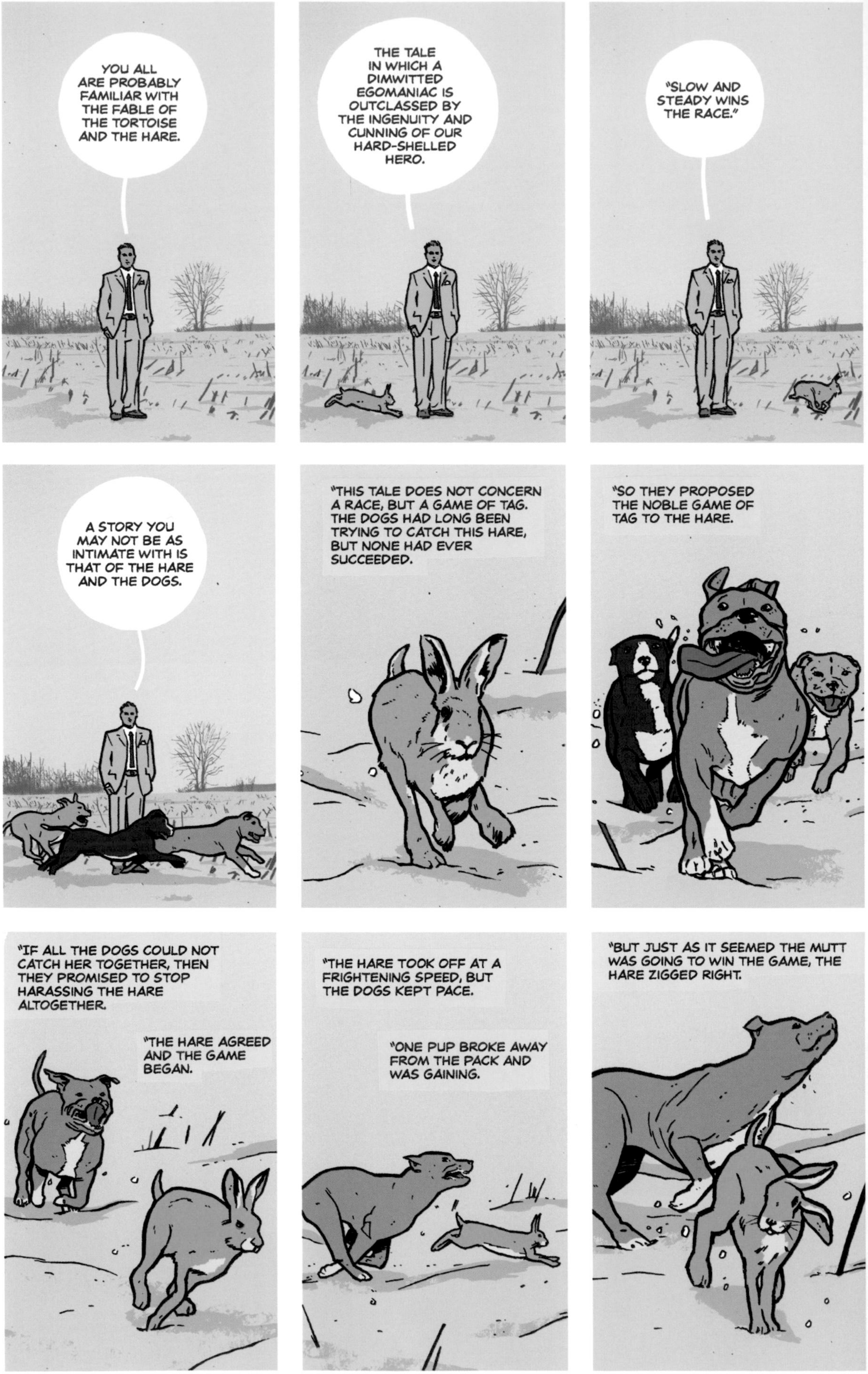
YOU ALL ARE PROBABLY FAMILIAR WITH THE FABLE OF THE TORTOISE AND THE HARE.
THE TALE IN WHICH A DIMWITTED EGOMANIAC IS OUTCLASSED BY THE INGENUITY AND CUNNING OF OUR HARD-SHELLED HERO.
"SLOW AND STEADY WINS THE RACE."
A STORY YOU MAY NOT BE AS INTIMATE WITH IS THAT OF THE HARE AND THE DOGS.
"THIS TALE DOES NOT CONCERN A RACE, BUT A GAME OF TAG. THE DOGS HAD LONG BEEN TRYING TO CATCH THIS HARE, BUT NONE HAD EVER SUCCEEDED.
"SO THEY PROPOSED THE NOBLE GAME OF TAG TO THE HARE.
"IF ALL THE DOGS COULD NOT CATCH HER TOGETHER, THEN THEY PROMISED TO STOP HARASSING THE HARE ALTOGETHER.
"THE HARE AGREED AND THE GAME BEGAN.
"THE HARE TOOK OFF AT A FRIGHTENING SPEED, BUT THE DOGS KEPT PACE.
"ONE PUP BROKE AWAY FROM THE PACK AND WAS GAINING.
"BUT JUST AS IT SEEMED THE MUTT WAS GOING TO WIN THE GAME, THE HARE ZIGGED RIGHT.

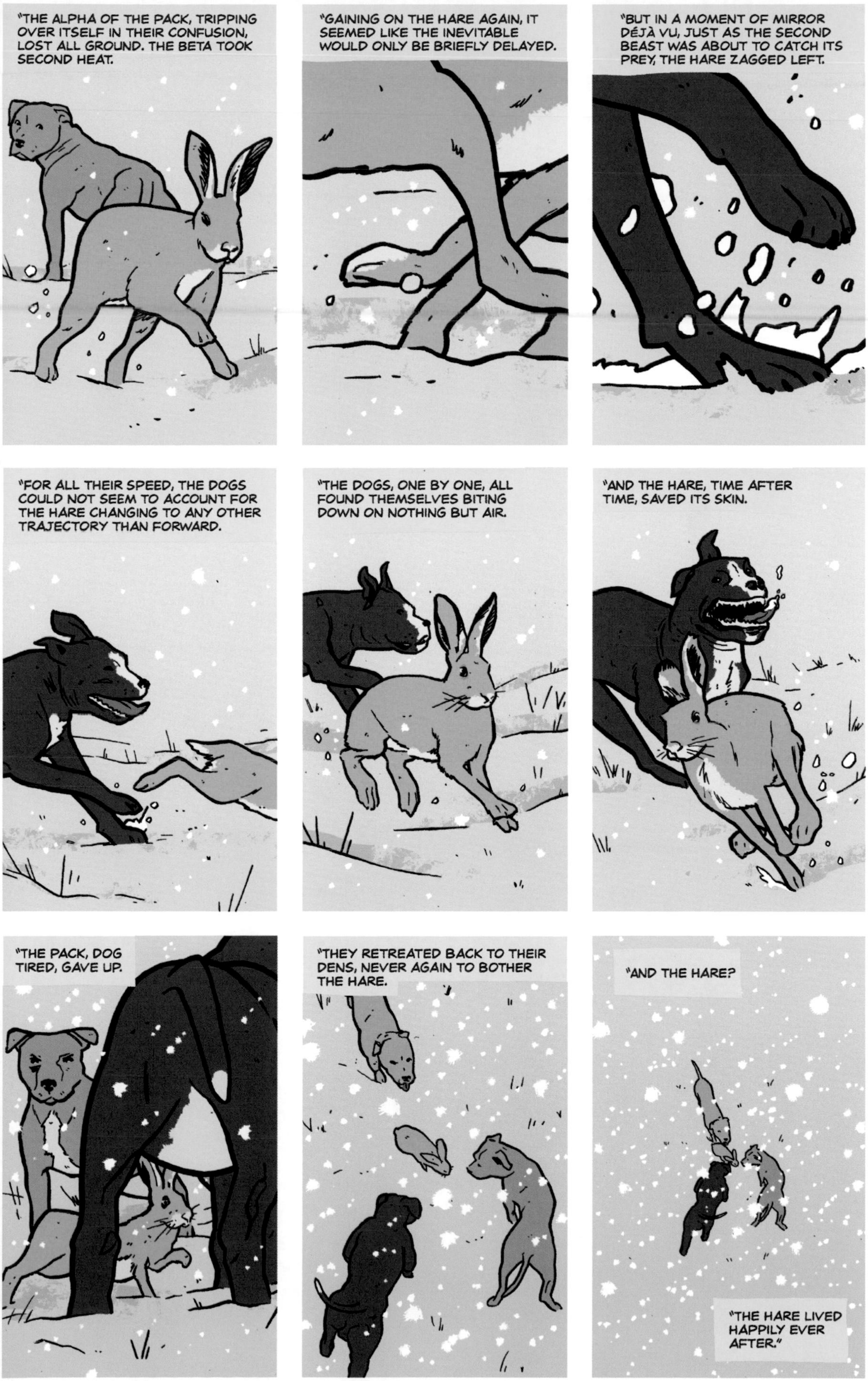
"THE ALPHA OF THE PACK, TRIPPING OVER ITSELF IN THEIR CONFUSION, LOST ALL GROUND. THE BETA TOOK SECOND HEAT.
"GAINING ON THE HARE AGAIN, IT SEEMED LIKE THE INEVITABLE WOULD ONLY BE BRIEFLY DELAYED.
"BUT IN A MOMENT OF MIRROR DÉJÀ VU, JUST AS THE SECOND BEAST WAS ABOUT TO CATCH ITS PREY, THE HARE ZAGGED LEFT.
"FOR ALL THEIR SPEED, THE DOGS COULD NOT SEEM TO ACCOUNT FOR THE HARE CHANGING TO ANY OTHER TRAJECTORY THAN FORWARD.
"THE DOGS, ONE BY ONE, ALL FOUND THEMSELVES BITING DOWN ON NOTHING BUT AIR.
"AND THE HARE, TIME AFTER TIME, SAVED ITS SKIN.
"THE PACK, DOG TIRED, GAVE UP.
"THEY RETREATED BACK TO THEIR DENS, NEVER AGAIN TO BOTHER THE HARE.
"AND THE HARE?
"THE HARE LIVED HAPPILY EVER AFTER."

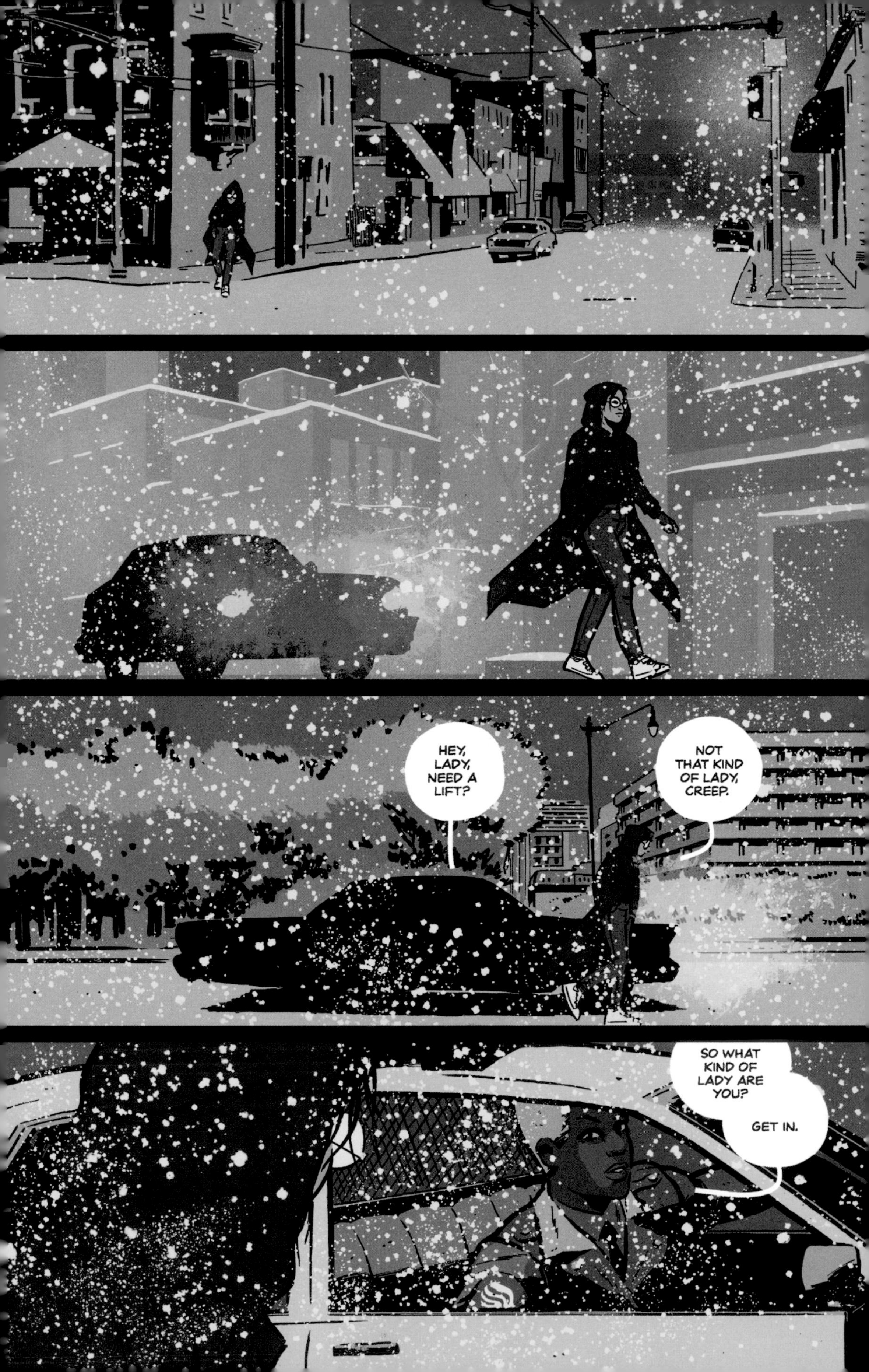
HEY, LADY, NEED A LIFT?
NOT THAT KIND OF LADY, CREEP.
SO WHAT KIND OF LADY ARE YOU?
GET IN.

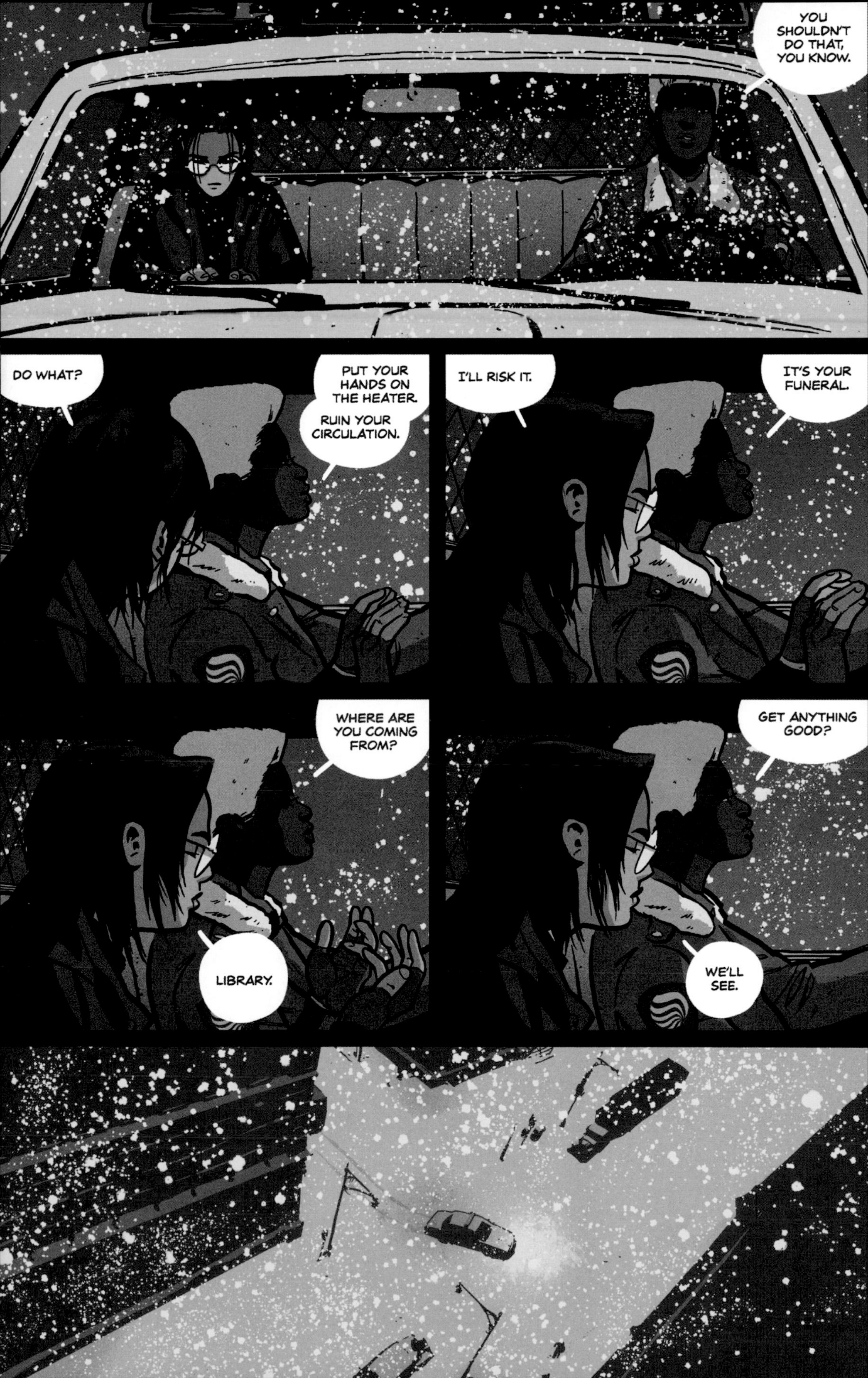
YOU SHOULDN'T DO THAT, YOU KNOW.
DO WHAT?
PUT YOUR HANDS ON THE HEATER.
RUIN YOUR CIRCULATION.
I'LL RISK IT.
IT'S YOUR FUNERAL.
WHERE ARE YOU COMING FROM?
LIBRARY.
GET ANYTHING GOOD?
WE'LL SEE.

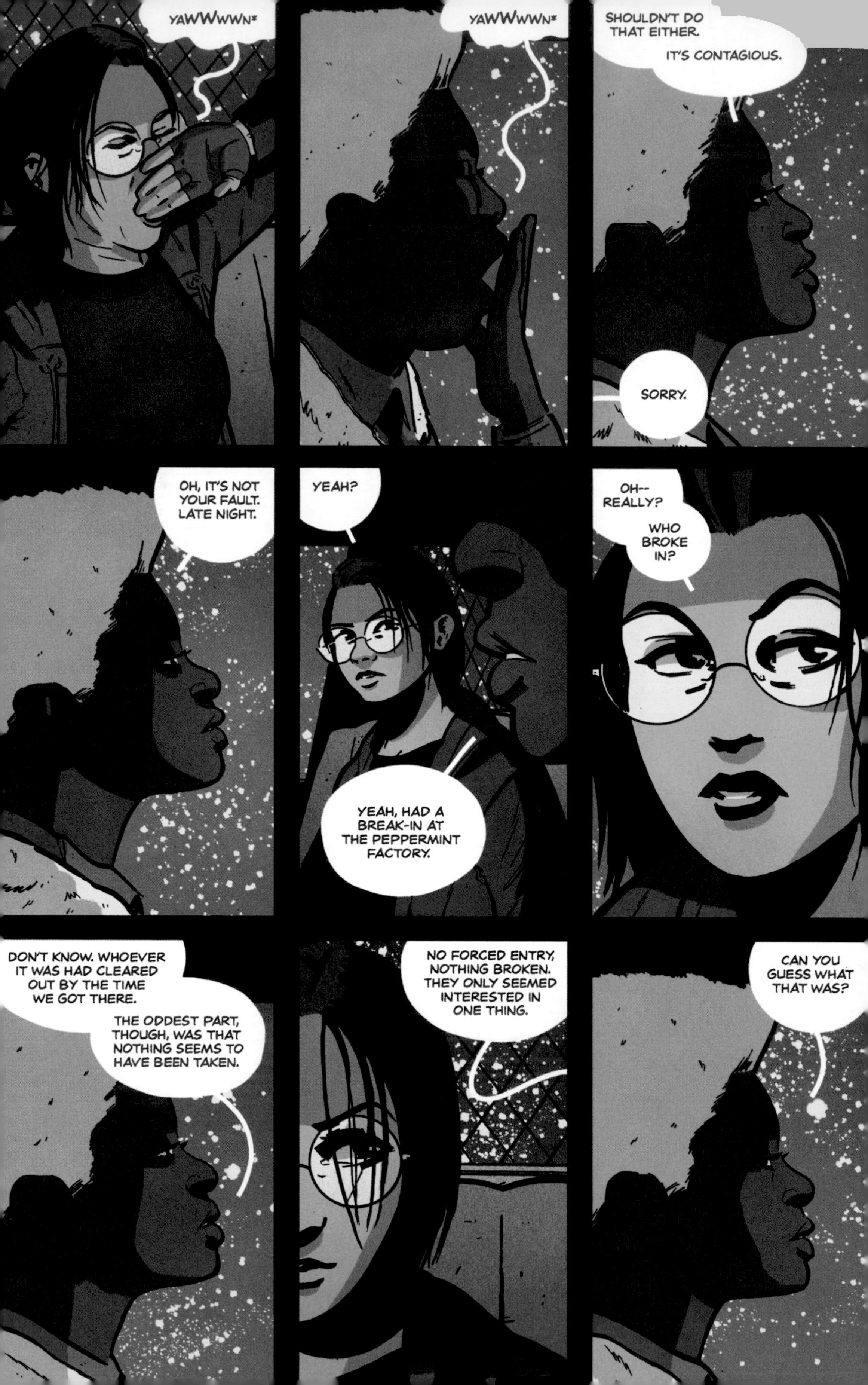
YAWWWWN*
YAWWWWN*
SHOULDN'T DO THAT EITHER.
IT'S CONTAGIOUS.
SORRY.
OH, IT'S NOT YOUR FAULT. LATE NIGHT.
YEAH?
YEAH, HAD A BREAK-IN AT THE PEPPERMINT FACTORY.
OH-- REALLY?
WHO BROKE IN?
DON'T KNOW. WHOEVER IT WAS HAD CLEARED OUT BY THE TIME WE GOT THERE.
THE ODDEST PART, THOUGH, WAS THAT NOTHING SEEMS TO HAVE BEEN TAKEN.
NO FORCED ENTRY, NOTHING BROKEN. THEY ONLY SEEMED INTERESTED IN ONE THING.
CAN YOU GUESS WHAT THAT WAS?

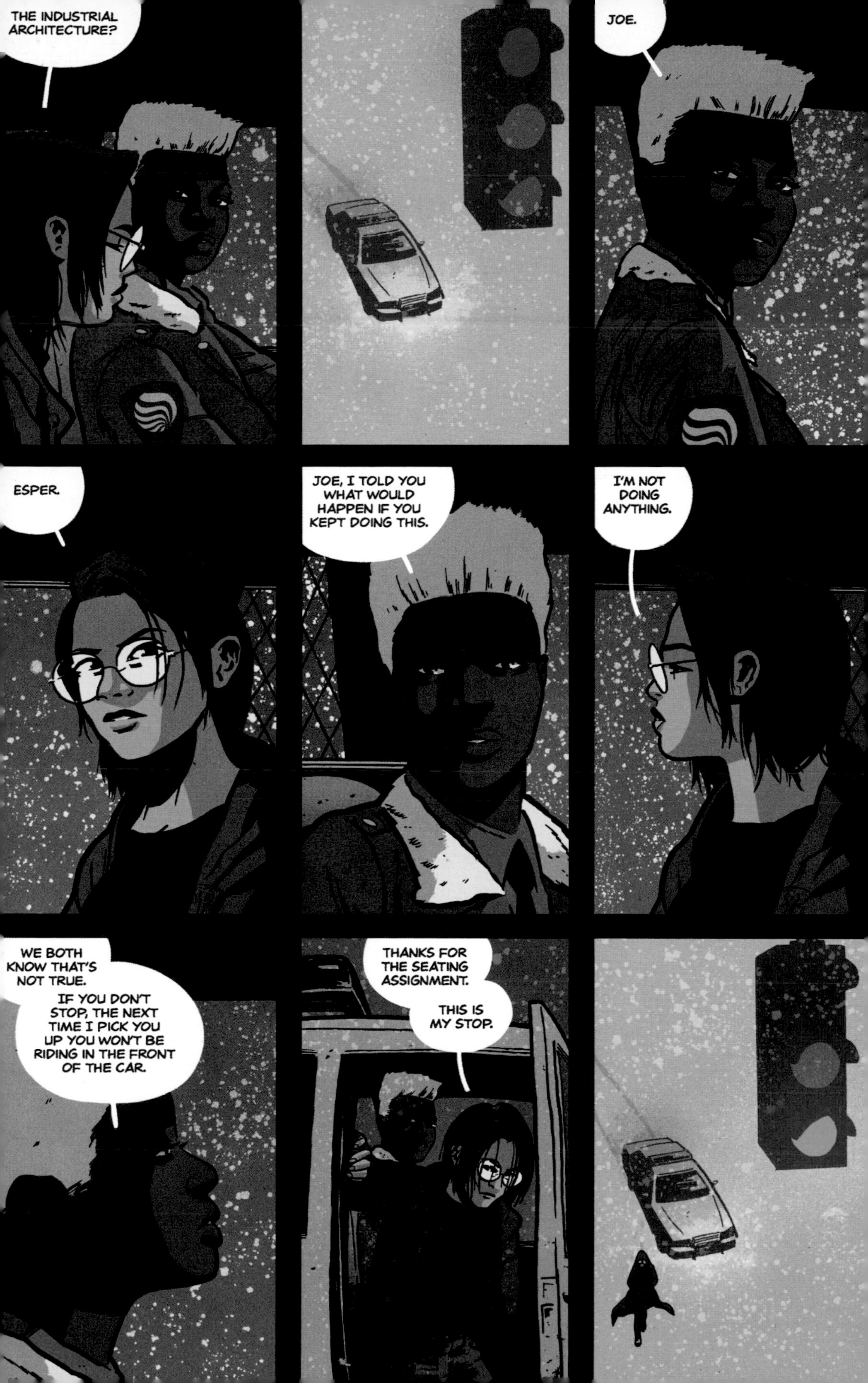
THE INDUSTRIAL ARCHITECTURE?
JOE.
ESPER.
JOE, I TOLD YOU WHAT WOULD HAPPEN IF YOU KEPT DOING THIS.
I'M NOT DOING ANYTHING.
WE BOTH KNOW THAT'S NOT TRUE.
IF YOU DON'T STOP, THE NEXT TIME I PICK YOU UP YOU WON'T BE RIDING IN THE FRONT OF THE CAR.
THANKS FOR THE SEATING ASSIGNMENT.
THIS IS MY STOP.

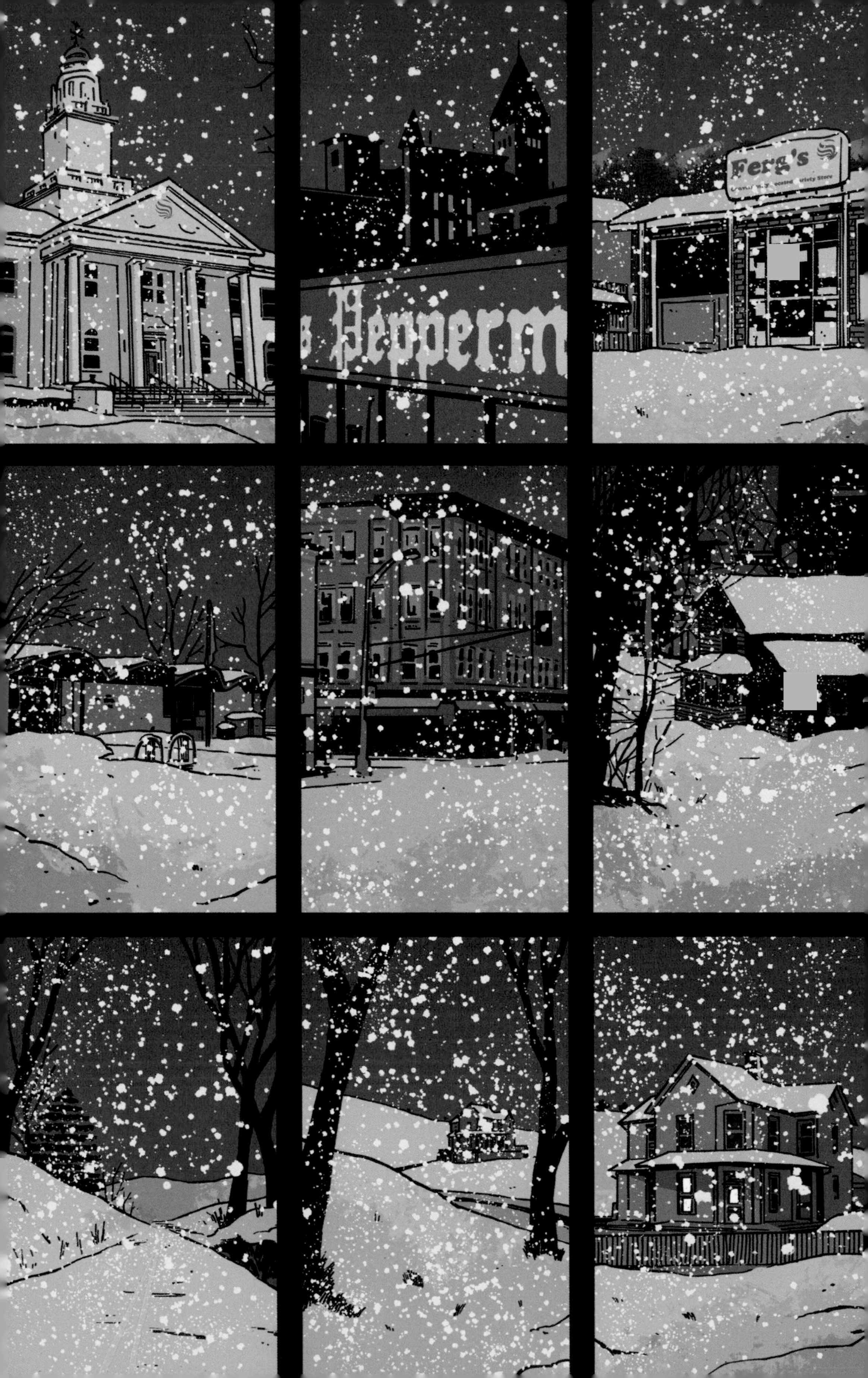
Pepperm
Ferg's

--SO GET YOUR SHOVELS READY BECAUSE IT DOESN'T LOOK LIKE THE SNOW IS GOING TO LET UP ANYTIME SOON.

IT WAS A LITTLE BIT OF A SLOW START THIS MORNING WITH ROUND ONE, BUT IT LOOKS LIKE THIS ONE COULD GO THE DISTANCE.

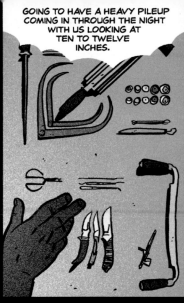

GOING TO HAVE A HEAVY PILEUP COMING IN THROUGH THE NIGHT WITH US LOOKING AT TEN TO TWELVE INCHES.

ROAD CONDITIONS ARE GOING TO BE LOOKING PRETTY ICY OUT THERE SO BETTER TO KEEP OFF THEM IF YOU CAN.

DING! DONG!

WE SUGGEST YOU STAY INSIDE, FIX YOURSELF A DRINK, AND KEEP IT RIGHT HERE AT W.P.P.B., YOUR HOME FOR--

***...

CLICK!

I'M COMING, I'M COMING.

DING! DONG!

HOLD YOUR HORSIES.

DING! DONG!

HI, MR. QUIL?

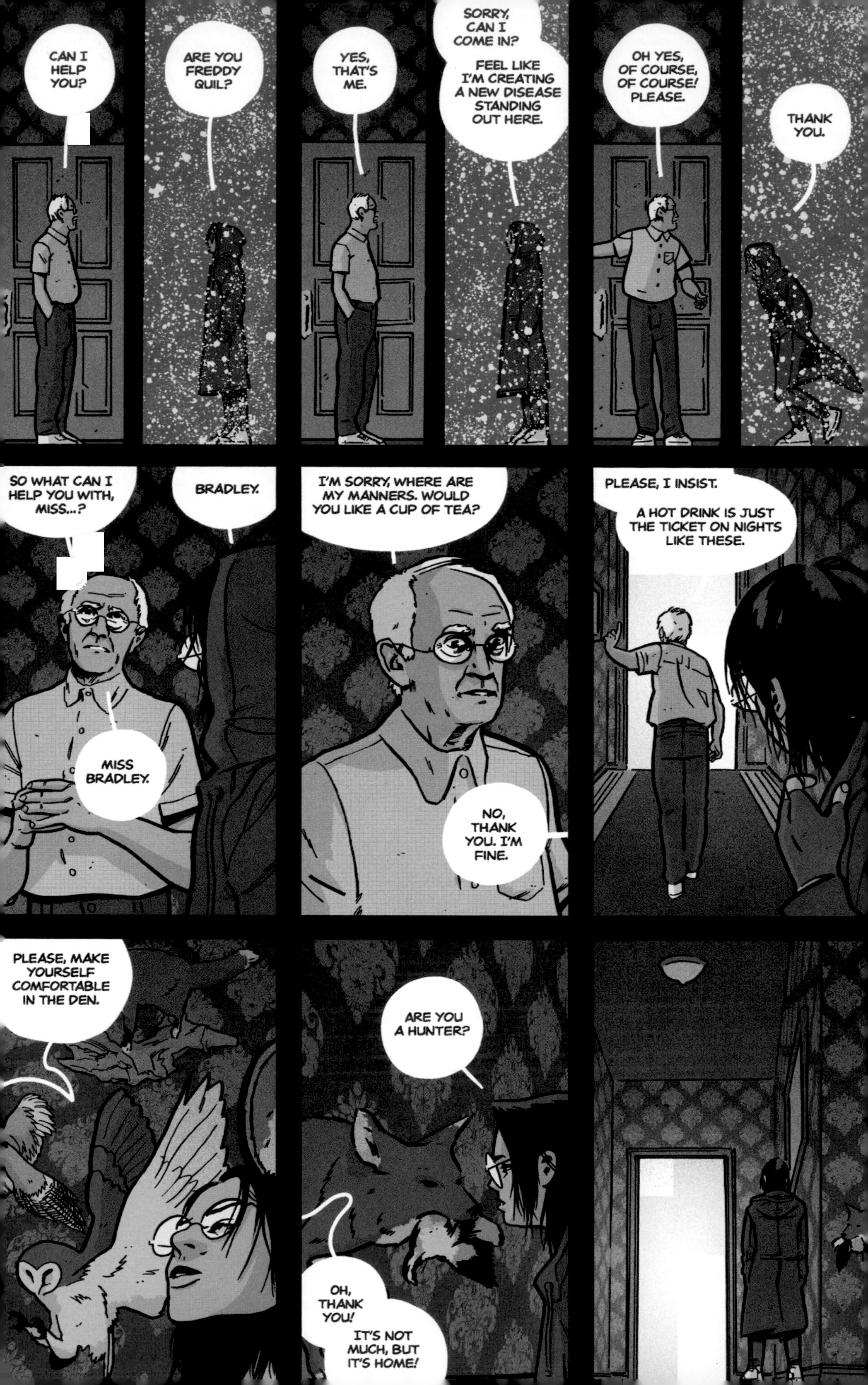
CAN I HELP YOU?
ARE YOU FREDDY QUIL?
YES, THAT'S ME.
SORRY, CAN I COME IN?
FEEL LIKE I'M CREATING A NEW DISEASE STANDING OUT HERE.
OH YES, OF COURSE, OF COURSE! PLEASE.
THANK YOU.
SO WHAT CAN I HELP YOU WITH, MISS...?
BRADLEY.
MISS BRADLEY.
I'M SORRY, WHERE ARE MY MANNERS. WOULD YOU LIKE A CUP OF TEA?
NO, THANK YOU. I'M FINE.
PLEASE, I INSIST.
A HOT DRINK IS JUST THE TICKET ON NIGHTS LIKE THESE.
PLEASE, MAKE YOURSELF COMFORTABLE IN THE DEN.
ARE YOU A HUNTER?
OH, THANK YOU!
IT'S NOT MUCH, BUT IT'S HOME!

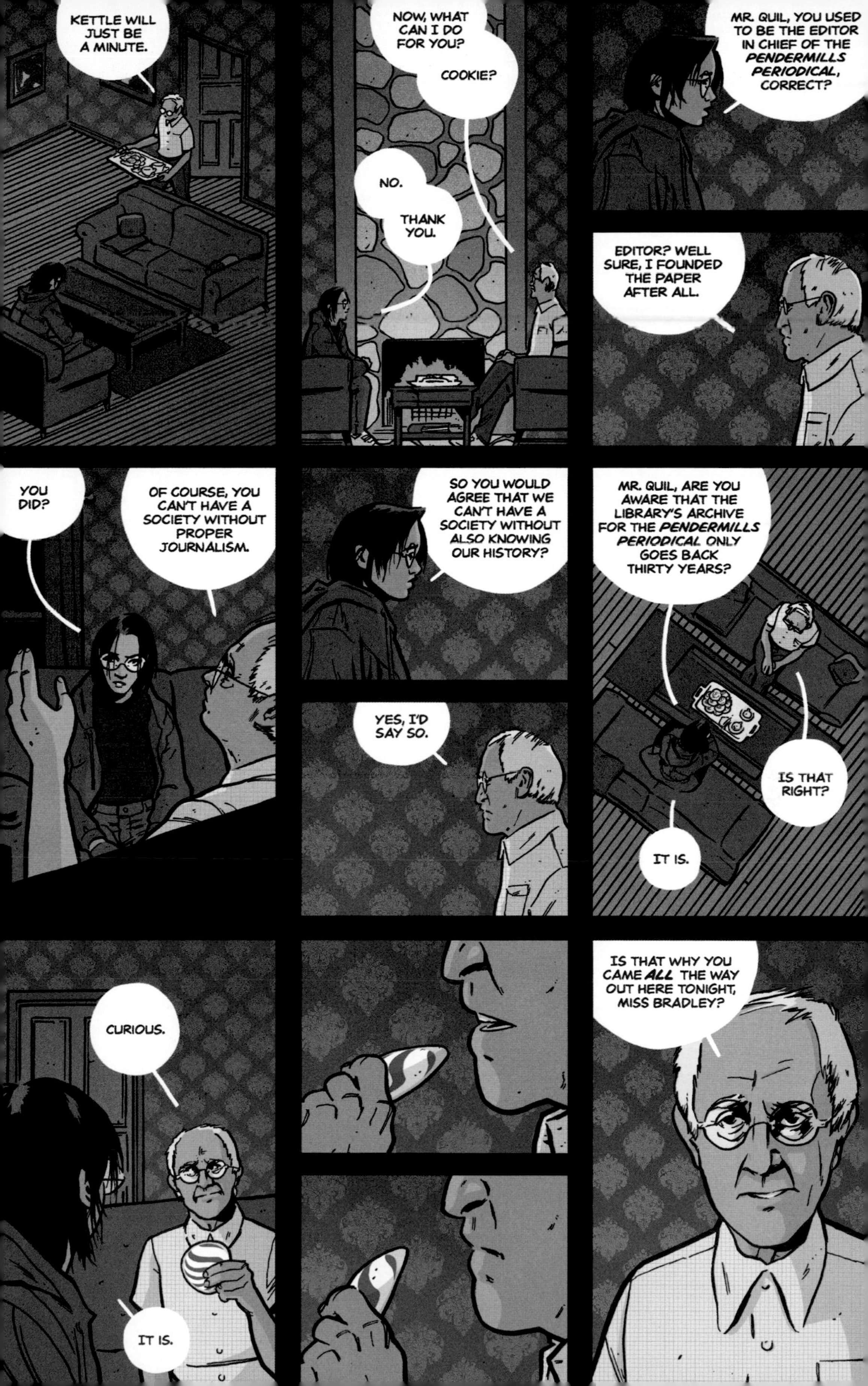
KETTLE WILL JUST BE A MINUTE.
NOW, WHAT CAN I DO FOR YOU?
COOKIE?
NO.
THANK YOU.
MR. QUIL, YOU USED TO BE THE EDITOR IN CHIEF OF THE *PENDERMILLS PERIODICAL*, CORRECT?
EDITOR? WELL SURE, I FOUNDED THE PAPER AFTER ALL.
YOU DID?
OF COURSE, YOU CAN'T HAVE A SOCIETY WITHOUT PROPER JOURNALISM.
SO YOU WOULD AGREE THAT WE CAN'T HAVE A SOCIETY WITHOUT ALSO KNOWING OUR HISTORY?
YES, I'D SAY SO.
MR. QUIL, ARE YOU AWARE THAT THE LIBRARY'S ARCHIVE FOR THE *PENDERMILLS PERIODICAL* ONLY GOES BACK THIRTY YEARS?
IS THAT RIGHT?
IT IS.
CURIOUS.
IT IS.
IS THAT WHY YOU CAME ***ALL*** THE WAY OUT HERE TONIGHT, MISS BRADLEY?

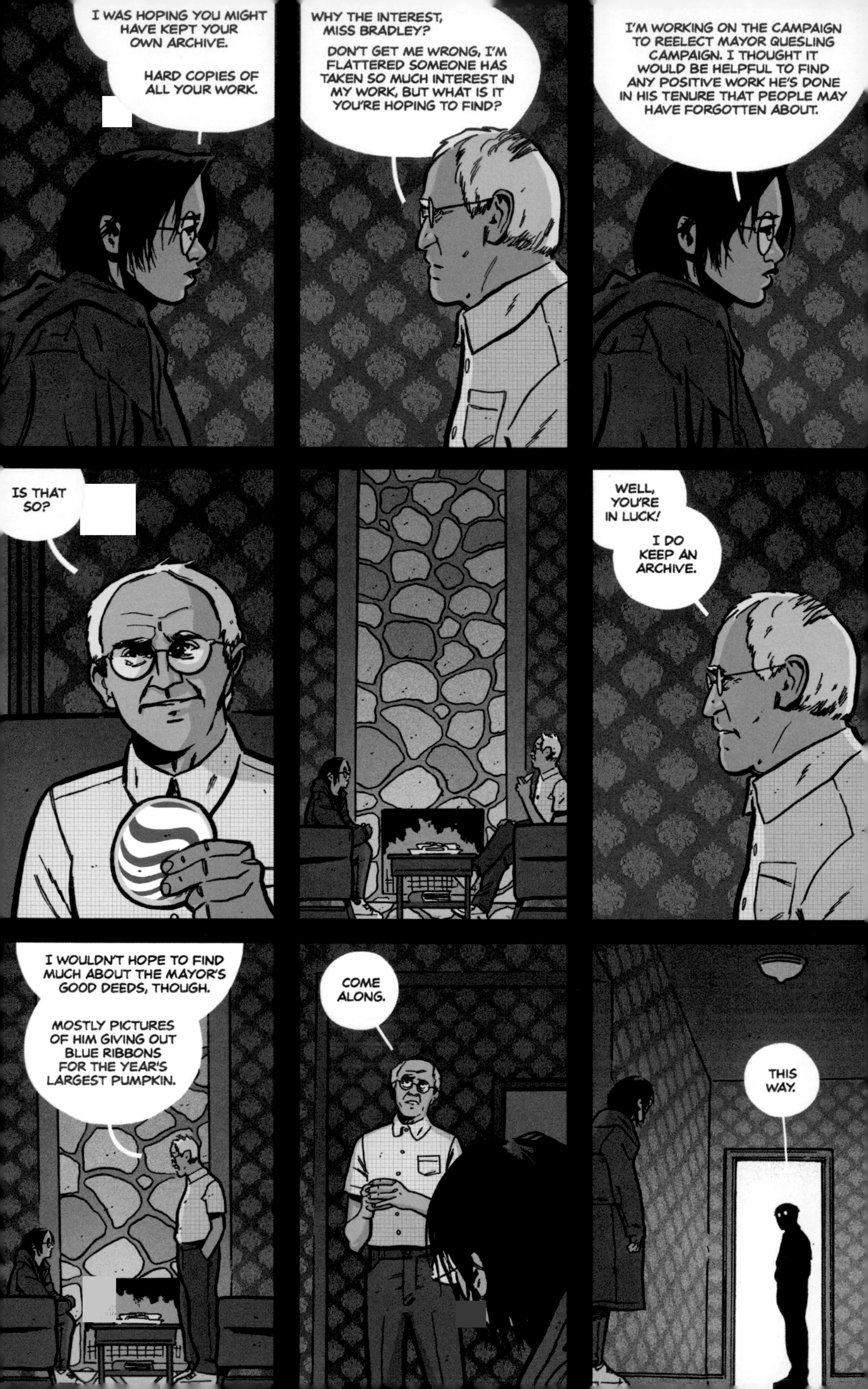
I WAS HOPING YOU MIGHT HAVE KEPT YOUR OWN ARCHIVE.
HARD COPIES OF ALL YOUR WORK.
WHY THE INTEREST, MISS BRADLEY?
DON'T GET ME WRONG, I'M FLATTERED SOMEONE HAS TAKEN SO MUCH INTEREST IN MY WORK, BUT WHAT IS IT YOU'RE HOPING TO FIND?
I'M WORKING ON THE CAMPAIGN TO REELECT MAYOR QUESLING CAMPAIGN. I THOUGHT IT WOULD BE HELPFUL TO FIND ANY POSITIVE WORK HE'S DONE IN HIS TENURE THAT PEOPLE MAY HAVE FORGOTTEN ABOUT.
IS THAT SO?
WELL, YOU'RE IN LUCK!
I DO KEEP AN ARCHIVE.
I WOULDN'T HOPE TO FIND MUCH ABOUT THE MAYOR'S GOOD DEEDS, THOUGH.
MOSTLY PICTURES OF HIM GIVING OUT BLUE RIBBONS FOR THE YEAR'S LARGEST PUMPKIN.
COME ALONG.
THIS WAY.

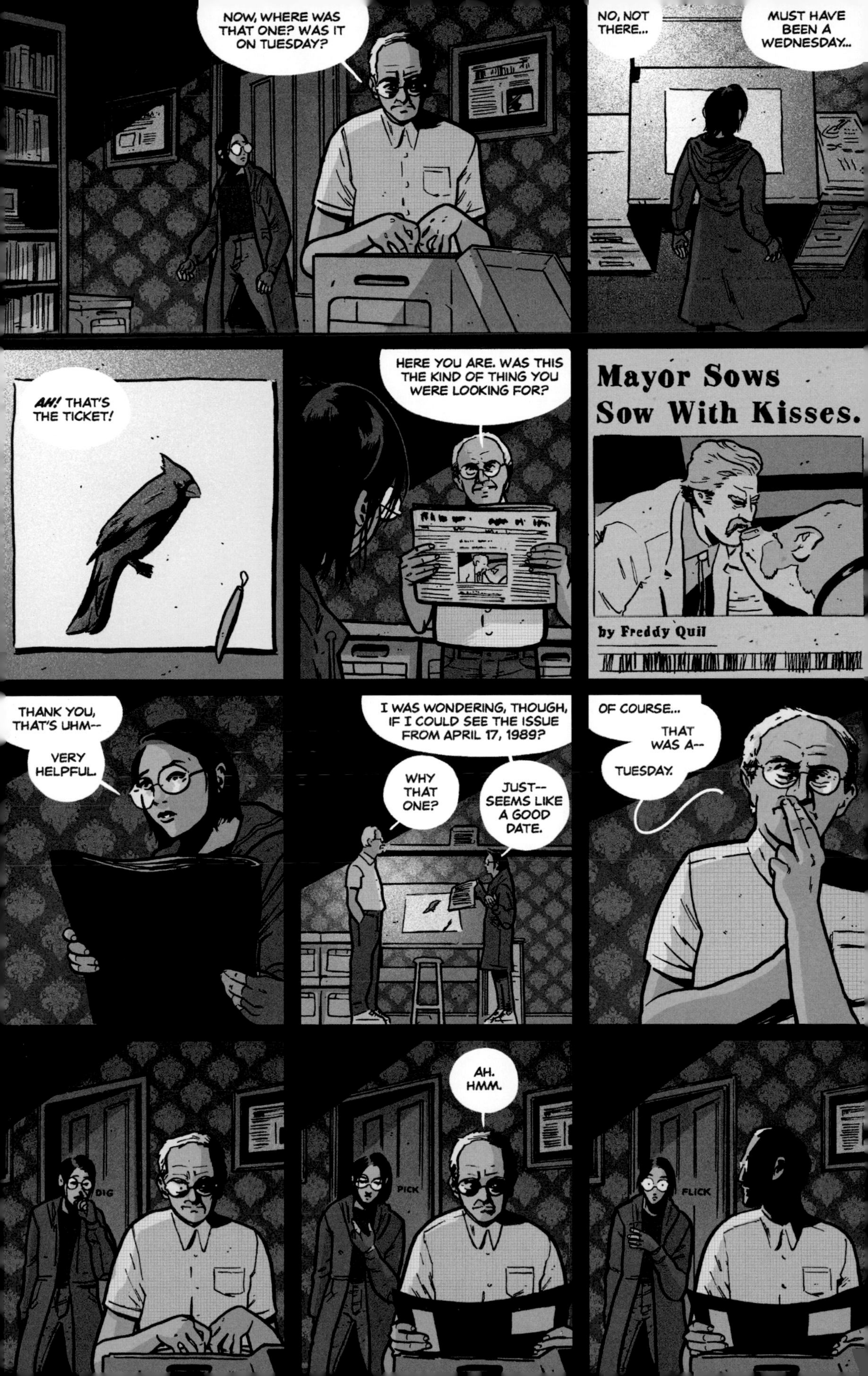
NOW, WHERE WAS THAT ONE? WAS IT ON TUESDAY?
NO, NOT THERE...
MUST HAVE BEEN A WEDNESDAY...
AH! THAT'S THE TICKET!
HERE YOU ARE. WAS THIS THE KIND OF THING YOU WERE LOOKING FOR?
Mayor Sows Sow With Kisses.
by Freddy Quil
THANK YOU, THAT'S UHM--
VERY HELPFUL.
I WAS WONDERING, THOUGH, IF I COULD SEE THE ISSUE FROM APRIL 17, 1989?
WHY THAT ONE?
JUST-- SEEMS LIKE A GOOD DATE.
OF COURSE...
THAT WAS A--
TUESDAY.
DIG
AH. HMM.
PICK
FLICK

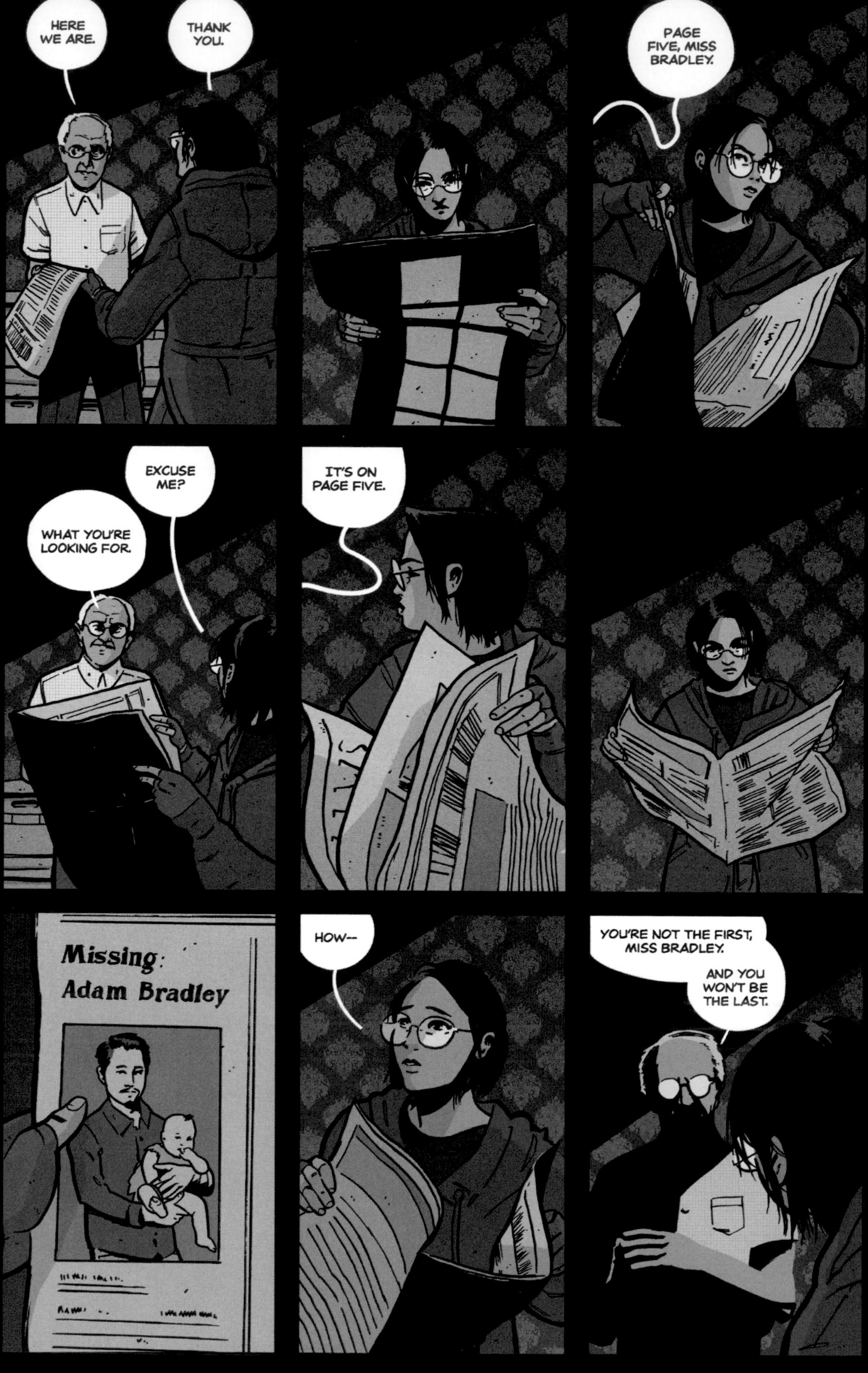
HERE WE ARE.
THANK YOU.
PAGE FIVE, MISS BRADLEY.
EXCUSE ME?
WHAT YOU'RE LOOKING FOR.
IT'S ON PAGE FIVE.
Missing: Adam Bradley
HOW--
YOU'RE NOT THE FIRST, MISS BRADLEY.
AND YOU WON'T BE THE LAST.

THIS IS ABOUT MISS GUFFIN, ISN'T IT?

YOU WERE FRIENDS?

OH, CHILD.

SHE'S GONE.

YOU DON'T KNOW THAT.

OH, BUT *I DO.* SAME AS YOU KNOW.

SCREEEEEEEEEE

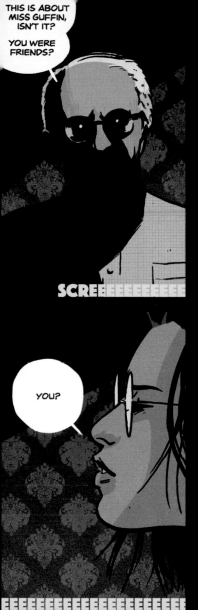

YOU?

ME? OH NO, NO, NO.

HER.

EEEEEEEEEEEEEEEEEEEE

ON THEIR EIGHTEENTH YEAR, THEY SIGNED IN RED, NEVER TO BE HEARD FROM AGAIN.

IT'S ALWAYS BEEN *HER.*

EEEEEEEEEEEEEEEEEEEE

CHILD?

WHERE ARE YOU GOING?

YOU HAVEN'T HAD YOUR TEA YET!

EEEEEEEEEEEEE

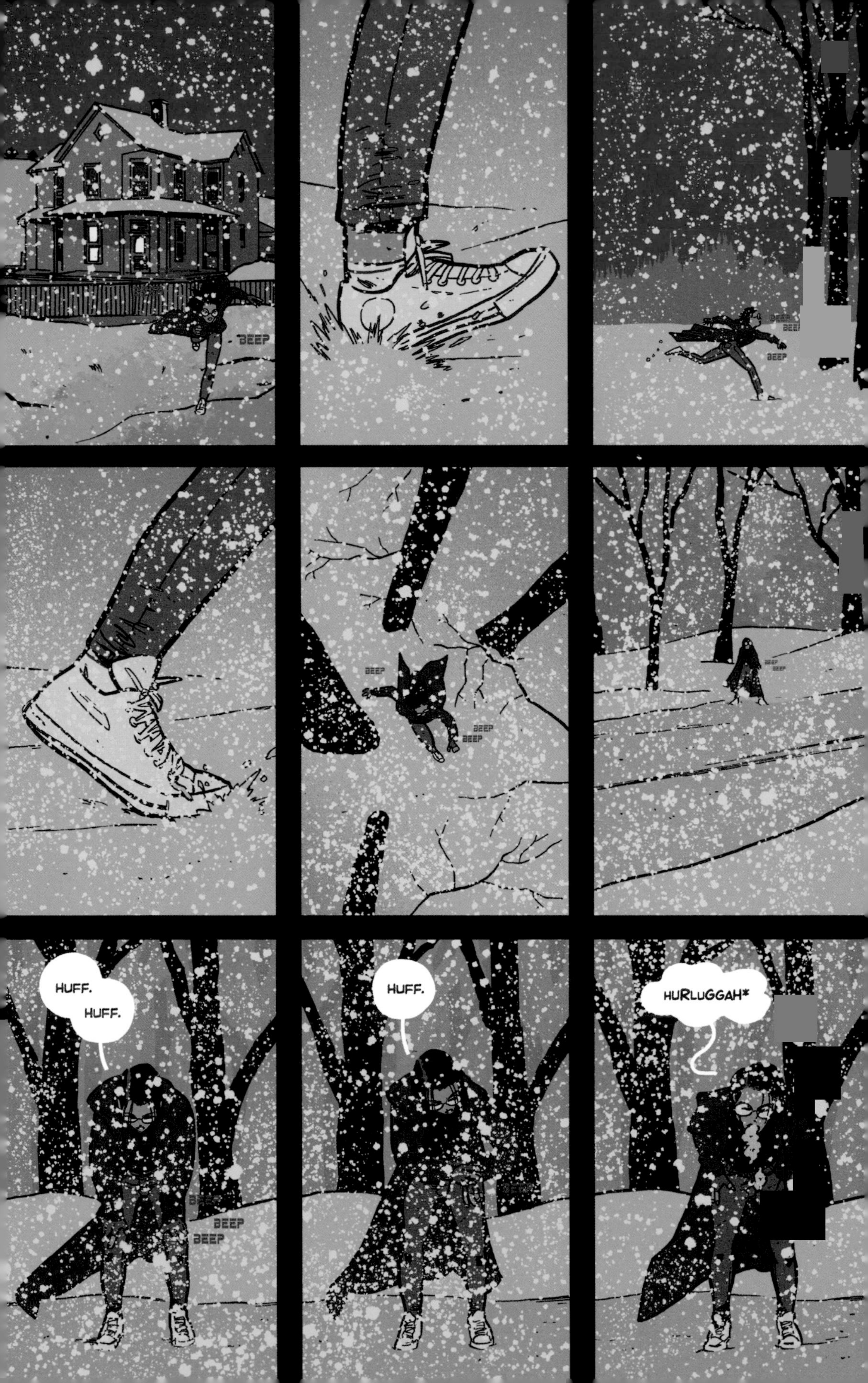

BEEP
BEEP
BEEP
BEEP
BEEP
BEEP
BEEP
BEEP
HUFF.
HUFF.
BEEP
BEEP
HUFF.
HURLUGGAH*

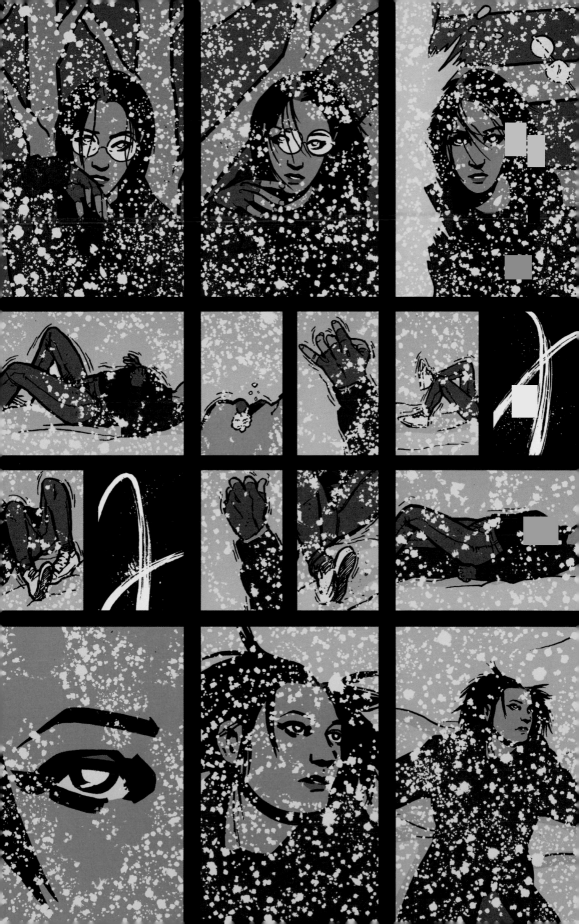

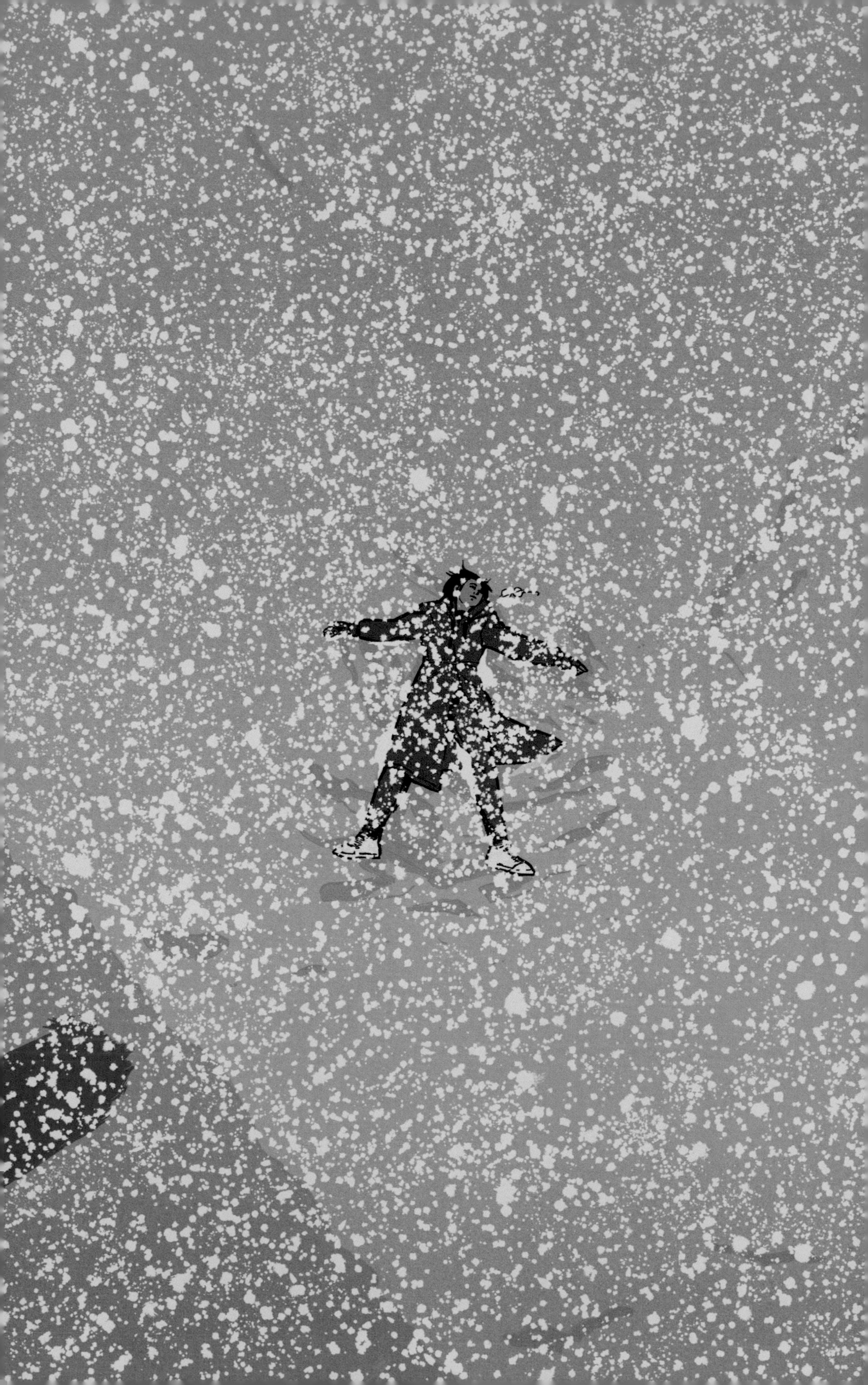

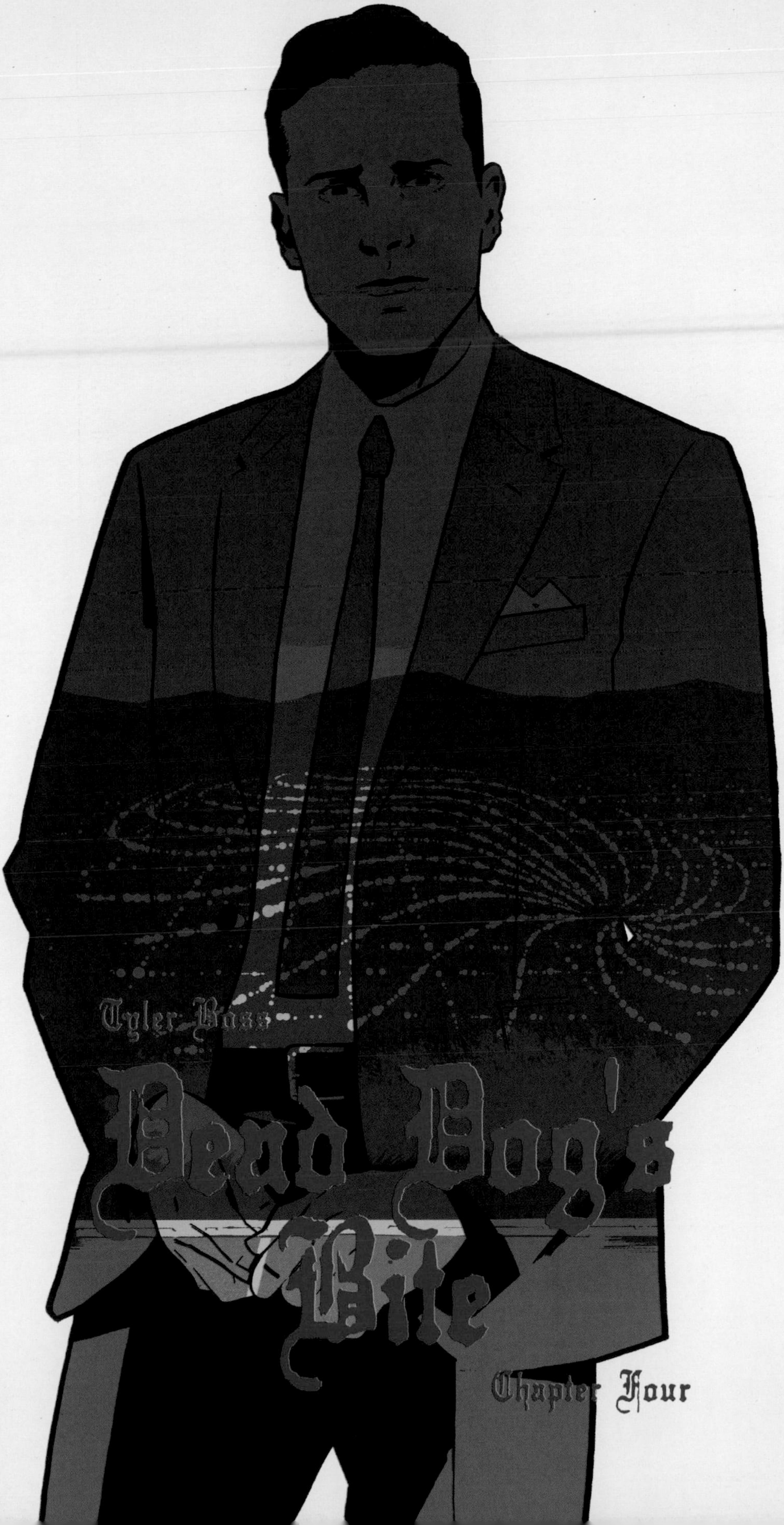
Tyler Boss
Dead Dog's Bite
Chapter Four

"You can never really trust
someone who remembers every
embarrassing detail of your
adolescence..."
                                  --D.C.

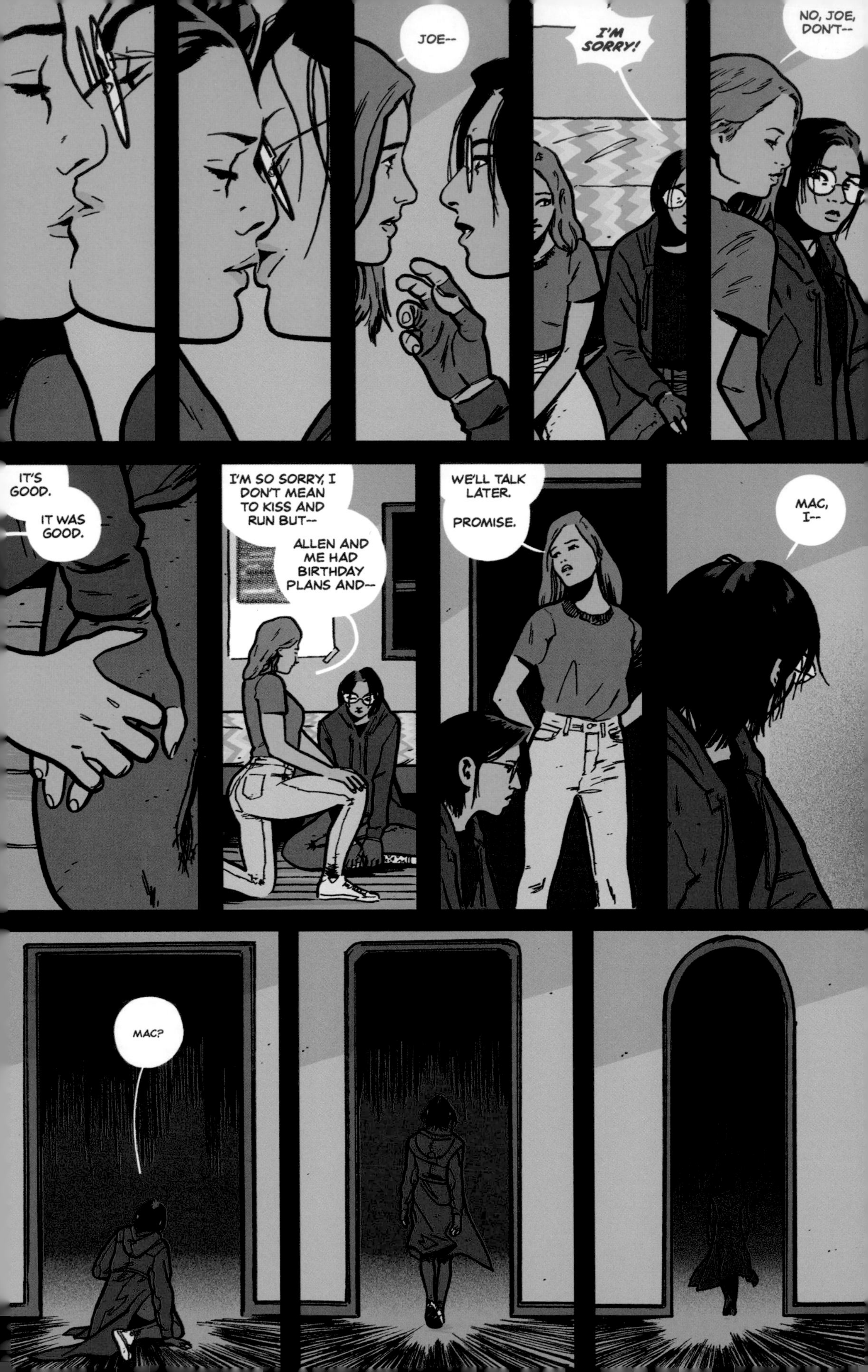
JOE--
I'M SORRY!
NO, JOE, DON'T--
IT'S GOOD.
IT WAS GOOD.
I'M SO SORRY, I DON'T MEAN TO KISS AND RUN BUT--
ALLEN AND ME HAD BIRTHDAY PLANS AND--
WE'LL TALK LATER.
PROMISE.
MAC, I--
MAC?

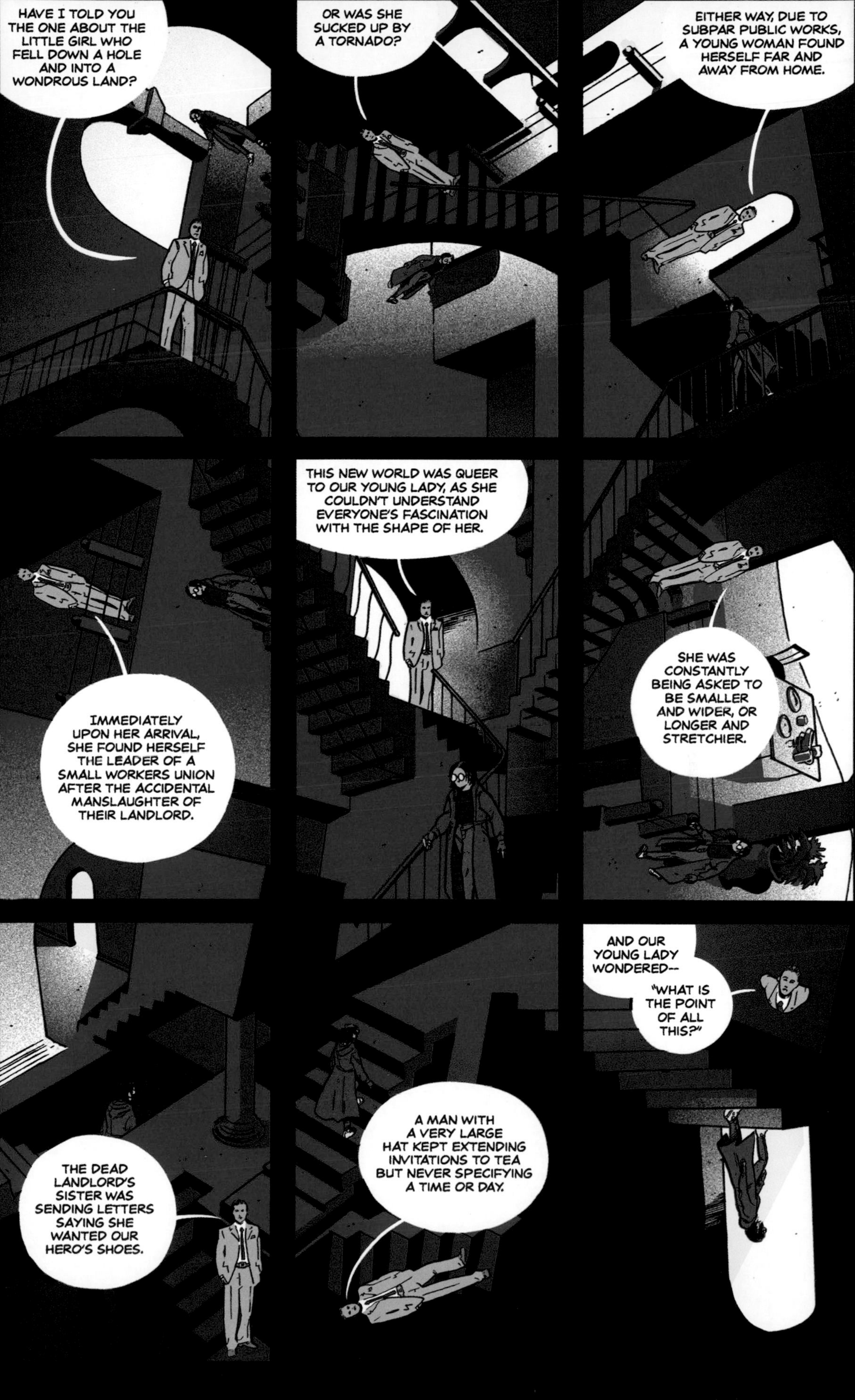
HAVE I TOLD YOU THE ONE ABOUT THE LITTLE GIRL WHO FELL DOWN A HOLE AND INTO A WONDROUS LAND?
OR WAS SHE SUCKED UP BY A TORNADO?
EITHER WAY, DUE TO SUBPAR PUBLIC WORKS, A YOUNG WOMAN FOUND HERSELF FAR AND AWAY FROM HOME.
IMMEDIATELY UPON HER ARRIVAL, SHE FOUND HERSELF THE LEADER OF A SMALL WORKERS UNION AFTER THE ACCIDENTAL MANSLAUGHTER OF THEIR LANDLORD.
THIS NEW WORLD WAS QUEER TO OUR YOUNG LADY, AS SHE COULDN'T UNDERSTAND EVERYONE'S FASCINATION WITH THE SHAPE OF HER.
SHE WAS CONSTANTLY BEING ASKED TO BE SMALLER AND WIDER, OR LONGER AND STRETCHIER.
THE DEAD LANDLORD'S SISTER WAS SENDING LETTERS SAYING SHE WANTED OUR HERO'S SHOES.
A MAN WITH A VERY LARGE HAT KEPT EXTENDING INVITATIONS TO TEA BUT NEVER SPECIFYING A TIME OR DAY.
AND OUR YOUNG LADY WONDERED--
"WHAT IS THE POINT OF ALL THIS?"

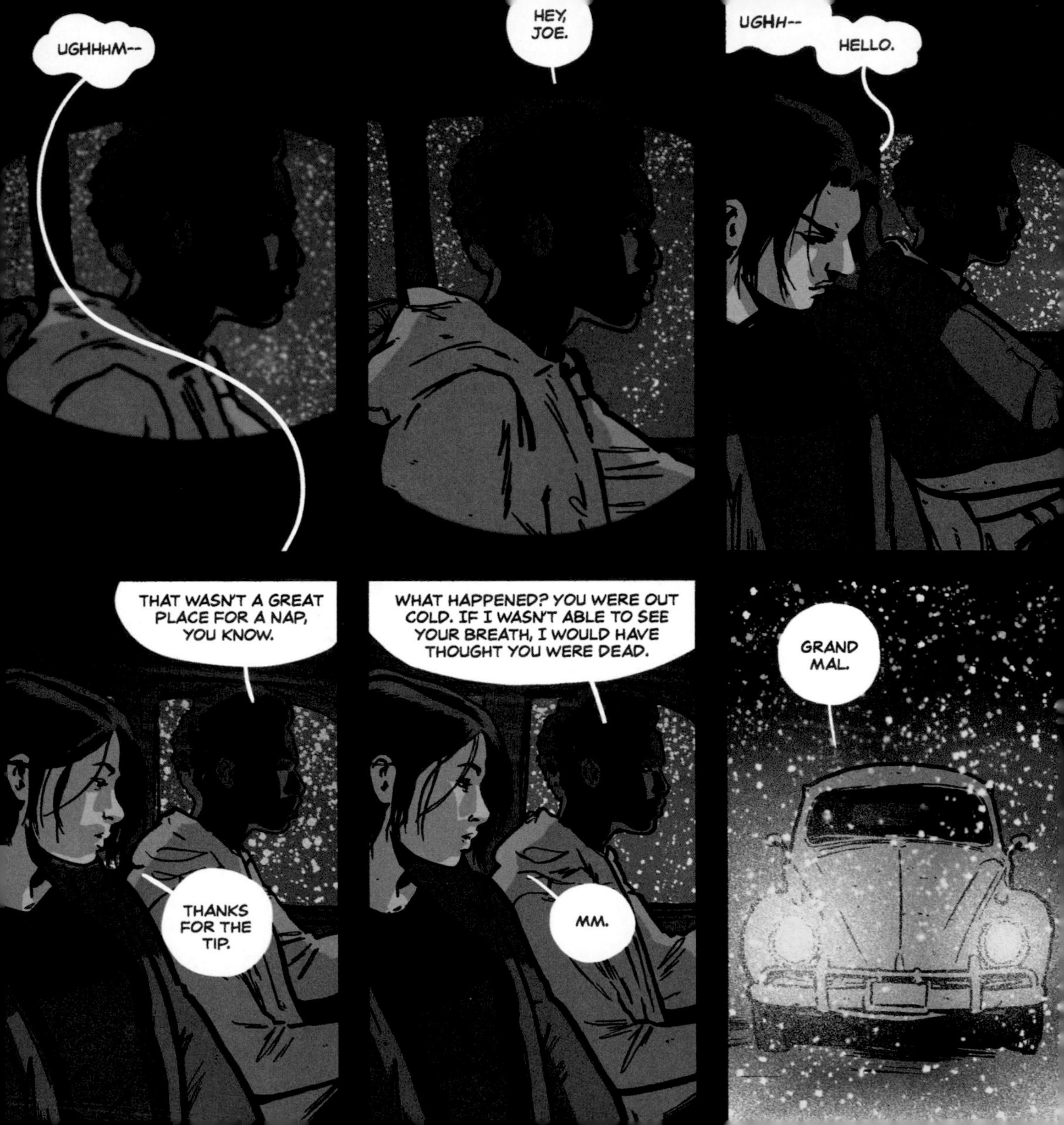
UGHHHM--
HEY, JOE.
UGHH--
HELLO.
THAT WASN'T A GREAT PLACE FOR A NAP, YOU KNOW.
THANKS FOR THE TIP.
WHAT HAPPENED? YOU WERE OUT COLD. IF I WASN'T ABLE TO SEE YOUR BREATH, I WOULD HAVE THOUGHT YOU WERE DEAD.
MM.
GRAND MAL.

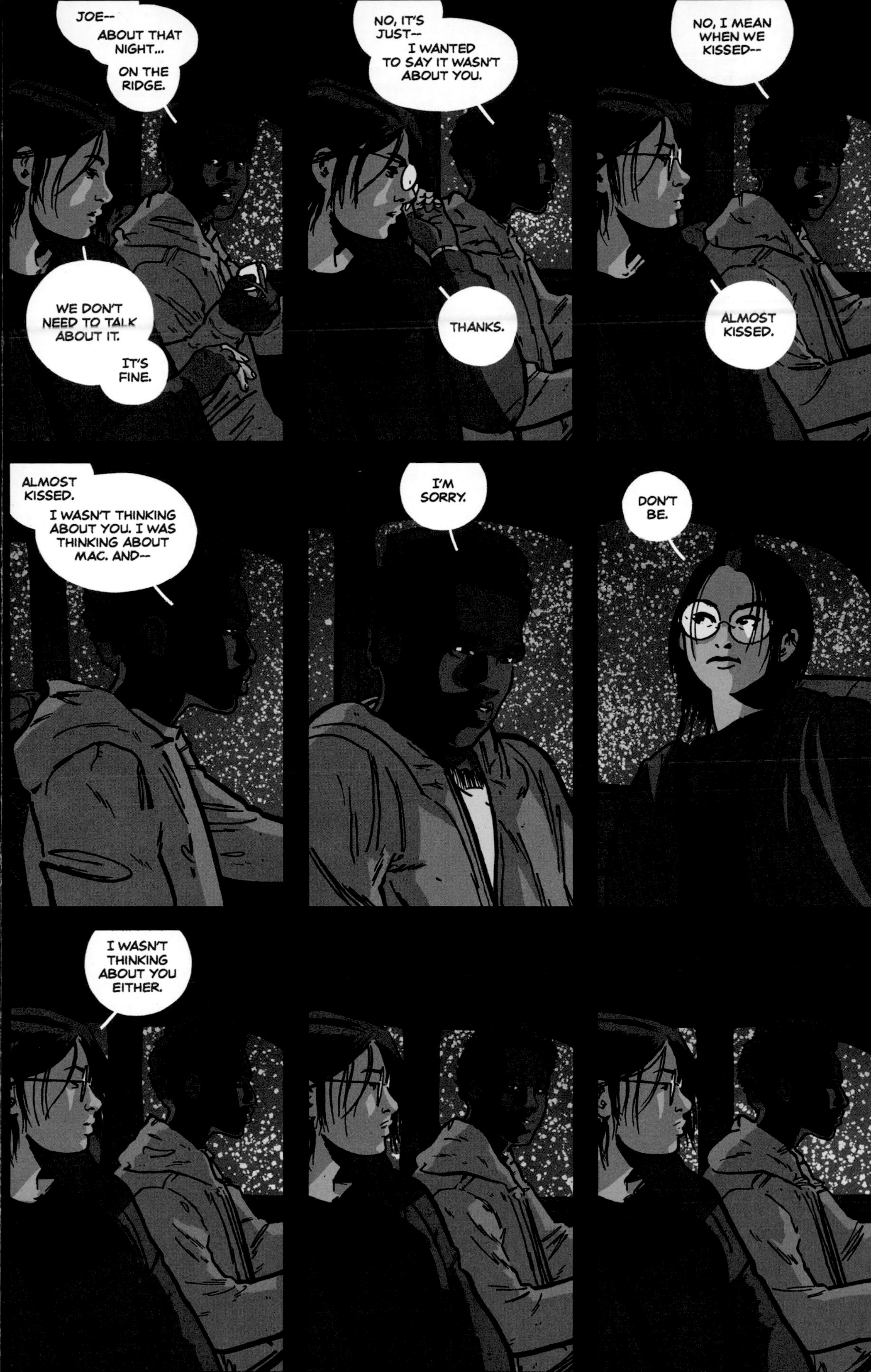
JOE-- ABOUT THAT NIGHT... ON THE RIDGE.
WE DON'T NEED TO TALK ABOUT IT. IT'S FINE.
NO, IT'S JUST-- I WANTED TO SAY IT WASN'T ABOUT YOU.
THANKS.
NO, I MEAN WHEN WE KISSED--
ALMOST KISSED.
ALMOST KISSED. I WASN'T THINKING ABOUT YOU. I WAS THINKING ABOUT MAC. AND--
I'M SORRY.
DON'T BE.
I WASN'T THINKING ABOUT YOU EITHER.

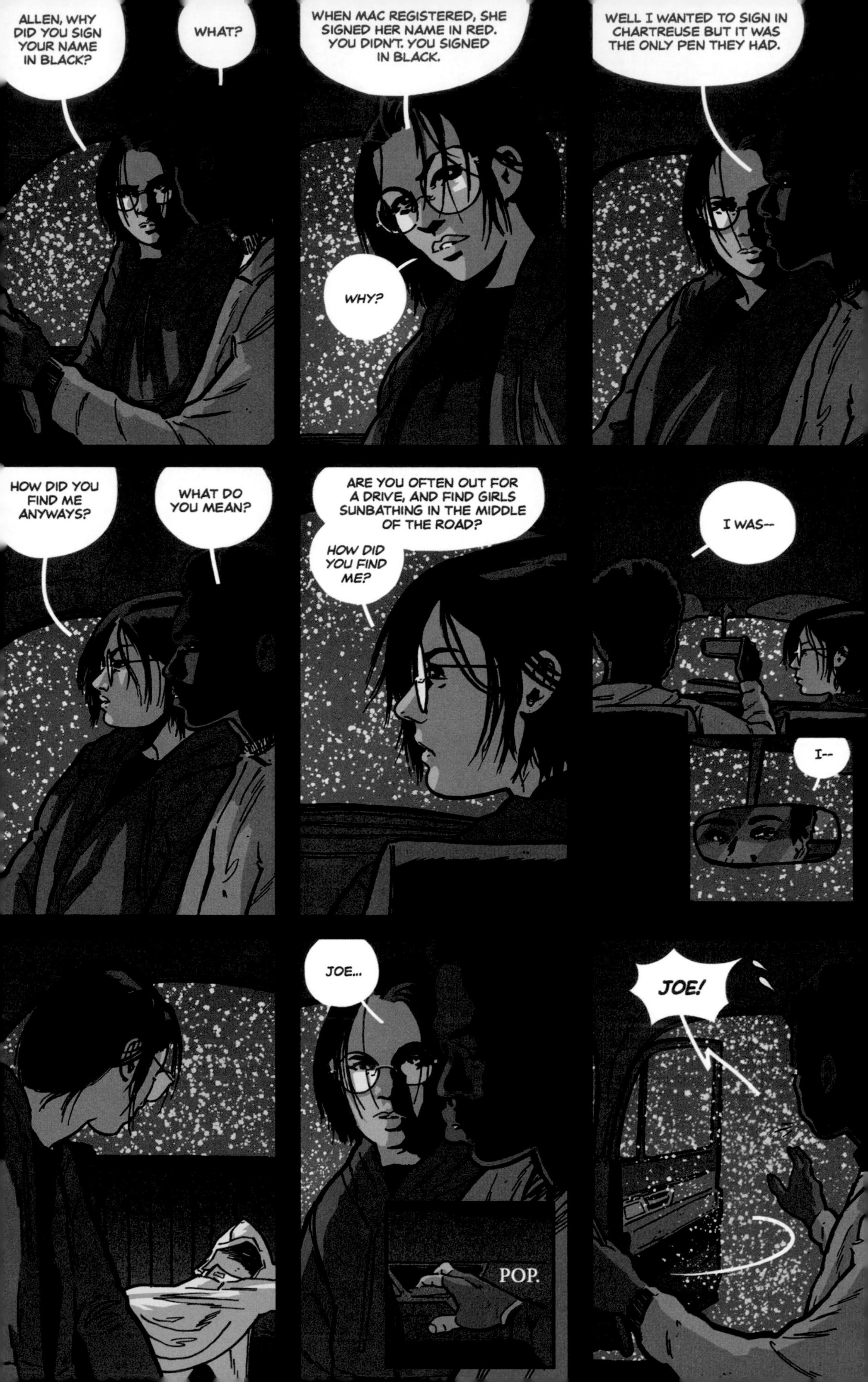
ALLEN, WHY DID YOU SIGN YOUR NAME IN BLACK?
WHAT?
WHEN MAC REGISTERED, SHE SIGNED HER NAME IN RED. YOU DIDN'T. YOU SIGNED IN BLACK.
WHY?
WELL I WANTED TO SIGN IN CHARTREUSE BUT IT WAS THE ONLY PEN THEY HAD.
HOW DID YOU FIND ME ANYWAYS?
WHAT DO YOU MEAN?
ARE YOU OFTEN OUT FOR A DRIVE, AND FIND GIRLS SUNBATHING IN THE MIDDLE OF THE ROAD?
HOW DID YOU FIND ME?
I WAS--
I--
JOE...
POP.
JOE!

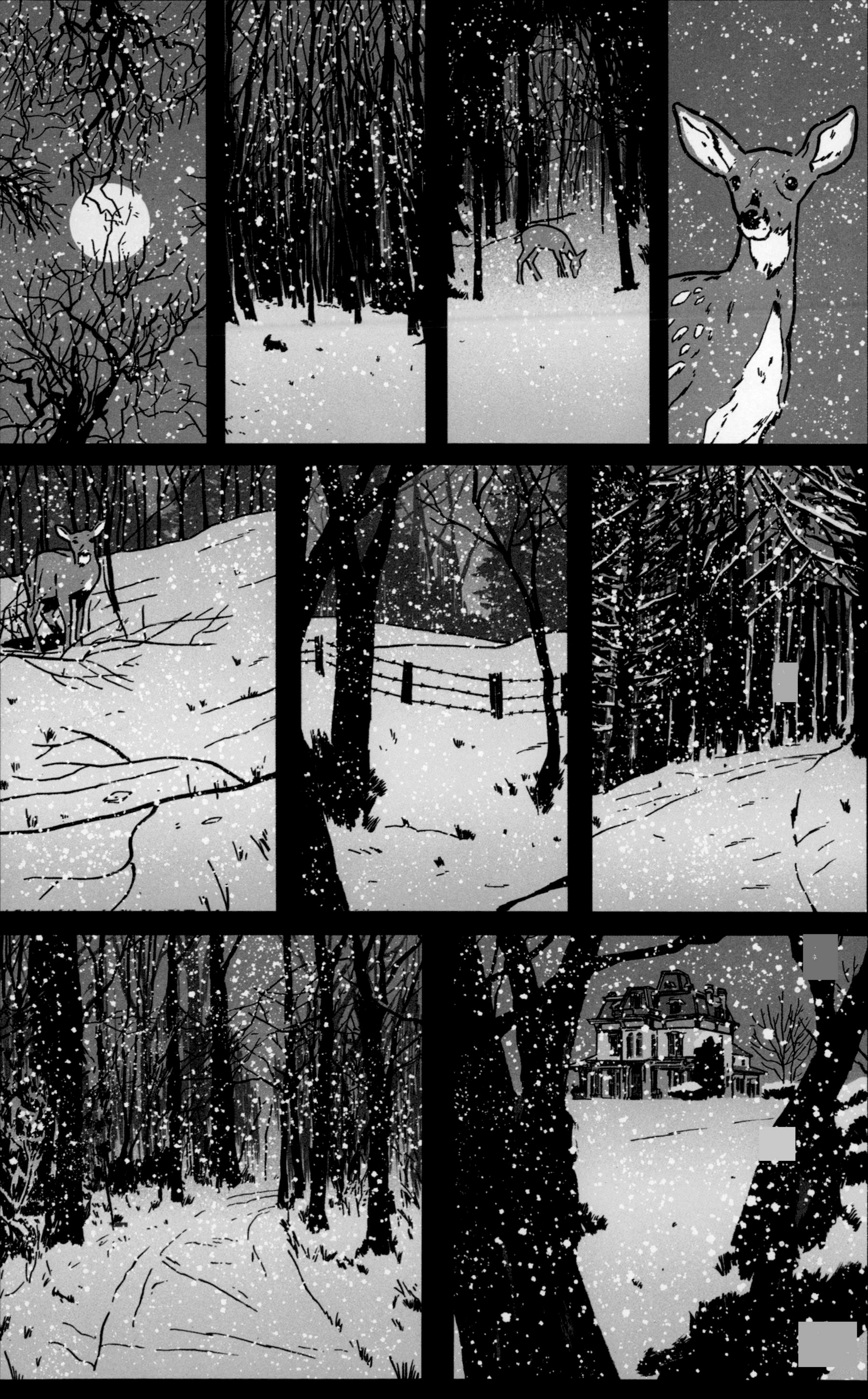

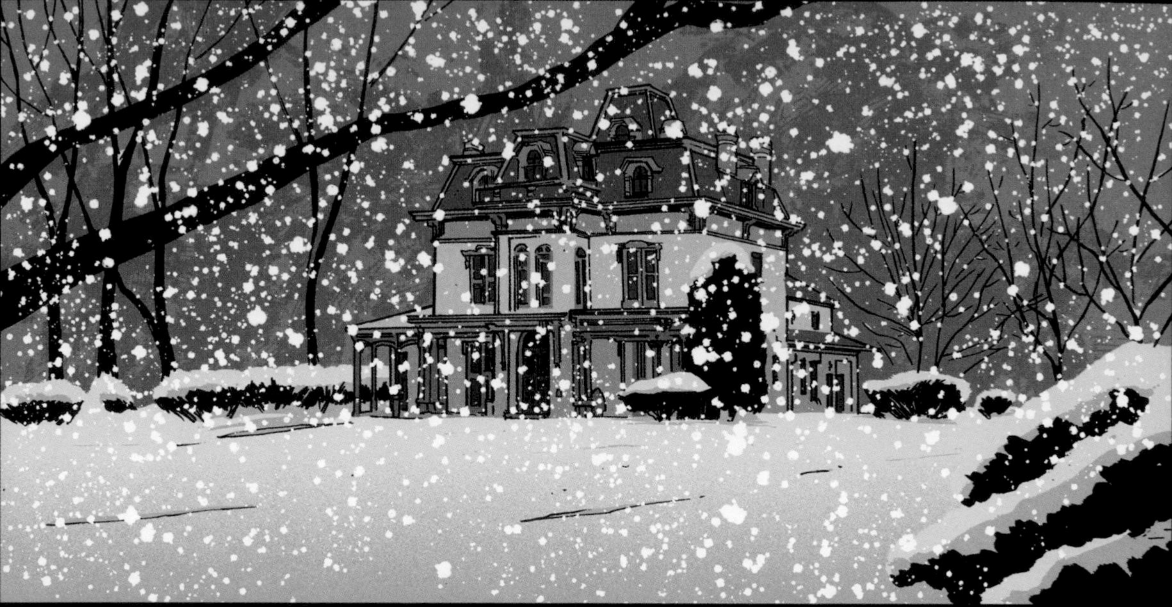
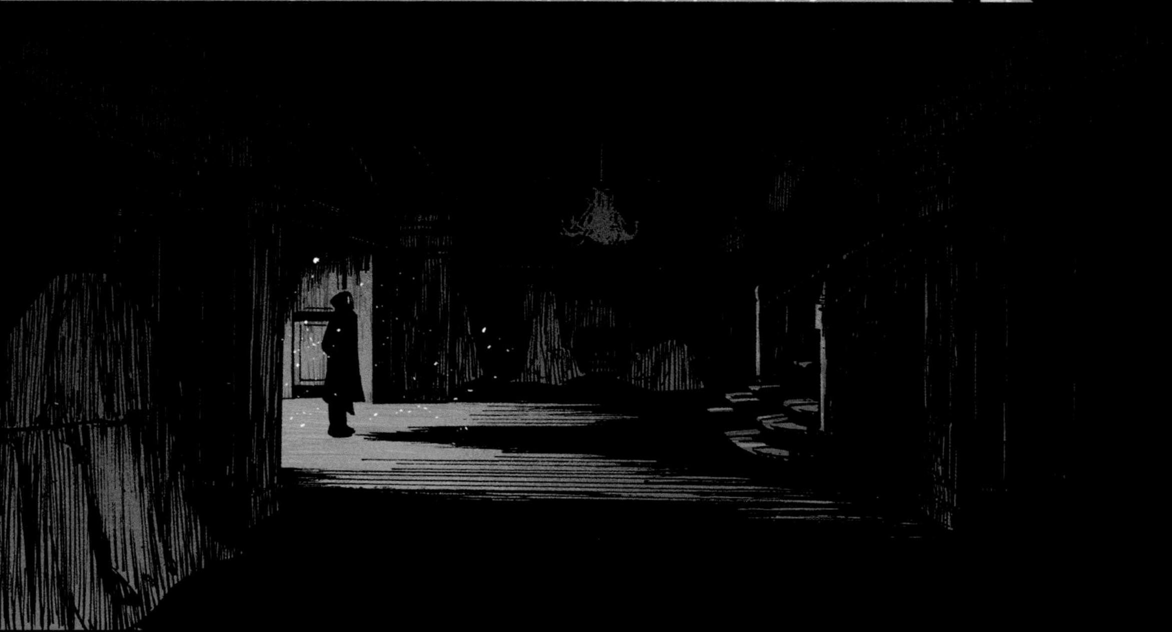

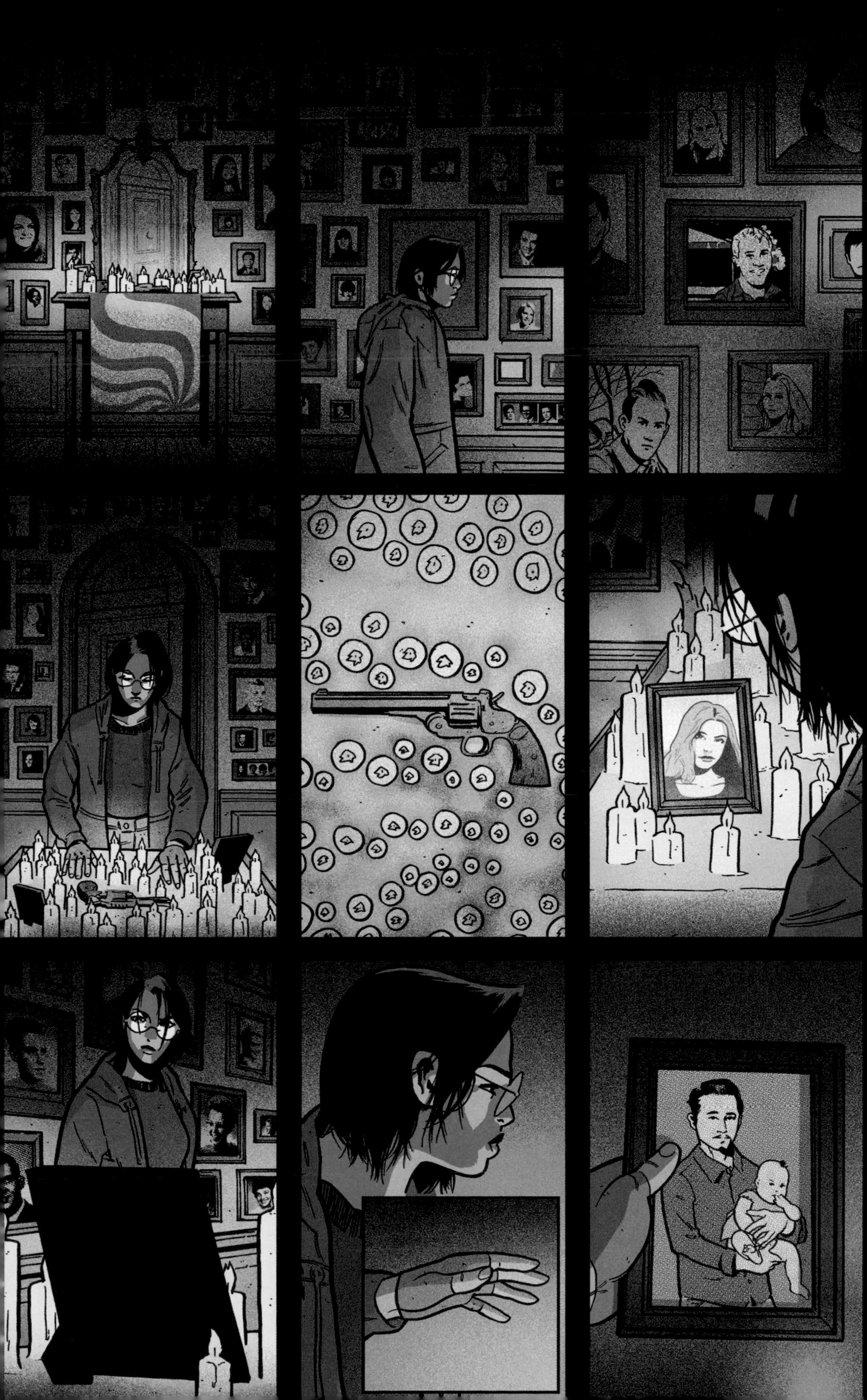

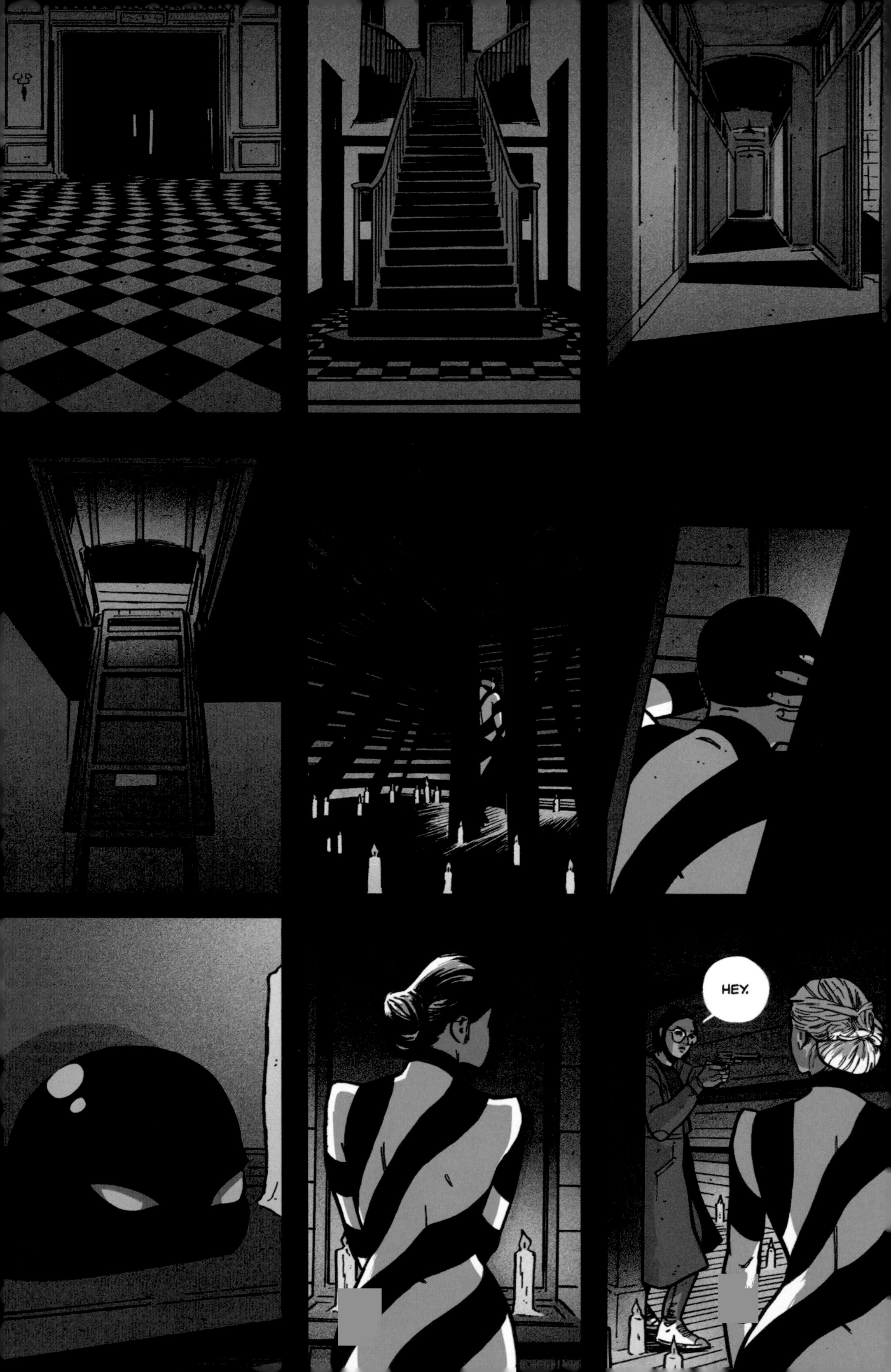
HEY.

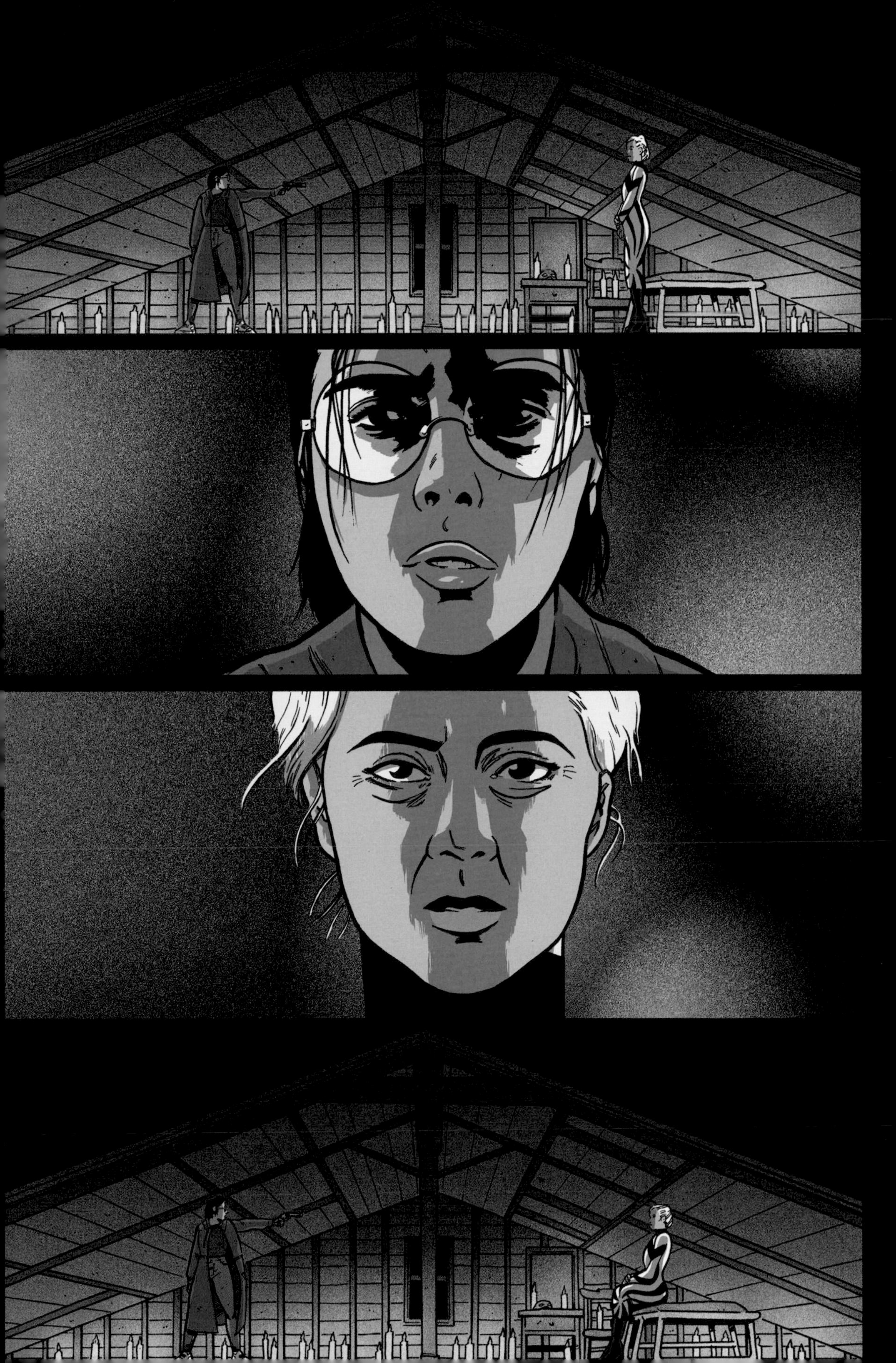

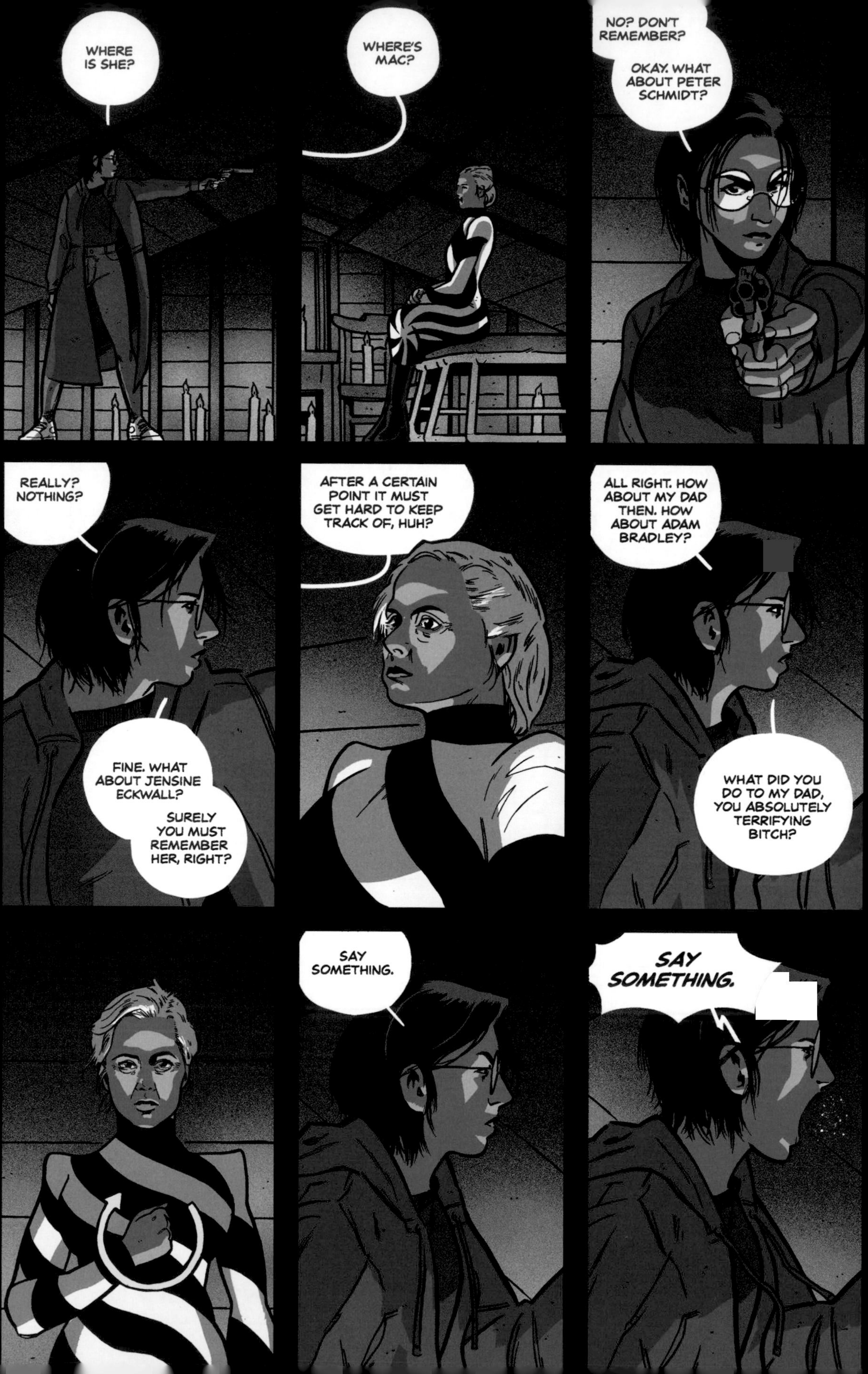
WHERE IS SHE?
WHERE'S MAC?
NO? DON'T REMEMBER?
OKAY. WHAT ABOUT PETER SCHMIDT?
REALLY? NOTHING?
FINE. WHAT ABOUT JENSINE ECKWALL?
SURELY YOU MUST REMEMBER HER, RIGHT?
AFTER A CERTAIN POINT IT MUST GET HARD TO KEEP TRACK OF, HUH?
ALL RIGHT. HOW ABOUT MY DAD THEN. HOW ABOUT ADAM BRADLEY?
WHAT DID YOU DO TO MY DAD, YOU ABSOLUTELY TERRIFYING BITCH?
SAY SOMETHING.
SAY SOMETHING.

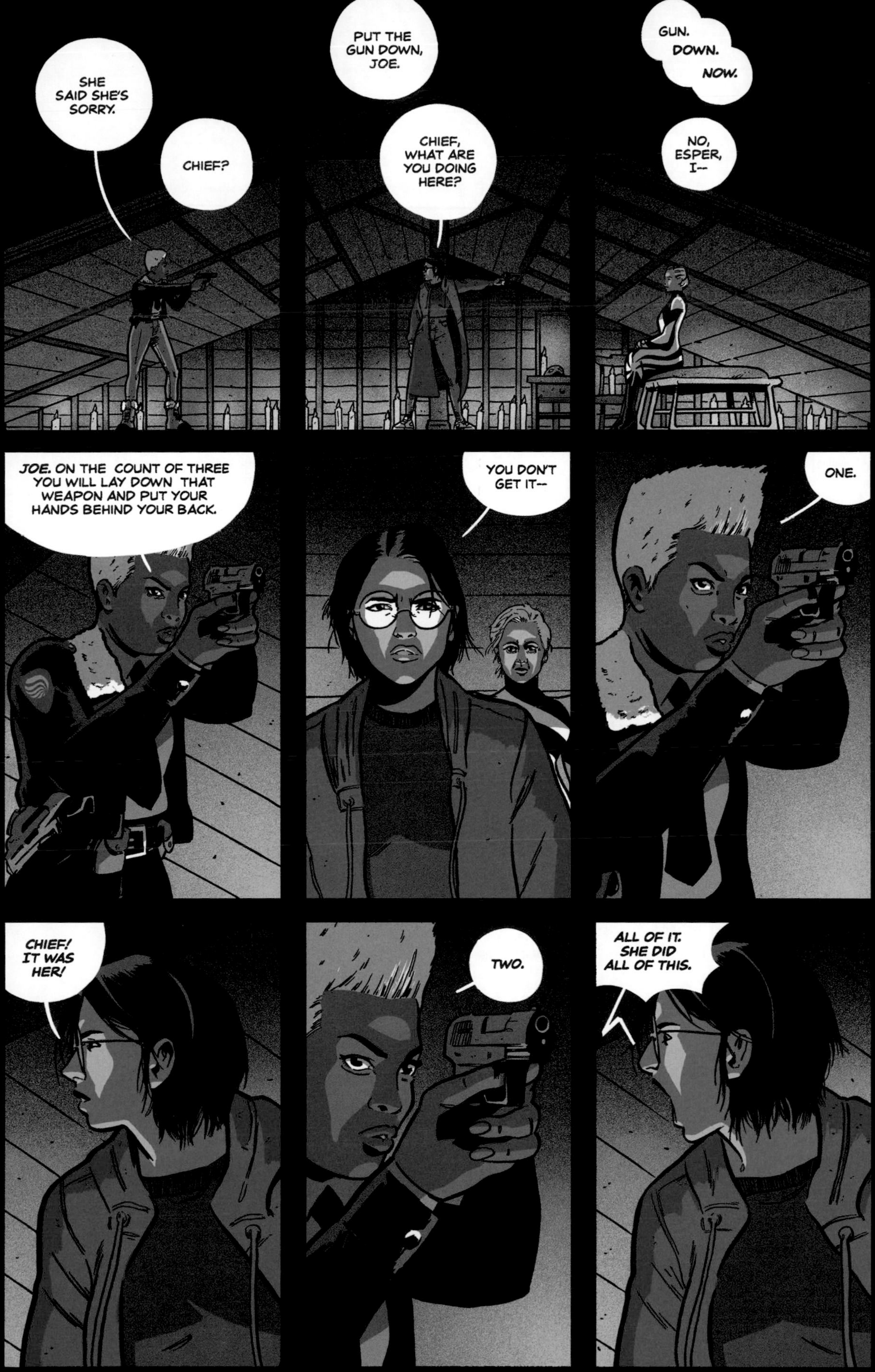
SHE SAID SHE'S SORRY.
CHIEF?
PUT THE GUN DOWN, JOE.
CHIEF, WHAT ARE YOU DOING HERE?
GUN.
DOWN.
NOW.
NO, ESPER, I--
JOE. ON THE COUNT OF THREE YOU WILL LAY DOWN THAT WEAPON AND PUT YOUR HANDS BEHIND YOUR BACK.
YOU DON'T GET IT--
ONE.
CHIEF! IT WAS HER!
TWO.
ALL OF IT. SHE DID ALL OF THIS.

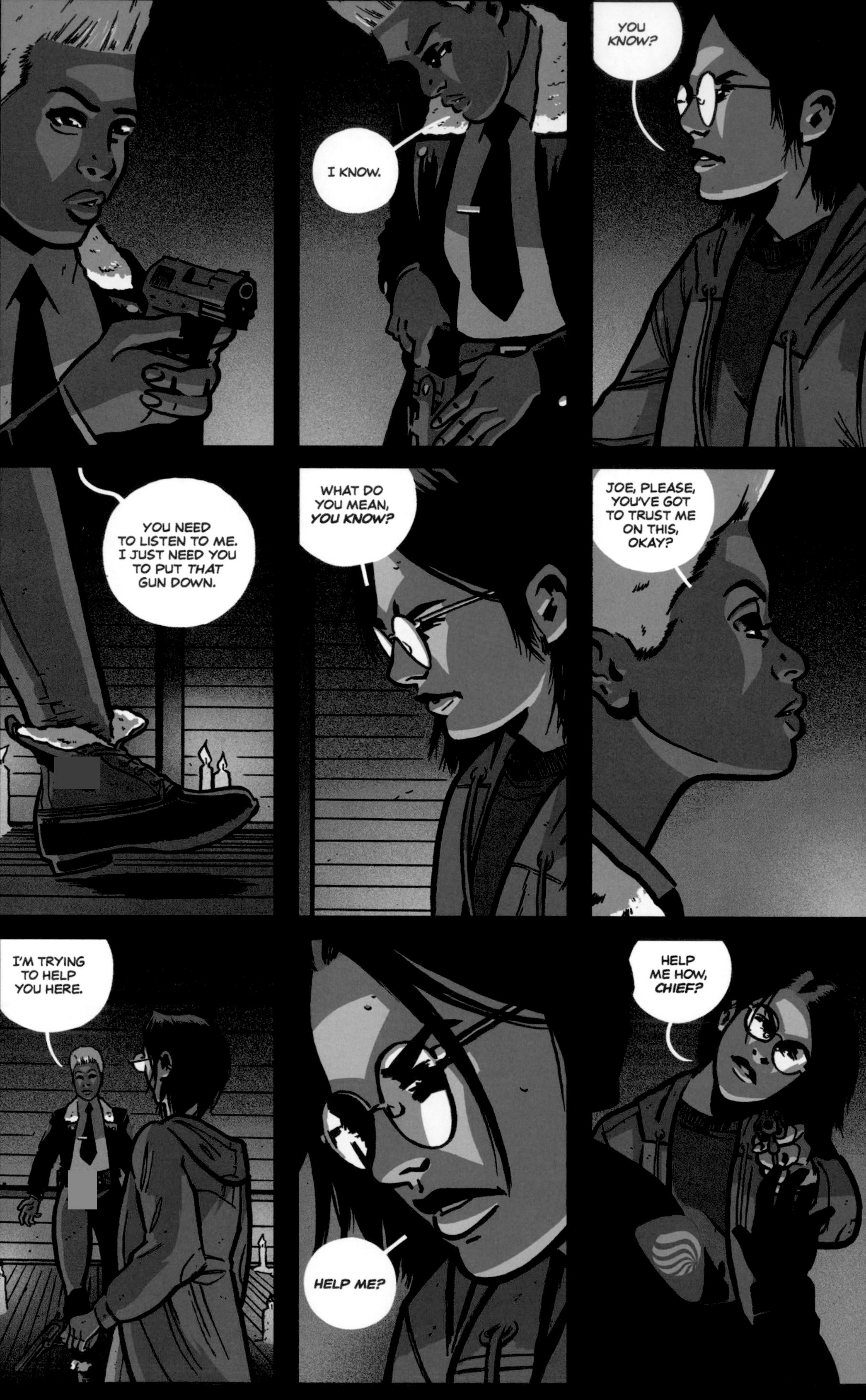
I KNOW.
YOU KNOW?
YOU NEED TO LISTEN TO ME. I JUST NEED YOU TO PUT *THAT* GUN DOWN.
WHAT DO YOU MEAN, *YOU KNOW?*
JOE, PLEASE, YOU'VE GOT TO TRUST ME ON THIS, OKAY?
I'M TRYING TO HELP YOU HERE.
HELP ME?
HELP ME HOW, *CHIEF?*

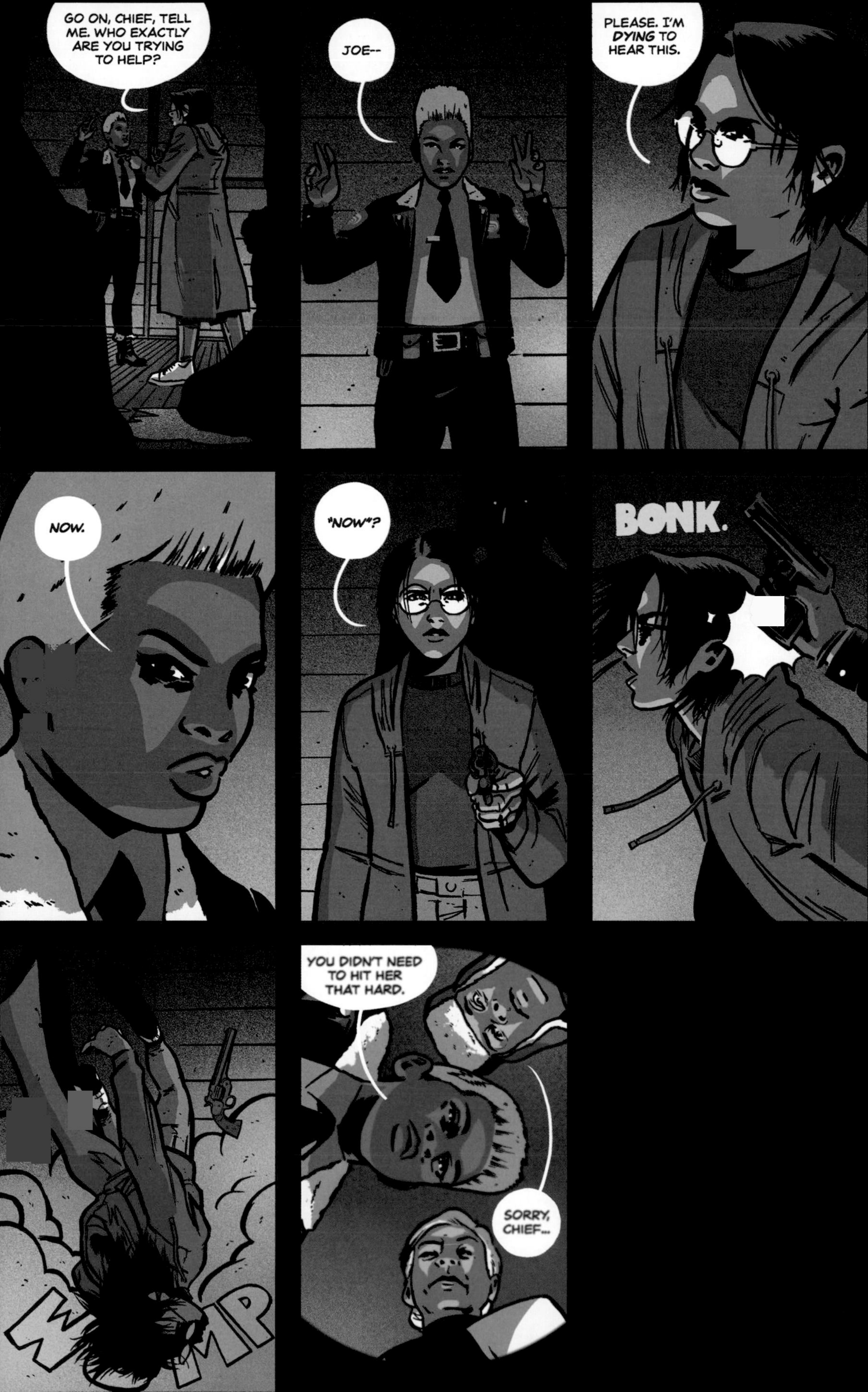
GO ON, CHIEF, TELL ME. WHO EXACTLY ARE YOU TRYING TO HELP?
JOE--
PLEASE. I'M *DYING* TO HEAR THIS.
NOW.
"NOW"?
BONK.
YOU DIDN'T NEED TO HIT HER THAT HARD.
SORRY, CHIEF...

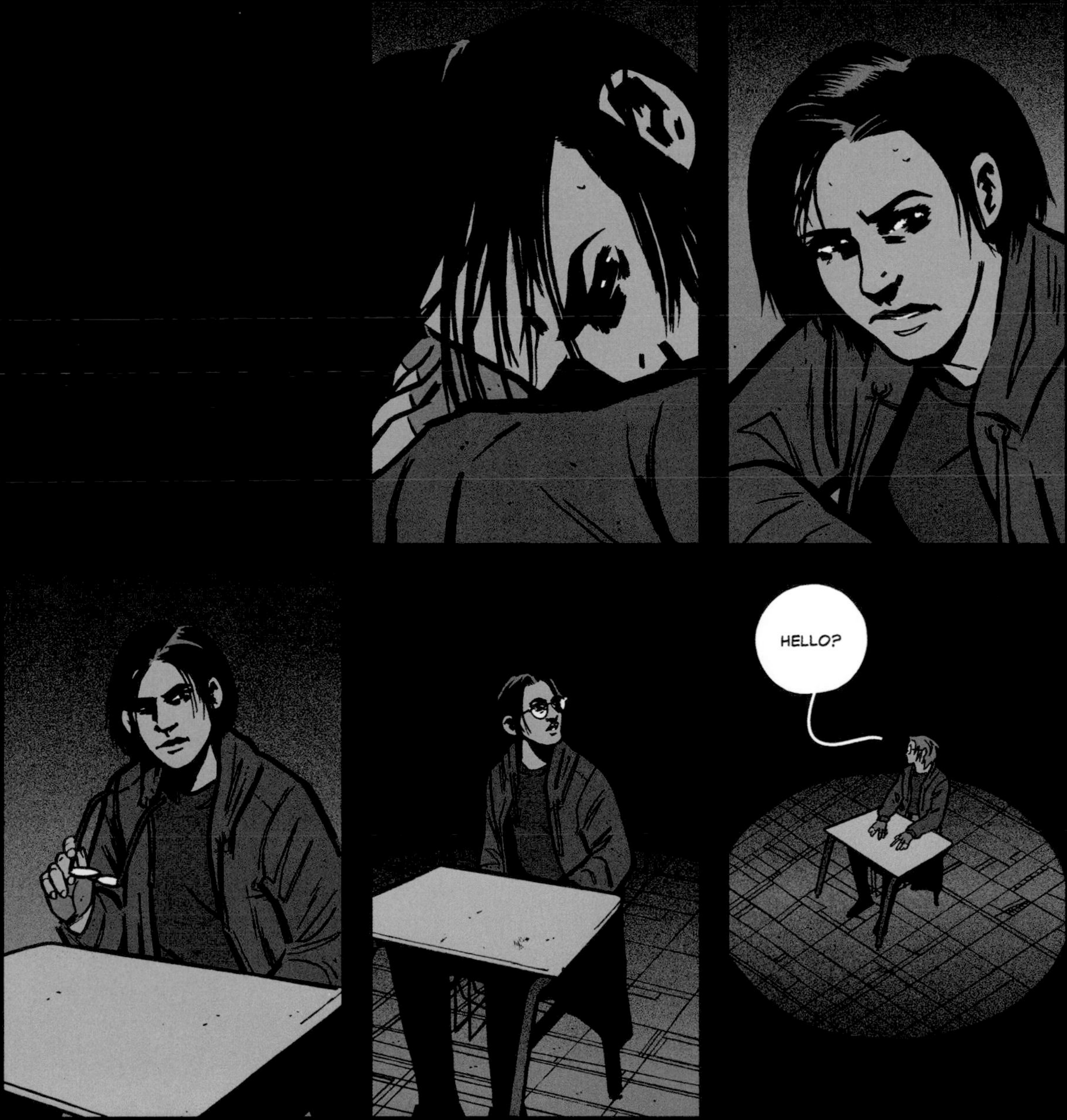
HELLO?

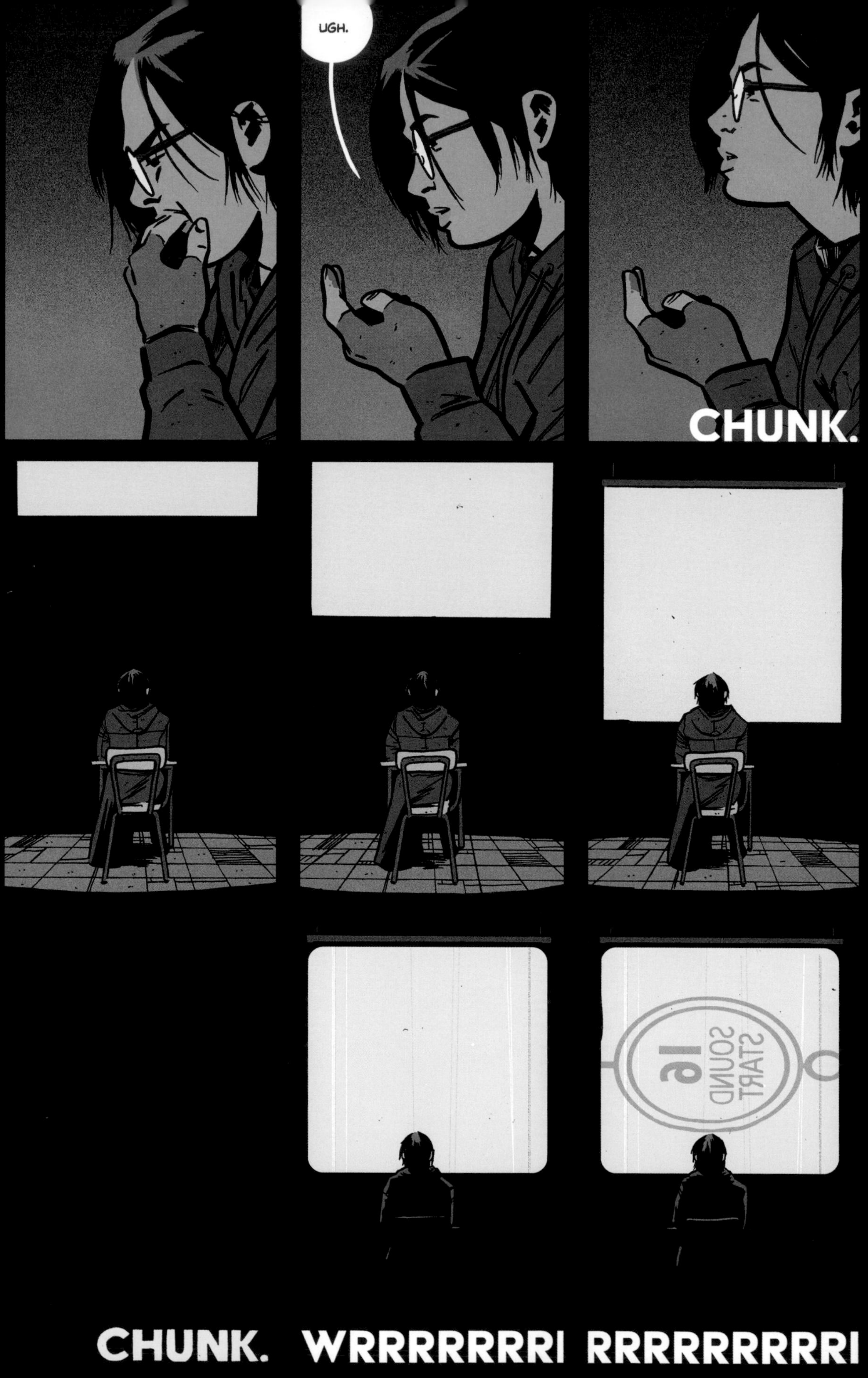
UGH.
CHUNK.
SOUND START 16
CHUNK.
WRRRRRRRI
RRRRRRRRRI

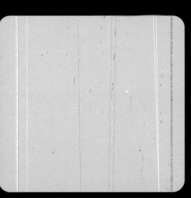

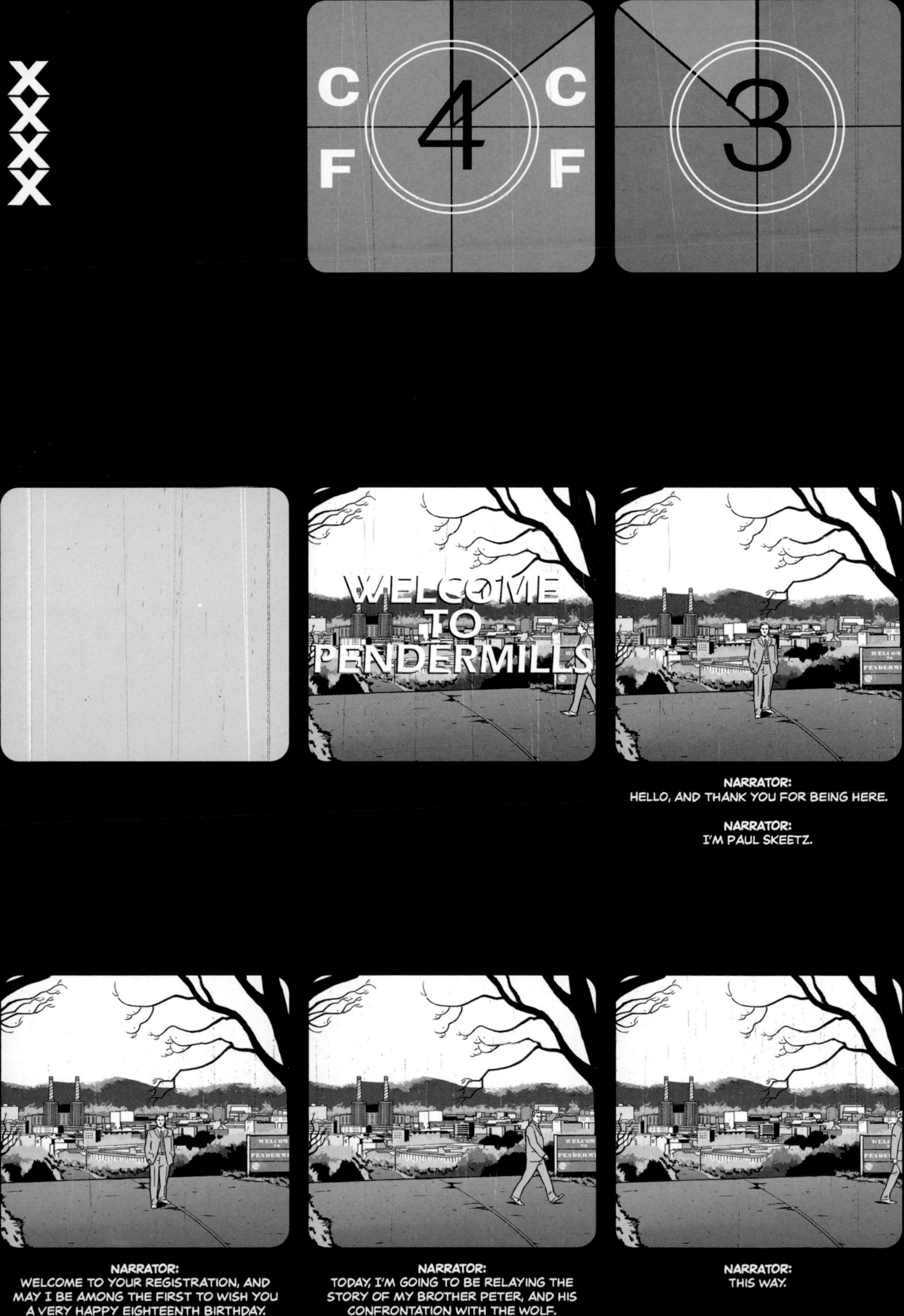
C
F
4
C
F
3
WELCOME TO PENDERMILLS
NARRATOR: HELLO, AND THANK YOU FOR BEING HERE.
NARRATOR: I'M PAUL SKEETZ.
NARRATOR: WELCOME TO YOUR REGISTRATION, AND MAY I BE AMONG THE FIRST TO WISH YOU A VERY HAPPY EIGHTEENTH BIRTHDAY.
NARRATOR: TODAY, I'M GOING TO BE RELAYING THE STORY OF MY BROTHER PETER, AND HIS CONFRONTATION WITH THE WOLF.
NARRATOR: THIS WAY.

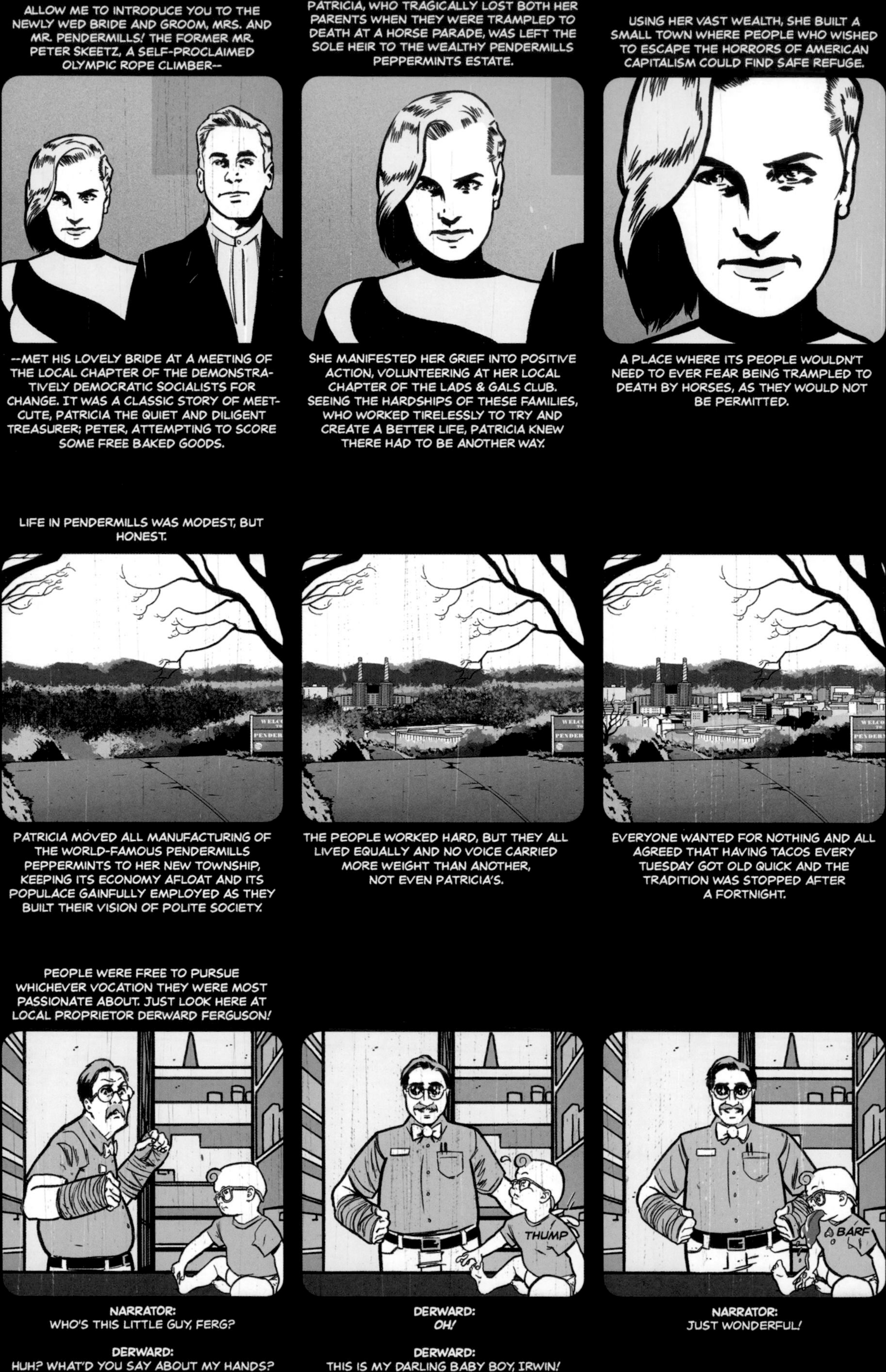
ALLOW ME TO INTRODUCE YOU TO THE NEWLY WED BRIDE AND GROOM, MRS. AND MR. PENDERMILLS! THE FORMER MR. PETER SKEETZ, A SELF-PROCLAIMED OLYMPIC ROPE CLIMBER--
--MET HIS LOVELY BRIDE AT A MEETING OF THE LOCAL CHAPTER OF THE DEMONSTRATIVELY DEMOCRATIC SOCIALISTS FOR CHANGE. IT WAS A CLASSIC STORY OF MEET-CUTE, PATRICIA THE QUIET AND DILIGENT TREASURER; PETER, ATTEMPTING TO SCORE SOME FREE BAKED GOODS.
PATRICIA, WHO TRAGICALLY LOST BOTH HER PARENTS WHEN THEY WERE TRAMPLED TO DEATH AT A HORSE PARADE, WAS LEFT THE SOLE HEIR TO THE WEALTHY PENDERMILLS PEPPERMINTS ESTATE.
SHE MANIFESTED HER GRIEF INTO POSITIVE ACTION, VOLUNTEERING AT HER LOCAL CHAPTER OF THE LADS & GALS CLUB. SEEING THE HARDSHIPS OF THESE FAMILIES, WHO WORKED TIRELESSLY TO TRY AND CREATE A BETTER LIFE, PATRICIA KNEW THERE HAD TO BE ANOTHER WAY.
USING HER VAST WEALTH, SHE BUILT A SMALL TOWN WHERE PEOPLE WHO WISHED TO ESCAPE THE HORRORS OF AMERICAN CAPITALISM COULD FIND SAFE REFUGE.
A PLACE WHERE ITS PEOPLE WOULDN'T NEED TO EVER FEAR BEING TRAMPLED TO DEATH BY HORSES, AS THEY WOULD NOT BE PERMITTED.
LIFE IN PENDERMILLS WAS MODEST, BUT HONEST.
PATRICIA MOVED ALL MANUFACTURING OF THE WORLD-FAMOUS PENDERMILLS PEPPERMINTS TO HER NEW TOWNSHIP, KEEPING ITS ECONOMY AFLOAT AND ITS POPULACE GAINFULLY EMPLOYED AS THEY BUILT THEIR VISION OF POLITE SOCIETY.
THE PEOPLE WORKED HARD, BUT THEY ALL LIVED EQUALLY AND NO VOICE CARRIED MORE WEIGHT THAN ANOTHER, NOT EVEN PATRICIA'S.
EVERYONE WANTED FOR NOTHING AND ALL AGREED THAT HAVING TACOS EVERY TUESDAY GOT OLD QUICK AND THE TRADITION WAS STOPPED AFTER A FORTNIGHT.
PEOPLE WERE FREE TO PURSUE WHICHEVER VOCATION THEY WERE MOST PASSIONATE ABOUT. JUST LOOK HERE AT LOCAL PROPRIETOR DERWARD FERGUSON!
NARRATOR: WHO'S THIS LITTLE GUY, FERG?
DERWARD: HUH? WHAT'D YOU SAY ABOUT MY HANDS?
THUMP
DERWARD: OH!
DERWARD: THIS IS MY DARLING BABY BOY, IRWIN!
BARF
NARRATOR: JUST WONDERFUL!

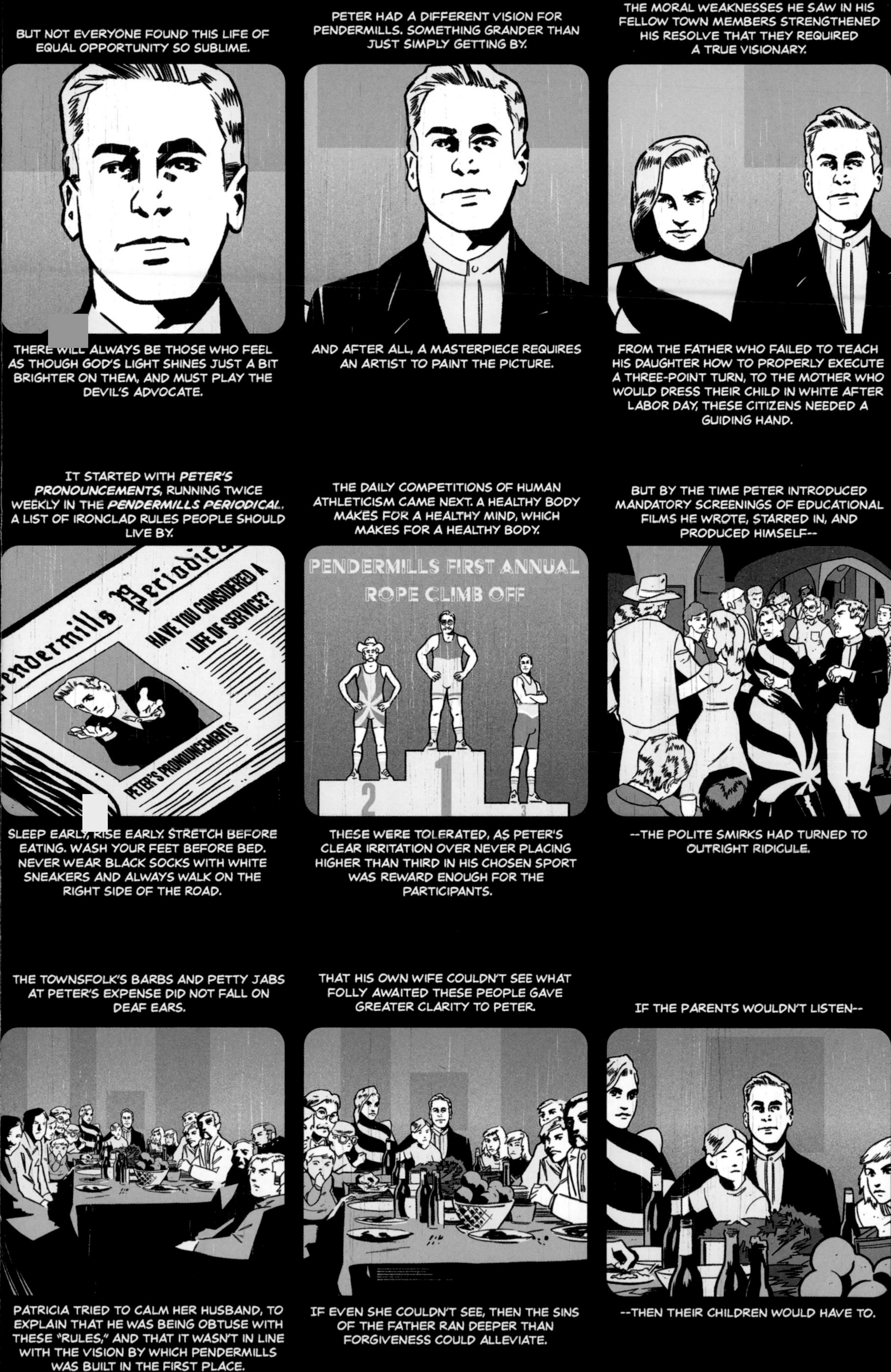
BUT NOT EVERYONE FOUND THIS LIFE OF EQUAL OPPORTUNITY SO SUBLIME.
THERE WILL ALWAYS BE THOSE WHO FEEL AS THOUGH GOD'S LIGHT SHINES JUST A BIT BRIGHTER ON THEM, AND MUST PLAY THE DEVIL'S ADVOCATE.
PETER HAD A DIFFERENT VISION FOR PENDERMILLS. SOMETHING GRANDER THAN JUST SIMPLY GETTING BY.
AND AFTER ALL, A MASTERPIECE REQUIRES AN ARTIST TO PAINT THE PICTURE.
THE MORAL WEAKNESSES HE SAW IN HIS FELLOW TOWN MEMBERS STRENGTHENED HIS RESOLVE THAT THEY REQUIRED A TRUE VISIONARY.
FROM THE FATHER WHO FAILED TO TEACH HIS DAUGHTER HOW TO PROPERLY EXECUTE A THREE-POINT TURN, TO THE MOTHER WHO WOULD DRESS THEIR CHILD IN WHITE AFTER LABOR DAY, THESE CITIZENS NEEDED A GUIDING HAND.
IT STARTED WITH *PETER'S PRONOUNCEMENTS*, RUNNING TWICE WEEKLY IN THE *PENDERMILLS PERIODICAL*, A LIST OF IRONCLAD RULES PEOPLE SHOULD LIVE BY.
Pendermills Periodical
HAVE YOU CONSIDERED A LIFE OF SERVICE?
PETER'S PRONOUNCEMENTS
SLEEP EARLY, RISE EARLY. STRETCH BEFORE EATING. WASH YOUR FEET BEFORE BED. NEVER WEAR BLACK SOCKS WITH WHITE SNEAKERS AND ALWAYS WALK ON THE RIGHT SIDE OF THE ROAD.
THE DAILY COMPETITIONS OF HUMAN ATHLETICISM CAME NEXT. A HEALTHY BODY MAKES FOR A HEALTHY MIND, WHICH MAKES FOR A HEALTHY BODY.
PENDERMILLS FIRST ANNUAL ROPE CLIMB OFF
2
1
3
THESE WERE TOLERATED, AS PETER'S CLEAR IRRITATION OVER NEVER PLACING HIGHER THAN THIRD IN HIS CHOSEN SPORT WAS REWARD ENOUGH FOR THE PARTICIPANTS.
BUT BY THE TIME PETER INTRODUCED MANDATORY SCREENINGS OF EDUCATIONAL FILMS HE WROTE, STARRED IN, AND PRODUCED HIMSELF--
--THE POLITE SMIRKS HAD TURNED TO OUTRIGHT RIDICULE.
THE TOWNSFOLK'S BARBS AND PETTY JABS AT PETER'S EXPENSE DID NOT FALL ON DEAF EARS.
PATRICIA TRIED TO CALM HER HUSBAND, TO EXPLAIN THAT HE WAS BEING OBTUSE WITH THESE "RULES," AND THAT IT WASN'T IN LINE WITH THE VISION BY WHICH PENDERMILLS WAS BUILT IN THE FIRST PLACE.
THAT HIS OWN WIFE COULDN'T SEE WHAT FOLLY AWAITED THESE PEOPLE GAVE GREATER CLARITY TO PETER.
IF EVEN SHE COULDN'T SEE, THEN THE SINS OF THE FATHER RAN DEEPER THAN FORGIVENESS COULD ALLEVIATE.
IF THE PARENTS WOULDN'T LISTEN--
--THEN THEIR CHILDREN WOULD HAVE TO.

EVERYONE COULD RECALL THE DAY WITH EASE, WHEN PATRICIA, WHO HAD ALWAYS BEEN THE FIRST TO ARRIVE AND LAST TO LEAVE THE PENDERMILLS PEPPERMINTS FACTORY, DIDN'T COME TO WORK.

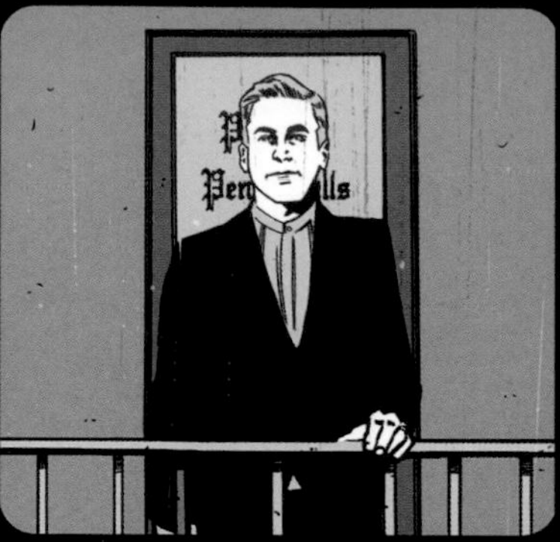

AS IF THIS LAPSE IN CONTINUITY WASN'T EGREGIOUS ENOUGH, HER SHOES WERE FILLED WITH THE FEET OF PETER.

WHEN INQUIRED AS TO HIS WIFE'S WHEREABOUTS, PETER WOULD SHRUG AND REPLY, "ON HOLIDAY."

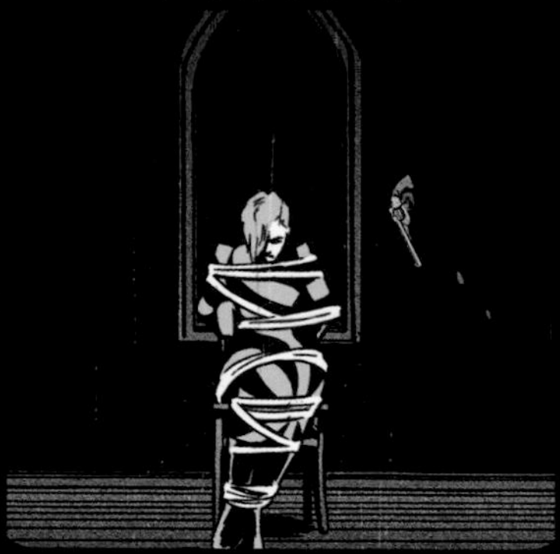

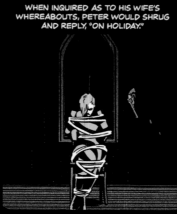

WHEN PRESSED AS TO WHERE, HE WOULD JUST SAY "ON HOLIDAY" LOUDER.

PETER'S ASCENDANCY AS THE FIGUREHEAD CAME WITH MORE BAD NEWS.

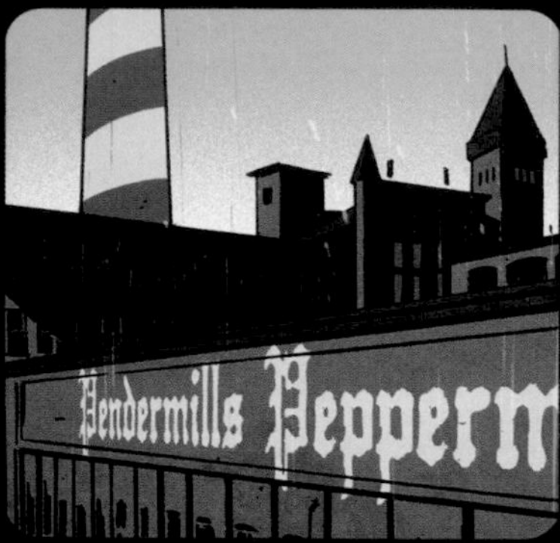
Pendermills

PETER INFORMED THE CITIZENS THAT SALES OF THE WORLD-FAMOUS PEPPERMINTS HAD PLUMMETED AND THAT THE TOWN WAS ON THE VERGE OF BANKRUPTCY AND RUIN.

LUCKILY FOR THEM, BEFORE PATRICIA LEFT, SHE HAD GIVEN HIM A NEW SECRET RECIPE THAT PEOPLE WOULD NOT BE ABLE TO RESIST.

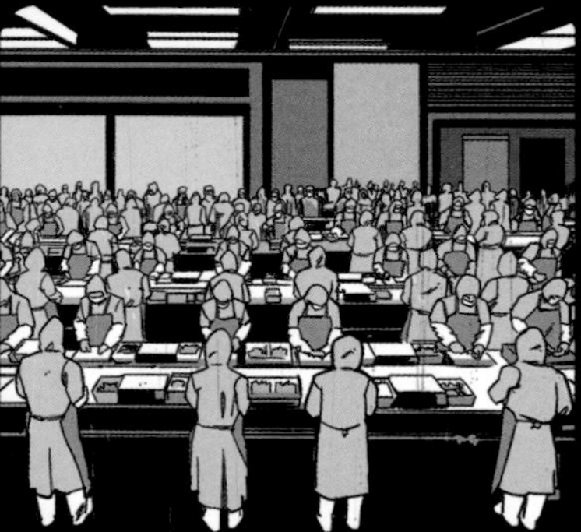

IMPLEMENTING A NEW TWELVE-HOUR WORKDAY, PETER TOLD THE WORKERS THEY WOULD HAVE TO WORK SEVEN DAYS A WEEK TO MEET THE INITIAL DEMAND FOR THEIR NEW SUCCULENT SWEETS.

BUT AFTER THREE LONG WEEKS, THE PEOPLE OF PENDERMILLS HAD HAD ENOUGH OF LIFE UNDER PETER'S TUTELAGE OF THE CANDY CONGLOMERATE.

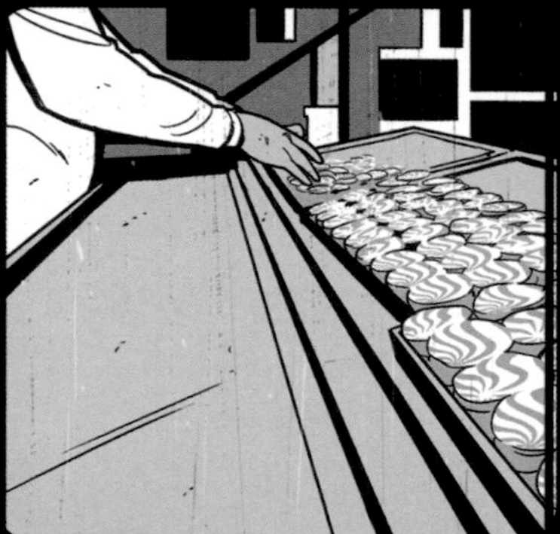

BANKRUPTCY OR NOT, THEY NEEDED A DAY OFF, AND MUCH TO EVERYONE'S SURPRISE, PETER AGREED.

HE TOLD THEM THAT THANKS TO ALL THEIR HARD WORK, THEY NOT ONLY HIT THEIR TARGET BUT EXCEEDED IT!

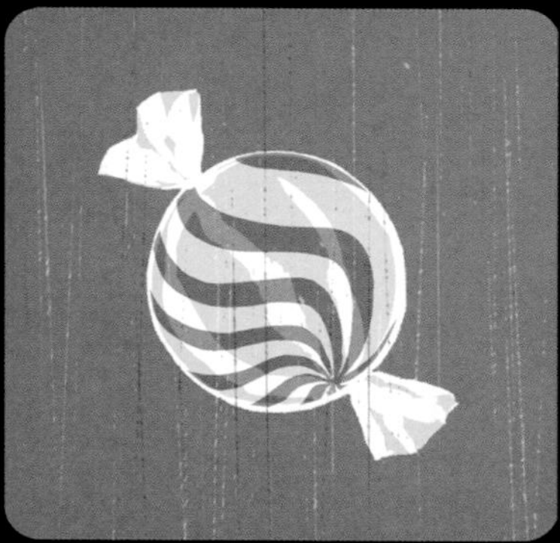

HE PROPOSED THEY CELEBRATE WITH A LARGE BANQUET WHERE THEY'D BE THE FIRST TO TRY THESE NEW PENDERMILLS PEPPERMINTS THAT WERE SURE TO TAKE THE WORLD BY STORM.

AFTER THE FOOD HAD BEEN EATEN, AND THE DRINKS HAD BEEN DRUNK, PETER STOOD AND RAISED HIS PROVERBIAL GLASS TO THE PEOPLE OF PENDERMILLS.

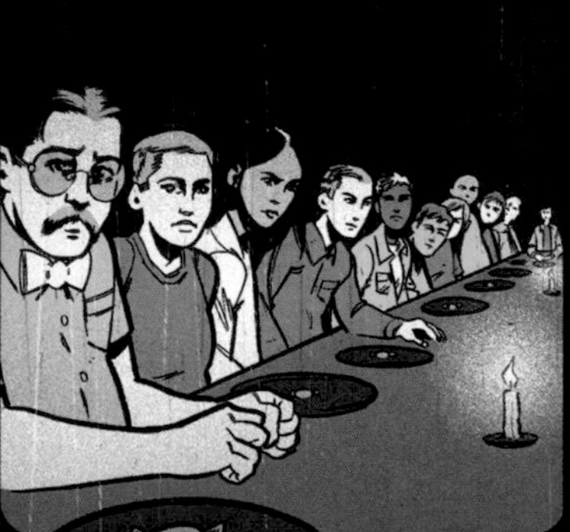

PETER:
IT'S BEEN HARD AND BACKBREAKING WORK BUT YOU DID IT. THROUGH YOUR SACRIFICE AND A LITTLE BIT OF GOOD OL'-FASHIONED ELBOW GREASE, YOU ARE NOW ON THE BRINK OF HAVING SAVED PENDERMILLS FROM RUIN.

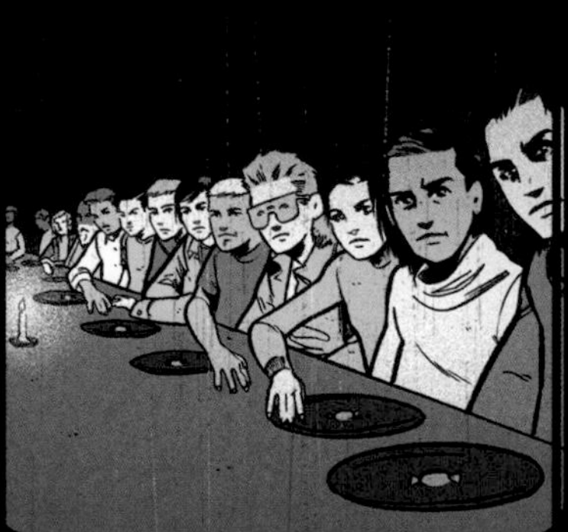

PETER:
I KNOW NONE OF YOU ARE BIG FANS OF MY PROCLAMATIONS SO I'LL KEEP THIS BRIEF. YOU'LL NEVER KNOW HOW MUCH I APPRECIATE WHAT YOU'VE DONE TO KEEP THE DREAM OF PENDERMILLS ALIVE. NOW--

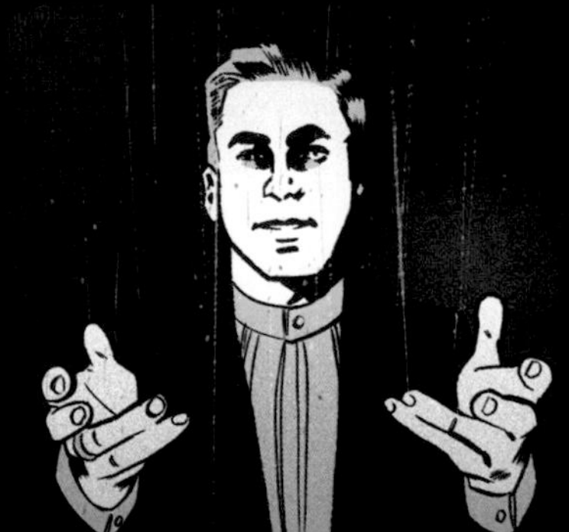

PETER:
--IT'S TIME TO TASTE THE FRUITS OF YOUR LABOR.

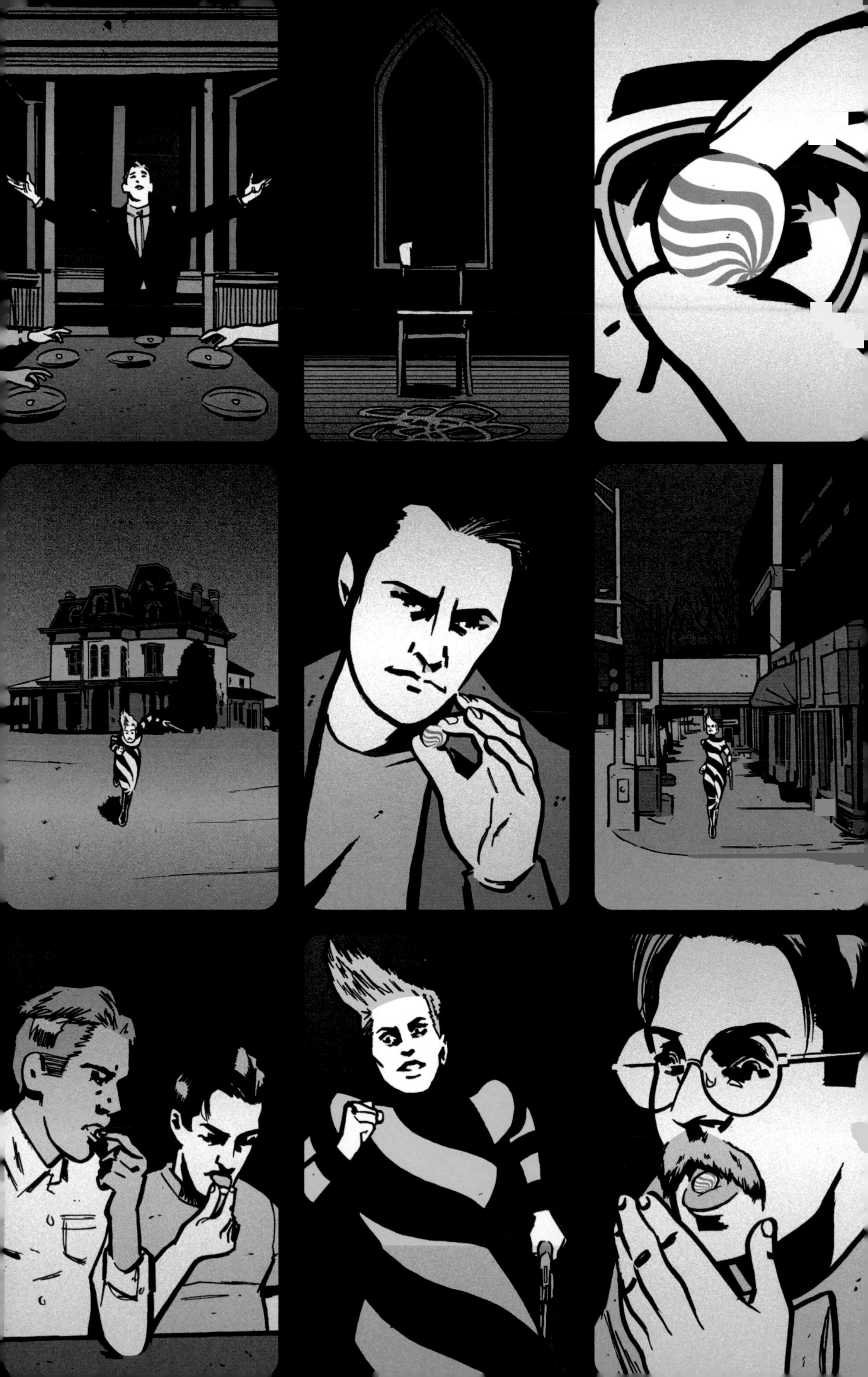

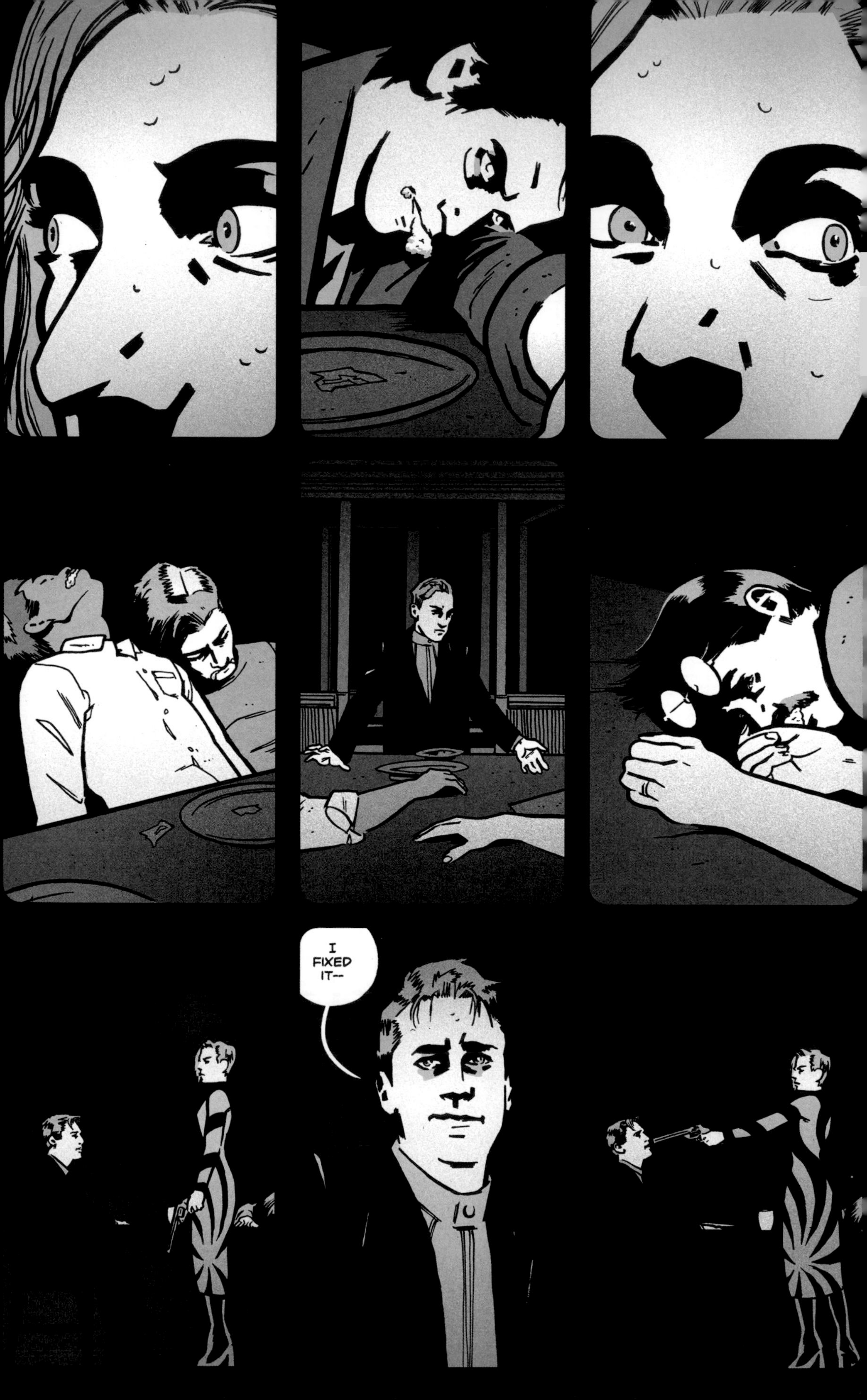
I FIXED IT--

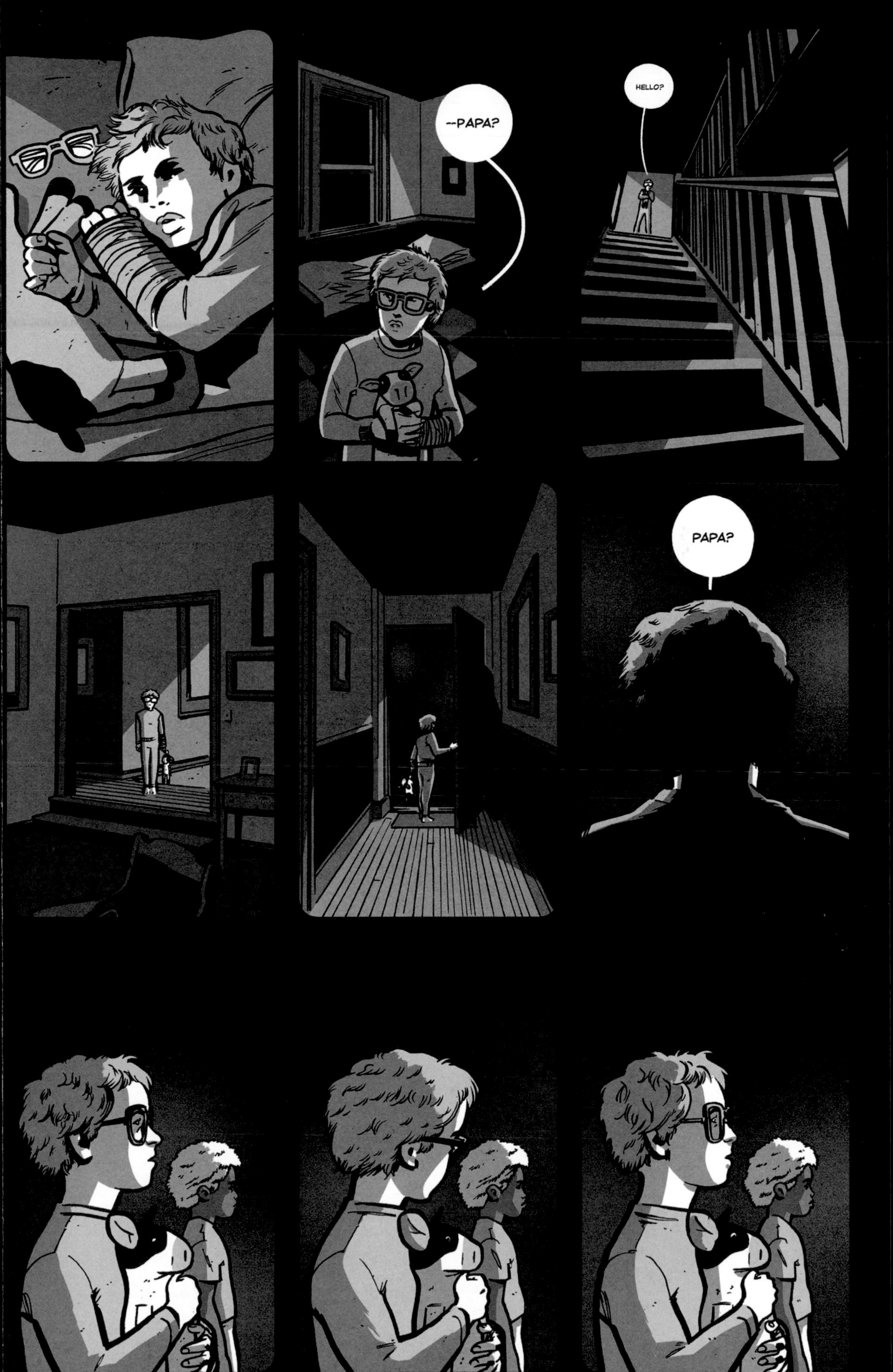
--PAPA?
HELLO?
PAPA?

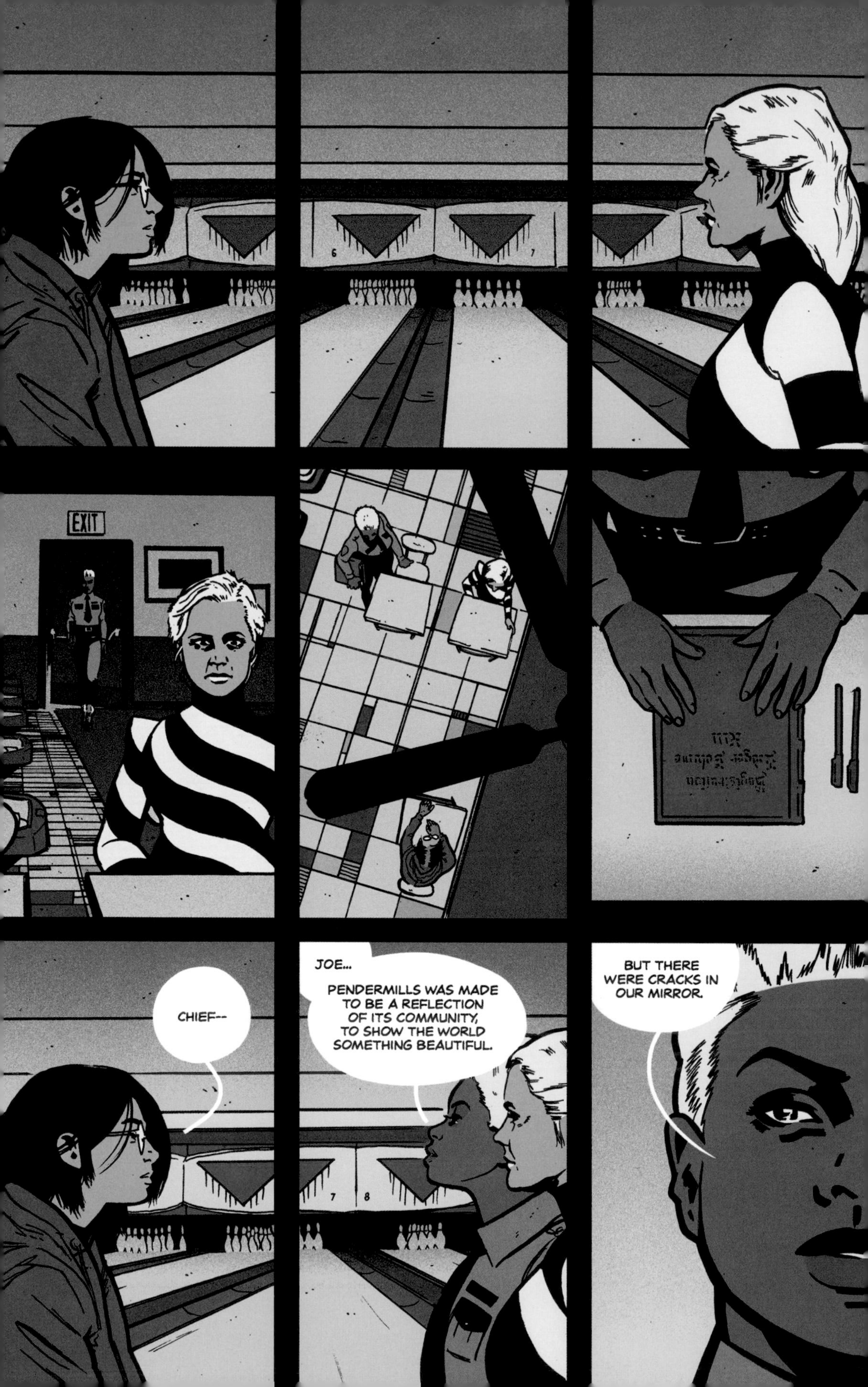
EXIT
CHIEF--
JOE...
PENDERMILLS WAS MADE TO BE A REFLECTION OF ITS COMMUNITY, TO SHOW THE WORLD SOMETHING BEAUTIFUL.
BUT THERE WERE CRACKS IN OUR MIRROR.

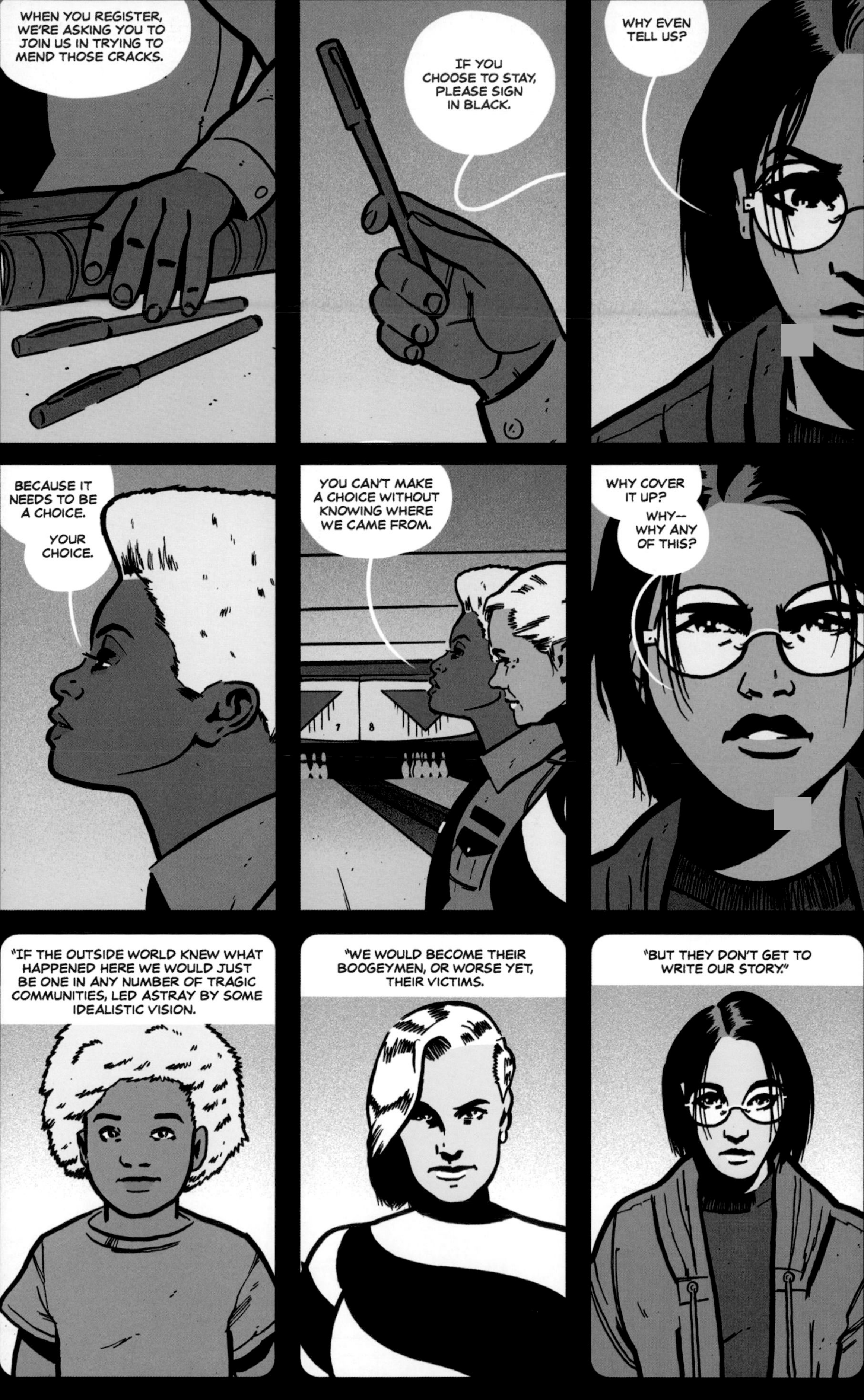
WHEN YOU REGISTER, WE'RE ASKING YOU TO JOIN US IN TRYING TO MEND THOSE CRACKS.
IF YOU CHOOSE TO STAY, PLEASE SIGN IN BLACK.
WHY EVEN TELL US?
BECAUSE IT NEEDS TO BE A CHOICE.
YOUR CHOICE.
YOU CAN'T MAKE A CHOICE WITHOUT KNOWING WHERE WE CAME FROM.
WHY COVER IT UP?
WHY-- WHY ANY OF THIS?
"IF THE OUTSIDE WORLD KNEW WHAT HAPPENED HERE WE WOULD JUST BE ONE IN ANY NUMBER OF TRAGIC COMMUNITIES, LED ASTRAY BY SOME IDEALISTIC VISION.
"WE WOULD BECOME THEIR BOOGEYMEN, OR WORSE YET, THEIR VICTIMS.
"BUT THEY DON'T GET TO WRITE OUR STORY."

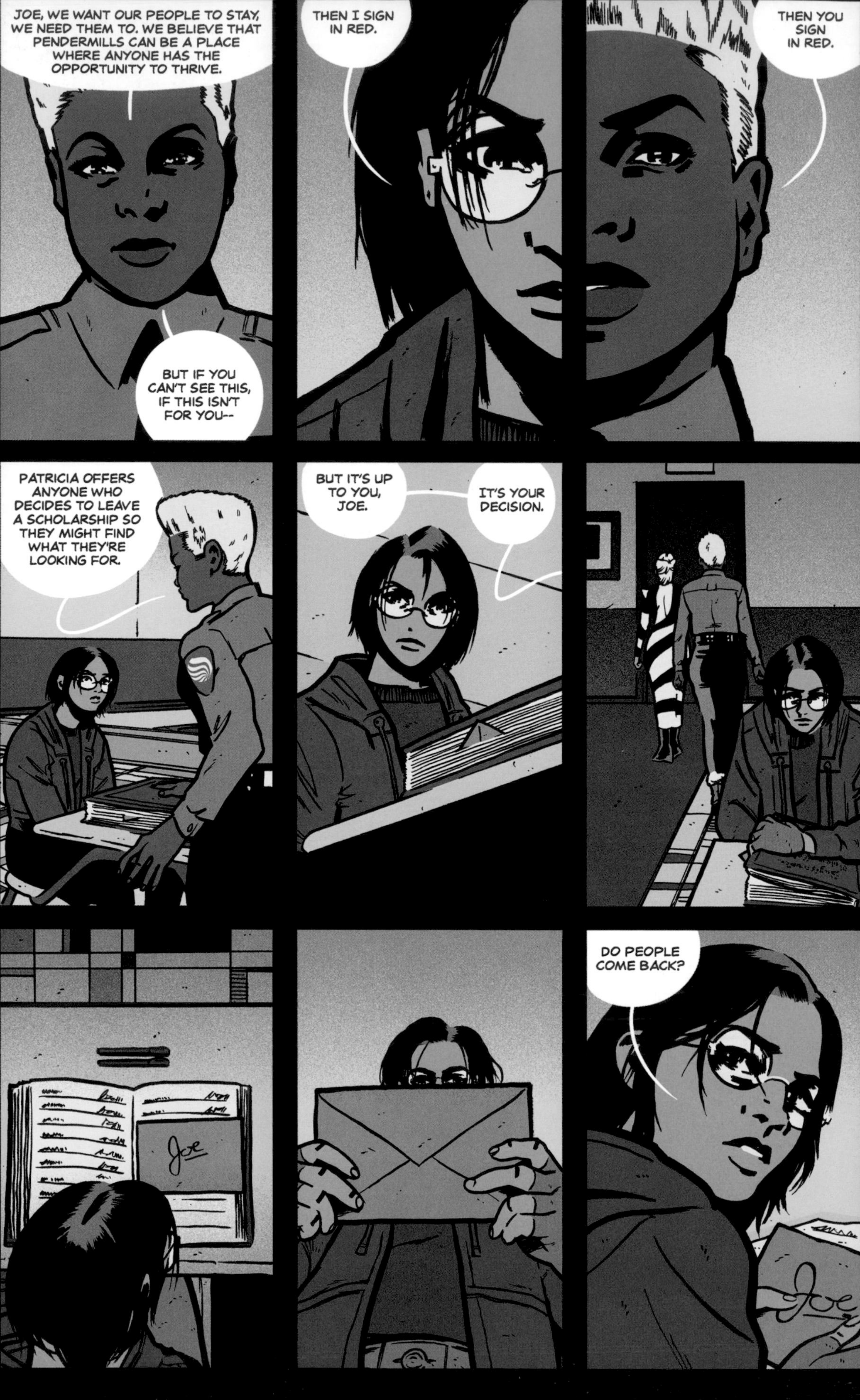
JOE, WE WANT OUR PEOPLE TO STAY, WE NEED THEM TO. WE BELIEVE THAT PENDERMILLS CAN BE A PLACE WHERE ANYONE HAS THE OPPORTUNITY TO THRIVE.
BUT IF YOU CAN'T SEE THIS, IF THIS ISN'T FOR YOU--
THEN I SIGN IN RED.
THEN YOU SIGN IN RED.
PATRICIA OFFERS ANYONE WHO DECIDES TO LEAVE A SCHOLARSHIP SO THEY MIGHT FIND WHAT THEY'RE LOOKING FOR.
BUT IT'S UP TO YOU, JOE.
IT'S YOUR DECISION.
Joe
DO PEOPLE COME BACK?

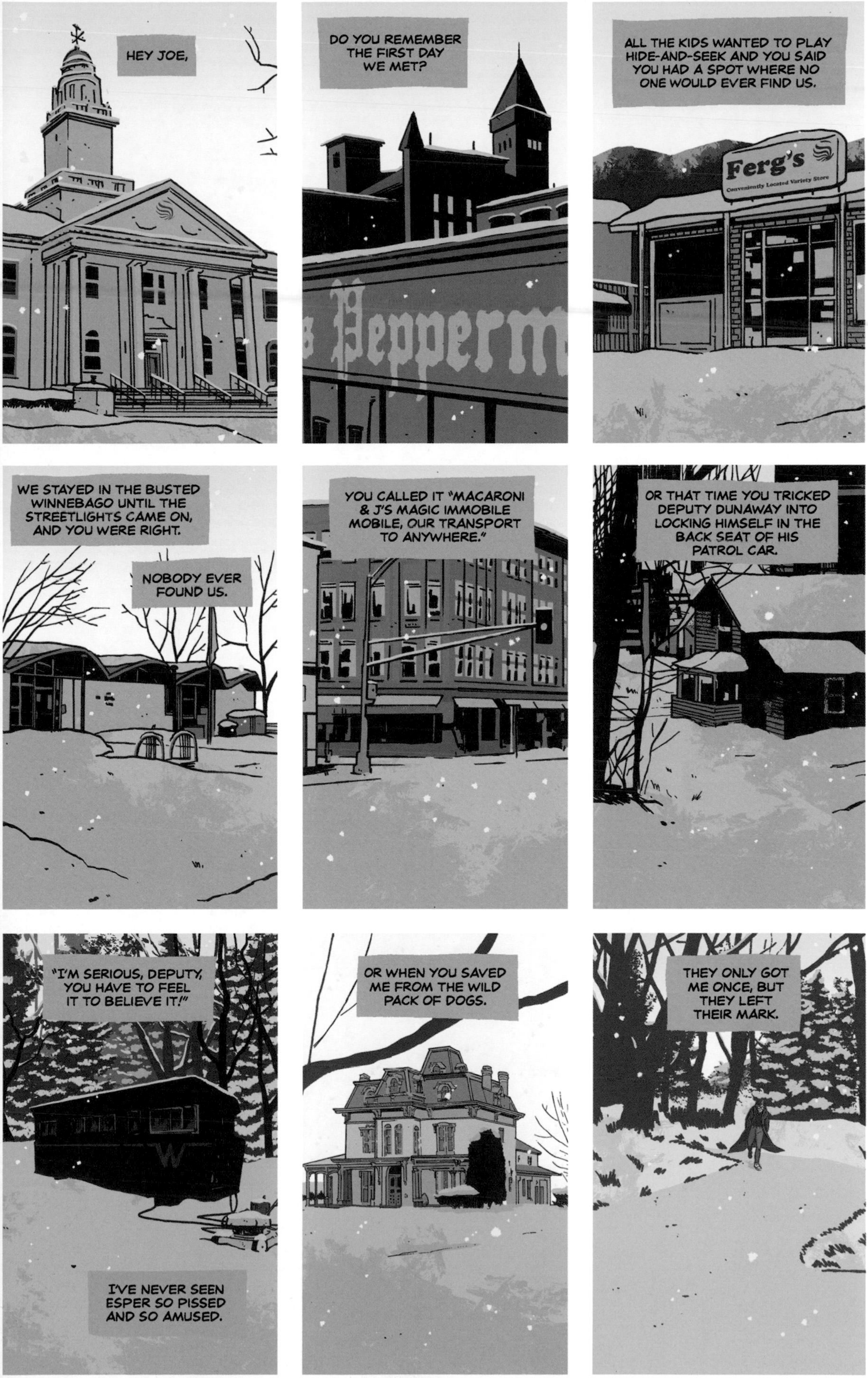
HEY JOE,
DO YOU REMEMBER THE FIRST DAY WE MET?
ALL THE KIDS WANTED TO PLAY HIDE-AND-SEEK AND YOU SAID YOU HAD A SPOT WHERE NO ONE WOULD EVER FIND US.
Ferg's
Conveniently Located Variety Store
WE STAYED IN THE BUSTED WINNEBAGO UNTIL THE STREETLIGHTS CAME ON, AND YOU WERE RIGHT.
NOBODY EVER FOUND US.
YOU CALLED IT "MACARONI & J'S MAGIC IMMOBILE MOBILE, OUR TRANSPORT TO ANYWHERE."
OR THAT TIME YOU TRICKED DEPUTY DUNAWAY INTO LOCKING HIMSELF IN THE BACK SEAT OF HIS PATROL CAR.
"I'M SERIOUS, DEPUTY, YOU HAVE TO FEEL IT TO BELIEVE IT!"
I'VE NEVER SEEN ESPER SO PISSED AND SO AMUSED.
OR WHEN YOU SAVED ME FROM THE WILD PACK OF DOGS.
THEY ONLY GOT ME ONCE, BUT THEY LEFT THEIR MARK.

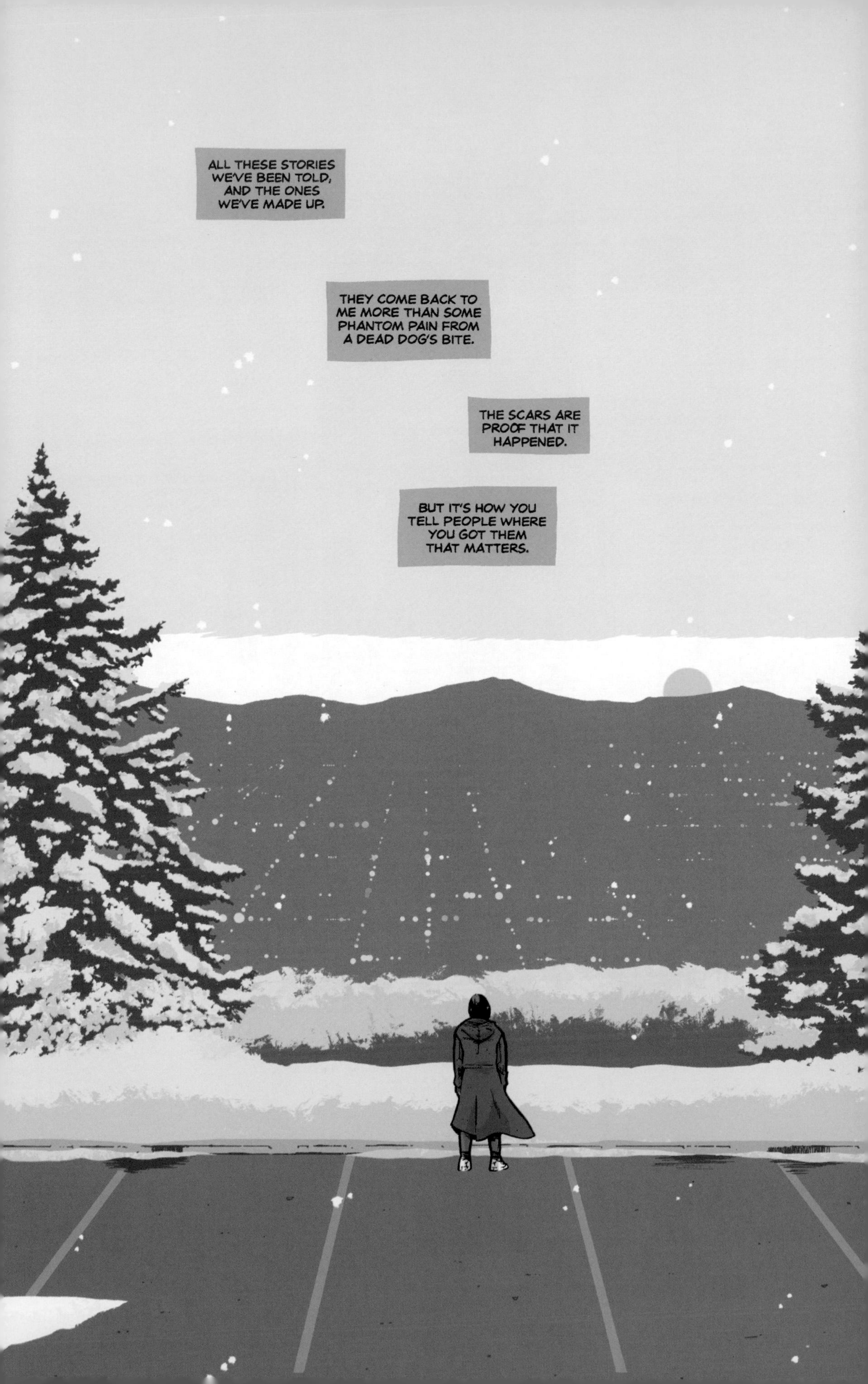
ALL THESE STORIES WE'VE BEEN TOLD, AND THE ONES WE'VE MADE UP.
THEY COME BACK TO ME MORE THAN SOME PHANTOM PAIN FROM A DEAD DOG'S BITE.
THE SCARS ARE PROOF THAT IT HAPPENED.
BUT IT'S HOW YOU TELL PEOPLE WHERE YOU GOT THEM THAT MATTERS.

Dead Guy's Bite™

SKETCHBOOK | Commentary by Tyler Boss

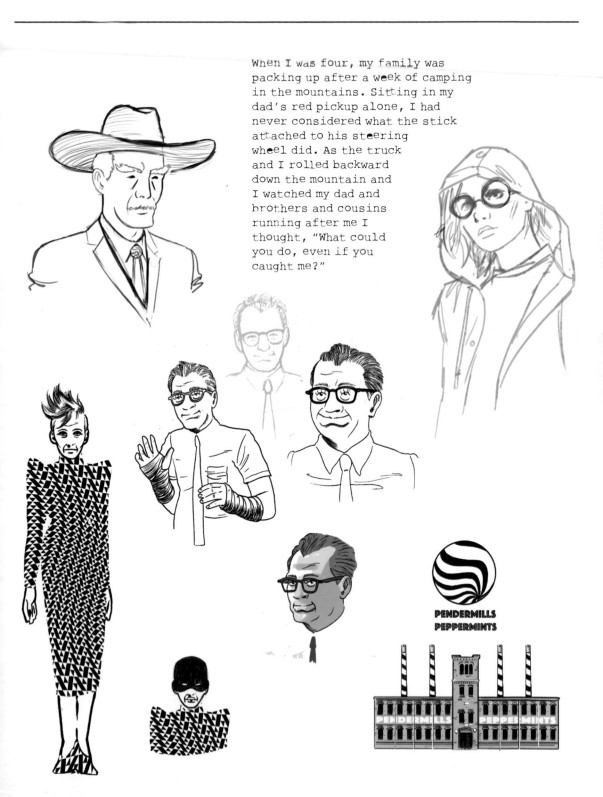

When I was four, my family was packing up after a week of camping in the mountains. Sitting in my dad's red pickup alone, I had never considered what the stick attached to his steering wheel did. As the truck and I rolled backward down the mountain and I watched my dad and brothers and cousins running after me I thought, "What could you do, even if you caught me?"

PENDERMILLS
PEPPERMINTS
PENDERMILLS
PEPPERMINTS

When I was five, I jumped into the shallow end of my neighbors' swimming pool. As my body sank to the bottom, I kept my eyes wide, staring up at the surface and the way the light broke on the waves my dive had made. When my mom dove in after me, she blocked out the sun.

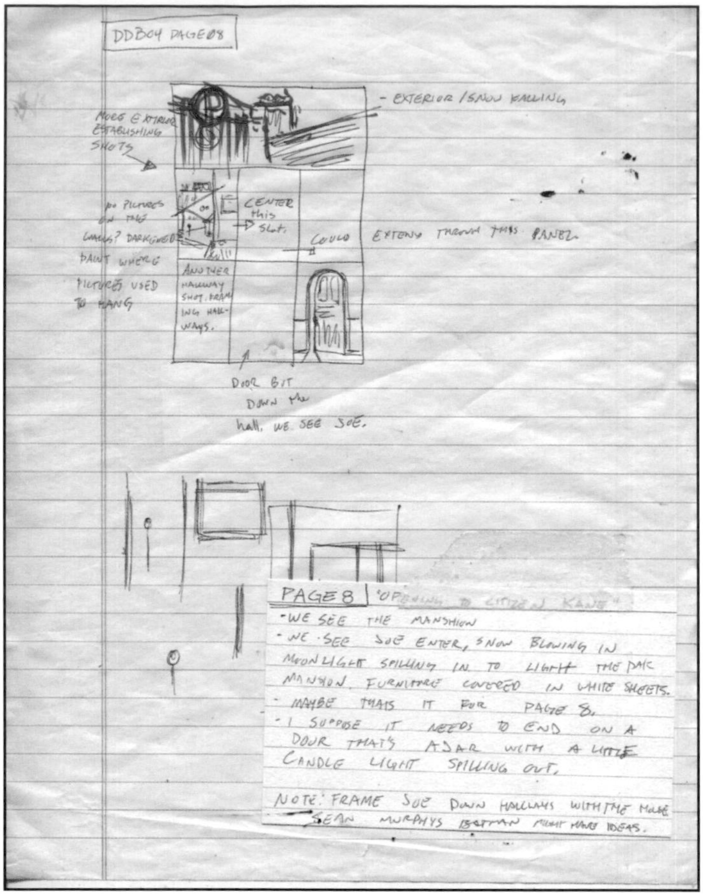

DDB04 PAGE08
- EXTERIOR / SNOW FALLING
MORE EXTERIOR ESTABLISHING SHOTS
CENTER this shot.
COULD EXTEND THROUGH THIS PANEL.
NO PICTURES ON THE WALLS? DARKENED PAINT WHERE PICTURES USED TO HANG
ANOTHER HALLWAY SHOT. FRAMING HALLWAYS.
DOOR BIT DOWN the hall. WE SEE SOE.
PAGE 8
"OPENING TO CITIZEN KANE"
- WE SEE THE MANSHION
- WE SEE SOE ENTER, SNOW BLOWING IN
MOONLIGHT SPILLING IN TO LIGHT THE DAK MANSION. FURNITURE COVERED IN WHITE SHEETS.
- MAYBE THATS IT FOR PAGE 8.
- I SUPPOSE IT NEEDS TO END ON A DOOR THAT'S AJAR WITH A LITTLE CANDLE LIGHT SPILLING OUT.
NOTE: FRAME SOE DOWN HALLWAYS WITH THE HOUSE
SEAN MURPHYS BATMAN MIGHT HAVE IDEAS.

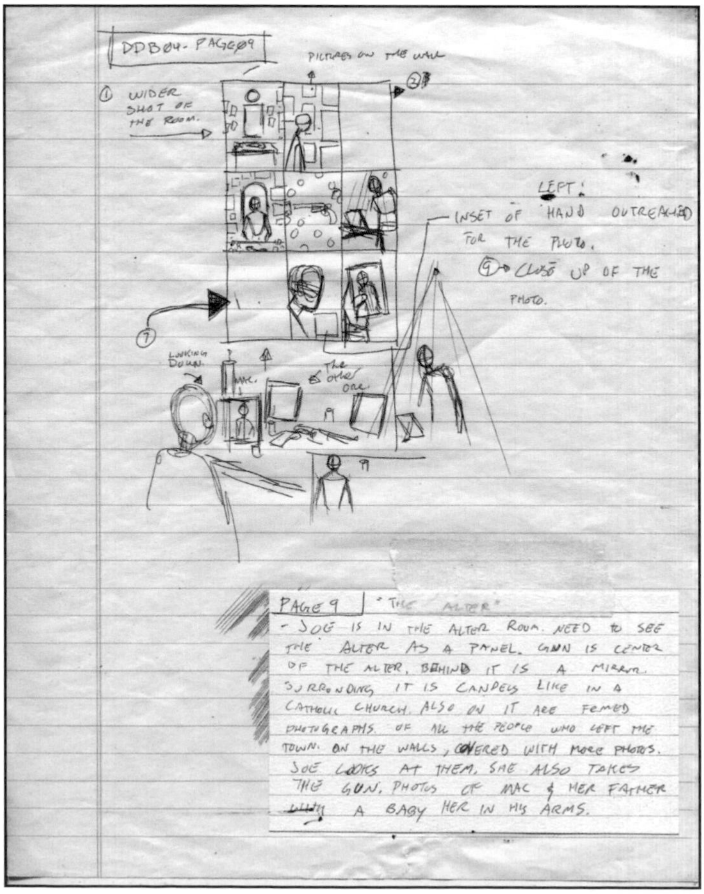

DDB04- PAGE09
PICTURES ON THE WALL
① WIDER SHOT OF THE ROOM.
LEFT: INSET OF HAND OUTREACHED FOR THE PHOTO.
④ CLOSE UP OF THE PHOTO.
LOOKING DOWN.
MAC.
The other one
PAGE 9
"THE ALTER"
- SOE IS IN THE ALTER ROOM. NEED TO SEE THE ALTER AS A PANEL. GUN IS CENTER OF THE ALTER, BEHIND IT IS A MIRROR. SURROUNDING IT IS CANDELS LIKE IN A CATHOLIC CHURCH. ALSO ON IT ARE FRAMED PHOTOGRAPHS OF ALL THE PEOPLE WHO LEFT THE TOWN. ON THE WALLS, COVERED WITH MORE PHOTOS. SOE LOOKS AT THEM. SHE ALSO TAKES THE GUN. PHOTOS OF MAC & HER FATHER A BABY HER IN HIS ARMS.

~~PAGES I'M ABLE TO USE~~ THIS HONESTLY PROBALY NEEDED.

8,9,10,11

- WE SEE A SHOT OF PENDERMILLS MANSION REALLY THINK THE OPENING TO CITIZEN KANE. MOVING IN SLOWLY ON THE SPACE.

- WE SEE JOE ENTER THE MANSION, SOME SNOW BLOWING IN FROM THE OPEN DOOR BEHIND HER. MOONLIGHT SPILLING IN TO LIGHT THE DARKENED MANSHION. ~~EVERYTHING~~ ALL THE FURNITURE IS COVERED IN WHITE SHEETS.

JOE IS WALKING THROUGH THE HOUSE. WE SHOULD SEE HER AT A DISTANCE. DOWN HALLWAYS, CONSTANTLY BEING FRAMED BY THE HOUSE.

SHE ENTERS A ROOM, THAT HAS AN ALTER OF CANDELS. OF SOME SORT. ON THE ALTER IS A GUN. SURRONDING THE GUN ARE PHOTOGRAPHS OF THE TOWN'S PEOPLE WHO LEFT. IT'S A LOT. WE SEE A PICTURE OF MAC. AND WE SEE A PICTURE OF A MAN IN CIRCLE GASSES HOLDING A BABY. JOE TAKES THE GUN.

JOE LEAVES THE ROOM & HEADS UPSTAIRS. SHE HEADS INTO A BEDROOM WHERE WE SEE PATRICIA. SHE TURNS TO LOOK AS JOE MAKES HER PRESENSE KNOWN.

NOTE: THE HALLWAY FROM THE ISSUE 03 OPEN SHOULD BE PATRICIA'S HALLWAYS IF POSSIBLE.

MAYBE WE DON'T SEE JOE MAKE IT TO THE ROOM. WE CUT TO PATRICIA IN HER ROOM LIKE WE DO WITH A P.O.V TYPE SHOT.

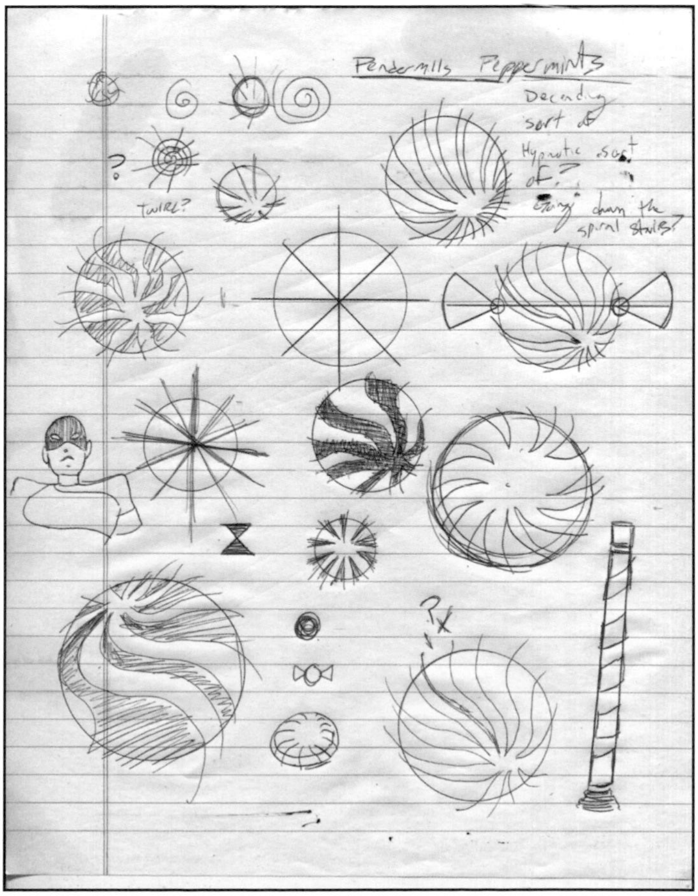

Pendermills Peppermints
Decending sort of Hypnotic sort of? Going down the spiral stairs?
Twirl?

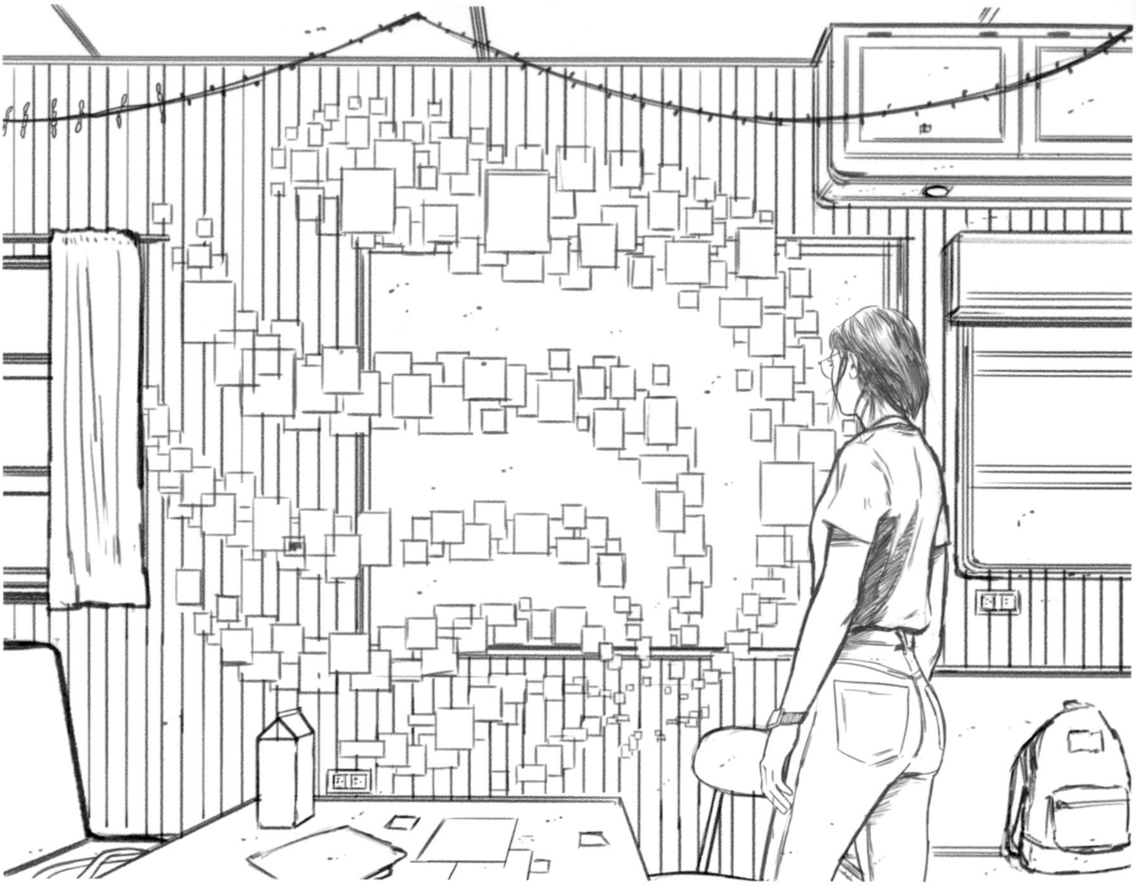

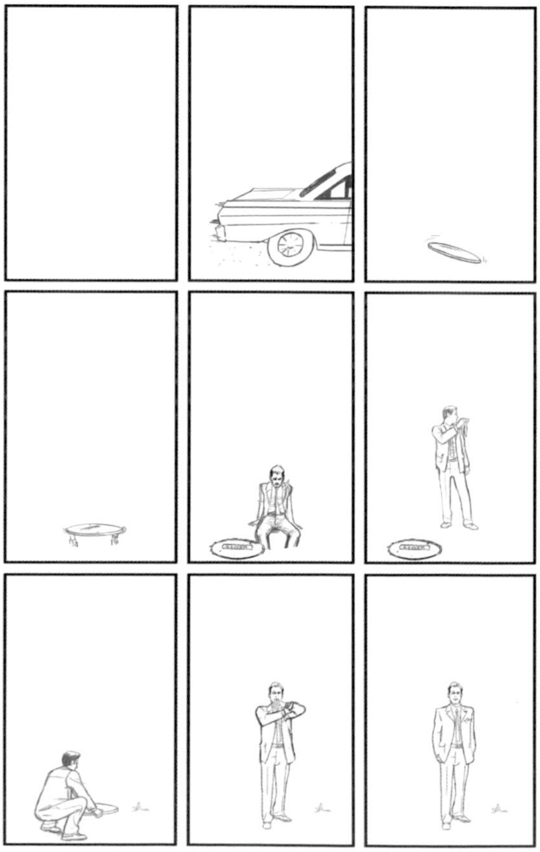

When I was fourteen, the other kids in the neighborhood convinced me to fight Brian. Lying on my back as Brian pummeled my head with his fists, I looked back and could see my dad's truck pulling into our driveway. He was putting his blue lunch bag onto his shoulder. I wonder if he still has that?

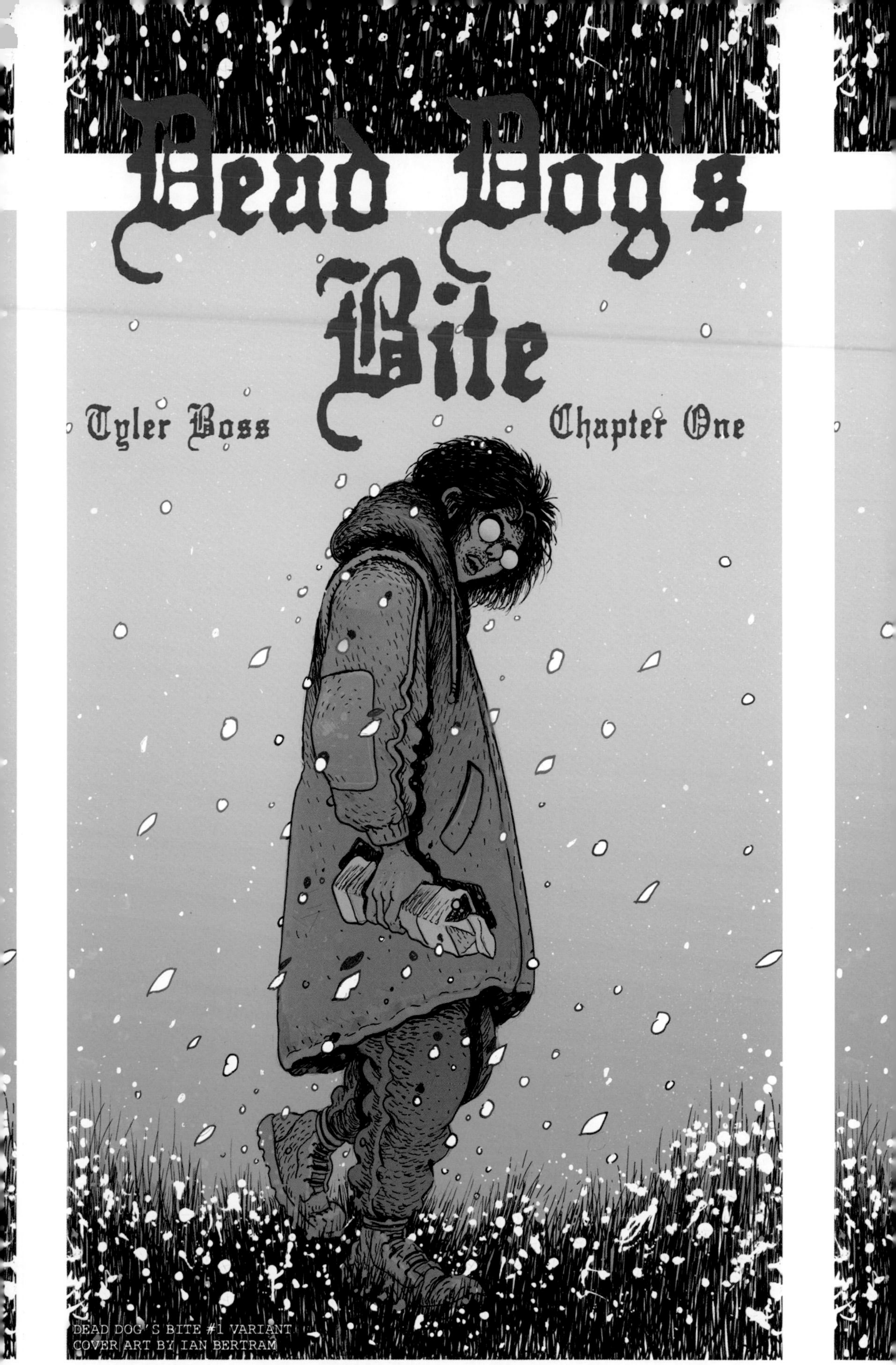
Dead Dog's Bite
Tyler Boss
Chapter One
DEAD DOG'S BITE #1 VARIANT
COVER ART BY IAN BERTRAM

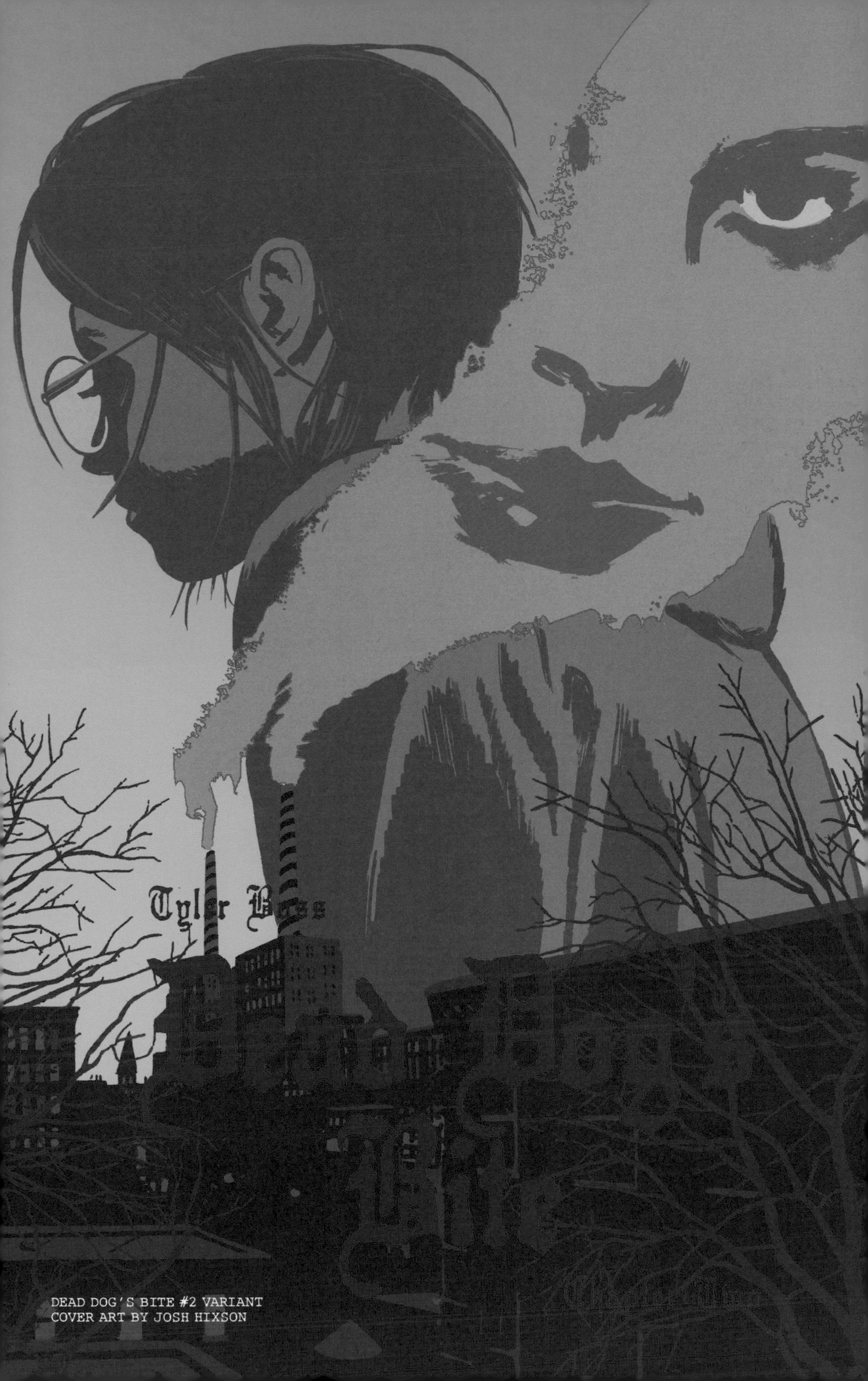

DEAD DOG'S BITE #2 VARIANT
COVER ART BY JOSH HIXSON

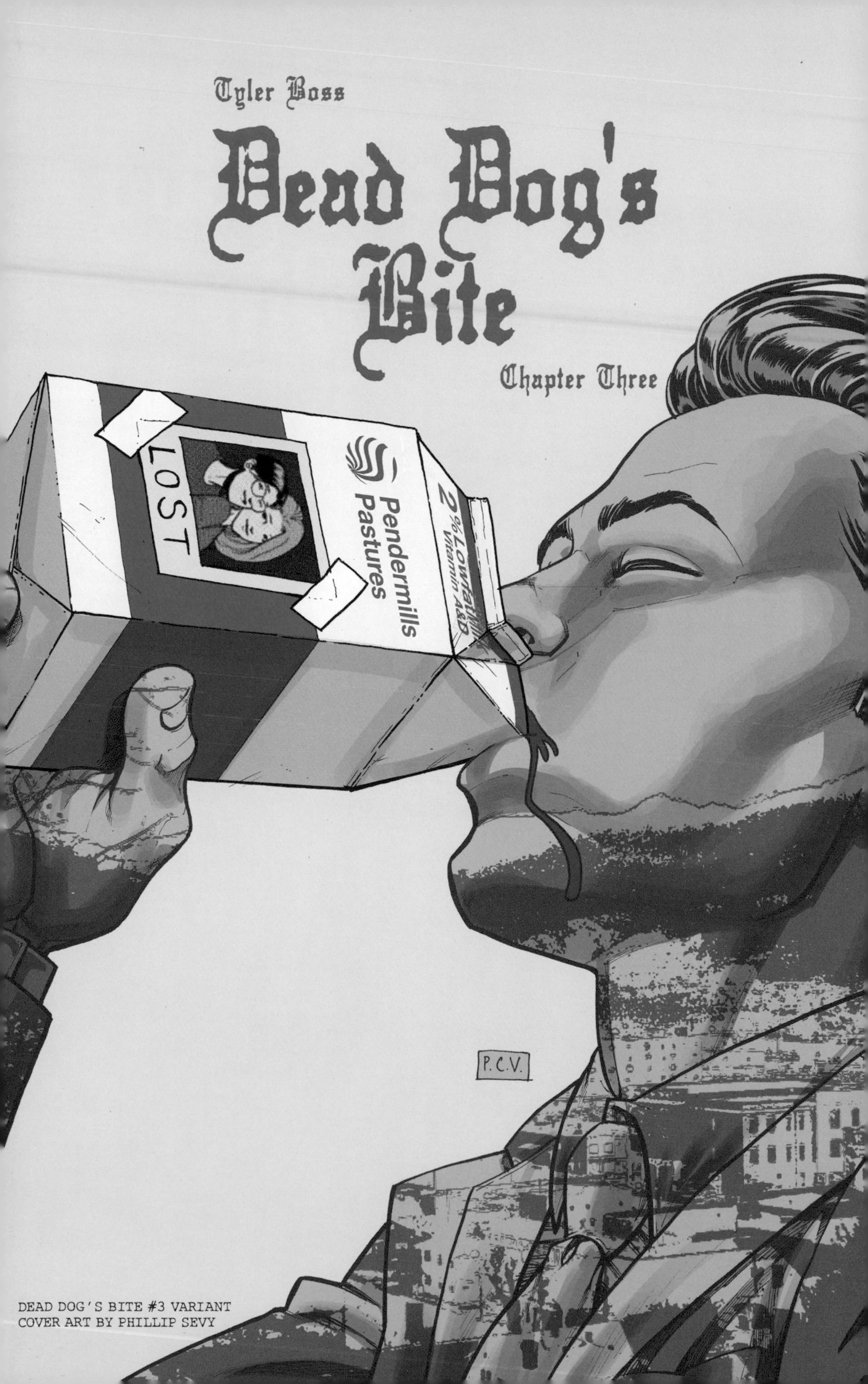
Tyler Boss
Dead Dog's Bite
Chapter Three
LOST
Pendermills Pastures
2% Lowfat
Vitamin A&D
P.C.V.
DEAD DOG'S BITE #3 VARIANT
COVER ART BY PHILLIP SEVY

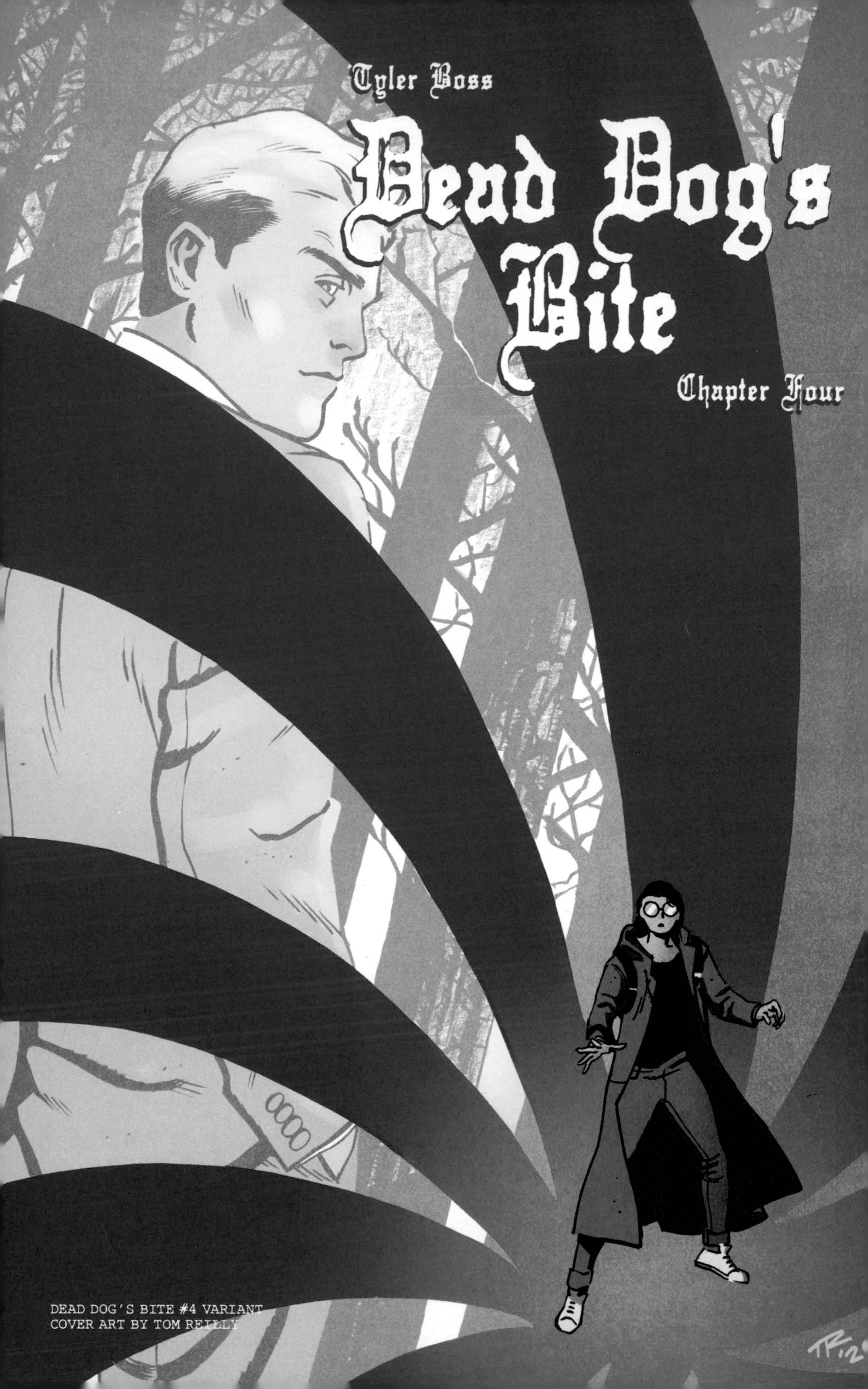
Tyler Boss
Dead Dog's Bite
Chapter Four
TR '12

DEAD DOG'S BITE #4 VARIANT
COVER ART BY TOM REILLY